CHOOSING JOY

A memoir of spiritual trauma survived

To: Danny and Morag
Blessings!

By John A. H. Dempster

COMMENDATIONS

What facets of the young Scot's family and cultural life most nourish the human spirit? What roles should education and religion play? How have we come to understand God in modern Scotland, and what price love and family ties?

A courageous John Dempster faces these alarming and brave questions as he describes a long and difficult navigation through his young life in late 20th century West Scotland, battling against an unrelenting and austere Christian legacy. As he emerges from darkness into the sunnier uplands of love and his own family life, we his readers find deep resonance with our own shadowy experiences of cultural conventions, family and institutional life.

Personally, I found this modern Scottish narrative both familiar and encouraging; but with the professional eye of a former psychiatrist and GP, John's courage, determination and ability to forgive as he relentlessly prioritises character development beyond mental illness, strike me as heroic. Forgive my mixture of Hanseatic languages, but *"Scots wha hae angst"* should read this book!

Dr Donald Mowat, Retired NHS GP and Psychiatrist

In *Choosing Joy*, John shares a story that is at once both ordinary and remarkable. Like many of his generation, he has been on a lifelong journey of reconsidering the faith he inherited in childhood. However, the honesty and sensitivity that characterise both his seeking and writing are remarkable. Through seven decades of wondering and wrestling we witness a gradually expanding vision and a deepening experience of the one he comes to know as the Great Love, the source of joy. *Choosing Joy* is a work of integrity and courage, soul-stirring and faith-enhancing.

Steve Aisthorpe, Church of Scotland Mission Development Worker, Author of *The Invisible Church* and *Rewilding the Church*

John's story, while centred primarily on his quest for spiritual certainty, is not just for those on similar journeys. At its heart, it's really the story of a young boy of the 1950s and 60s, seeking to find his way through the perils of challenging parental relationships, recurring waves of crippling self-doubt and anxiety, and a desire to find a way to meet the demands of others while retaining his own sense of his identity.

Will he find the love he most desperately seeks? You'll find yourself shouting to him across the pages, urging him on, warning him, wanting him to break out of the cycles in which he is caught and emerge from his journey unharmed.

The intellectual, self-deprecating charm of his writing and the beautifully chosen anecdotes and observations enhance the telling of his story, a universal, humane and genuinely moving one.

Graham Bullen, Novelist. Author of *The Quarant* and *The Broch*

ABOUT THE AUTHOR

John A.H. Dempster, born in 1952, studied at Wishaw High School and Glasgow and Strathclyde Universities. He worked in school and public libraries, ultimately specialising in library IT. He has been involved in churches for most of his life and is married with two adult children.

Matador
Unit E2 Airfield Business Park,
Harrison Road, Market Harborough,
Leicestershire. LE16 7UL
Tel: 0116 2792299
Email: books@troubador.co.uk
Web: www.troubador.co.uk/matador
Twitter: @matadorbooks

ISBN 978 1803132 242

British Library Cataloguing in Publication Data.
A catalogue record for this book is available from the British Library.

Printed and bound in the UK by TJ Books, Padstow, Cornwall
Typeset in 11pt Adobe Jenson Pro by Troubador Publishing Ltd, Leicester, UK

Matador is an imprint of Troubador Publishing Ltd

Remembering
William H. Dempster (2/10/1921 – 3/07/2011)
Helen L. Dempster (née Jackson) (18/3/1923 – 31/5/2005)
in love

Joy does not simply happen to us.
We have to choose joy and keep choosing it every day.
Henri Nouwen

The winter long,
All uncomplaining stand the trees.
God make my life,
Through all its strife.
As true to Spring as one of these.
Geoffrey Studdert Kennedy

Yet I am not silenced by the darkness,
by the thick darkness that covers my face
Job 23:17

CONTENTS

FOREWORD

I met John Dempster on Good Friday, 2011. Our friend Duncan MacPherson the Church of Scotland minister at Hilton Church in Inverness had recommended us to one another. As I look back that seemed an appropriate time for us to meet. For Christians, it is a day of deep reflection on the redemptive power of suffering; Christ's suffering on his cross, and the personal cross each one of us is called to take up in Christian discipleship. It is a day that assures us that even the worst that can happen is used by God to bring about the best. It assures us that our own suffering, bound to Christ's, is never meaningless but is used to make us more the people we were always meant to be. Somehow, these assurances seem to fit well with both of us and the journeys that we have both been on over the past ten years.

I remember the first meeting well. I found that day a fellow Christian, a kindred spirit and a comrade enquirer. We have been good friends for over ten years now, meeting regularly, usually over a cup of coffee, talking freely about the things that concern us deeply, and listening one another into a place of mutual acceptance and greater understanding. Typical of John, he describes our own meetings very much in terms of what I was able to offer him. I wonder if John realises the extent to which his own journey and searching has been such an encouragement to me. I warmly welcome his spiritual autobiography as something to which I know I will return from time to time in the future, reminding me of my friend and his journey. I also welcome it as a tremendously affirming offering to people of faith everywhere, encouraging us all to 'trust the process' and engage with our own spiritual journeys, wherever they take us. I am reminded as I read this book of several of John's qualities that I hugely admire.

First, there is his gentle positivity. John is a great noticer of the good in other people and in what they have to say. He is capable of homing in on the most positive and helpful aspects of a sermon, or an act of worship, or an individual, where perhaps others have been more distracted by what was awful! Often, he underscores these positive things and offers them back to the original giver in the most encouraging and upbuilding of ways. The same is true of this personal narrative. With aspects of church, or of life, that others might find difficult, or challenging, or just plain wrong, John sees these simply as a part of his journey and treats them with huge generosity and gentle acceptance. Without them, he would not be as he is today.

Second, there is his great honesty. I have always appreciated John's dissatisfaction with the glib and the clichéd. He asks honest, searching questions and in asking them recalls me to my own attempts to answer these as well as my own working conclusions. Sometimes he asks questions that haven't even occurred to me and that is a great gift in any friendship. In this book, the reader will notice the questions that John deals with on his journey and the answers he finds. We also notice the answers he does not find and the questions that so far go unanswered. Sometimes these will resonate deeply with our own enquiries. Always, they help us appreciate the value and the rewards of honesty and integrity in dealing with life's hard questions.

Finally, there is John's courage. I know that John worries, as we all do. I know that he has periods of despair as so many of us do. Some of these worries are about what others will say or think about us if the truth is known. Some of the despair is about ourselves and whether we will ever live and grow and change through the circumstances we are given. John has decided, with great courage, to choose joy and to make it a daily choice in the face of those things which worry us and bedevil us and tempt us to despair. In this sometimes defiant act of choosing joy John affirms for himself and for us all that life is meaningful from the centre out, that even our suffering is redeemed, and that this is true because the God who made us loves us; only loves us and loves us always, and we can rest secure in the knowledge of this love.

So, who would find this book helpful? First of all, those who, like John, experience periods of anxiety and depression. John is very open about this and it is his openness that gives such hope. John demonstrates a willingness and a way to talk about mental health issues that makes it easier for others, experiencing similar issues to do the same. He shows us that it is okay not to feel great all the time and it is okay to say so.

This book will also be of use to people who are struggling with faith (and that is most of us from time to time). He affirms that it is worth the struggle. He affirms that it is possible to grow through the precious faith we were given as children, acknowledging its importance and worth, but acknowledging also that there are aspects of that faith that are no longer helpful; that are, in fact harmful to us. He shows us what it has been like, with huge courage and integrity, to ask the questions and to make the journey out of what was given into what is now owned. He shows us the possibility not just of struggling to save a remnant of what we once believed, but of moving (through questioning and searching) into a place of strong and nourishing faith where he doesn't have to pretend to be anything, to feel anything or believe anything he is not, or does not feel or does not believe.

Finally, this book is definitely for those whose current beliefs are not helping their mental health. As a Mental Healthcare Chaplain, I found myself often saying to people, 'But if I believed that, I think I would be highly anxious/depressed too!' I strongly believe that good theology is good psychology and vice versa. This book may give some people the encouraging nudge that is needed to move from faith positions that really aren't helping to that place where not only can joy be a daily choice, but this choice can be made in the knowledge of a loving, generous and caring God, who wants us to be whole and well and active and content.

Thank you, John, for writing your story for us.

Rev Dr Iain Macritchie
Priest at St Michael and All Angels Church, Inverness.
Former Head of Programme for Spiritual Care and
Chaplaincy, NHS Education for Scotland.
18th October 2021.

INTRODUCTION

'Choose joy.'

I often whisper these words as I begin a new day.

But what do I mean? By 'choosing joy' do I mean simply making the best of the situation, seeking what's in the interests of others while denying the sense of de-realisation I sometimes feel because of mental health issues, the toxic hum of sadness? 'Choosing joy' certainly does mean refusing to dwell in the negative, though I certainly don't deny the pain either to myself or to those I share deeply with. But I opt as far as it is within my power to live as if joy is dominant and enduring and pain transitory by comparison. Joy I have found, is not identical to happiness, for in fact joy can provide a bedrock at times of great unhappiness.

This gives rise to many questions. Is my belief in joy no more than desperate delusional optimism? Isn't sadness in fact a more appropriate response to a pain-shadowed world? What is the source of the haunting, wistful anxiety which so frequently accompanies me? Has religious faith – specifically the brand of evangelicalism in which I was raised – been part of the problem, part of the solution, or both? How did I learn to choose joy? Has my life been a journey into a better way of living with the given of my emotional makeup, or into the transformation I hoped for, the healing and freedom?

Beginning in childhood, there have been moments when joy has broken through. And when joy comes, the transparent screen evaporates. I am free, knowing myself at one with the loveliness of things. Joy comes unexpectedly, its coming beyond my power to summon or control. Comes like the poet's muse, touching me briefly, leaving a waning afterglow. Joy also comes more predictably and less strongly as I'm immersed in writing, open to the deep overflowing well at the centre of my being. Joy at its purest brings a sense of wholeness and peace, an overwhelming knowledge that I am loved, that there is a transcendent joy which will endure, that joy is personal, another name for the Great Love we call (for want of a better word) God. The Christian story in which I locate my life centres on Jesus who was no stranger to suffering, but 'for the joy set before him he endured the cross, scorning its shame'. (Hebrews 12:2)

This book is the story of my life over the last seven decades, as son, friend, husband, father, librarian, church leader, outsider perpetually seeking the way in. It is not a 'misery memoir': my life has been challenging but I have for the most part remained positive and hopeful, knowing myself blessed and graced.

When I was a would-be evangelical Christian back in the 1960s, you were expected to be ready to speak about your faith, to give your 'testimony' – your personal account of coming to believe in Christ. I typed up a testimony on a couple of sheets of paper and kept it folded inside my Bible in case I was asked to share it at a meeting. But the truth was, I was simply saying what I thought was expected of me. The things of which I spoke were not I felt 'real' in my experience.

Since then I have learned to live and tell my story in terms which my earlier Baptist and Brethren listeners might not fully understand. But this too, I believe, is a story of salvation, a story of spiritual trauma survived, and a safe place found in the Great Love.

This is my true testimony.

The journey begins in the early 1950s.

*

You can contact the author at choosingjoybook@gmail.com
Some names and situations have been altered to protect people's privacy.

PART ONE

PART ONE

ONE

THE HANDWORK PROJECT

A chilly January morning in my tenth year. It's the first day back at school after the holidays and I am gloom-burdened because the carnival is over.

As I prepare to leave the house, my mother is taking the decorations off the Christmas tree which sits on the writing bureau in our living-room. Accidently she knocks it off-balance and although she catches it as it falls, strips of lametta twirl to the floor and a bauble shatters. I laugh, falsely.

Mum scowls at me.

On the way up the steep path to the school playground, I describe this incident to a friend.

'Why did you laugh?' he asks.

And I said (or thought), but I think I spoke, rather portentously, 'It is better to laugh than to cry'.

Crying was what I felt like doing, a wretched sobbing as the fall of the tree symbolised the dissolution of Christmas joy, and the grey mist of wintry angst.

*

Now that might be a good place to start. Dramatic opening, proof that I was fingered by sadness even in childhood. But not, I feel, the most honest starting point. In looking back I have too often viewed my childhood through the lens of what came afterwards, allowing memories of mental pain to obscure the many joys of my early years.

And so I suppose the handwork project in Miss Johnston's classroom is a better place to begin.

Miss Johnston from Canada, lovliest and most loving of my Primary School teachers. Miss Johnston from whom I learned of Christopher Columbus sailing the ocean blue in fourteen hundred, ninety-two and the Dutch boy who plugged the dyke with his finger, thereby averting catastrophe. Miss Johnston, who gave me my first taste of maple syrup as she walked round the Primary 3 classroom with a bottle of this exquisite elixir from her native land, kneeling beside each desk with a single spoon and never a thought of health and safety.

Our classroom led off the main hall in the Bearsden Academy primary department. The artwork hanging on the wall beside the door impressed me. I described it to my parents – a long grey building, with an imposing spire, towering over sylvan parkland. 'Sounds like Glasgow University,' they told me. 'You'll go there one day.'

For a handwork lesson, Miss Johnston gave each of us a circular piece of cardboard with thick spokes radiating from its hub. We were going to make a table-mat she said encouragingly. She hung lengths of brightly-coloured wool on a cupboard door and told us to take one piece at a time and wind it in and out of the spokes, working from centre to circumference.

Choosing the next piece of wool gave me a particular joy. I would approach the cupboard mesmerised by the panoply of colour. I relished the freedom to choose as I wished so that the pattern developed exactly as I wanted it. No teacher interrupting or making suggestions, no directions shouted from the desks behind me, no pieces of wool labelled for my attention. Just me and the wool, a sacred moment. I always selected the brightest colours vivid with joy and life.

Freedom to choose was at the centre of another epiphany a few years later. My parents and I were half-way through our annual fortnight's holiday at Seamill Hydro on the Ayrshire coast. These holidays were always relaxed, but one particular morning as I came out of the Annex where our bedrooms were located into the car-park, I realised that the hours until lunch-time stretched ahead and I was free, utterly free to do whatever I wanted.

I'm not sure what option I chose but I'm certain that whatever it was did not bring the transcendent joy of that initial revelation.

*

Though it was by far the most traumatic event of my childhood it did not to my knowledge affect me significantly. Further down the street there stood a house in which we kids knew a boy called Julian had died. I'd scurry past, eyes glued to the pavement ahead, a ritual designed to protect from the long tentacles of death. It never occurred to me that other neurotic children might be doing exactly the same thing as they passed 13 Maxwell Avenue.

My ten-week-old brother, William Hodge Dempster, died as he slept in his cot one summer Wednesday morning when I was three. I think I remember my parents' tears that day but of William himself I have no recollection. There is a photo of me sitting in the garden on a white-painted chair supporting a stern-faced baby on a second chair beside me. (Apparently mum was squatting behind to ensure that there were no accidents.) But I do not know how deeply if at all I was wounded by this separation from my sole sibling, nor how his death affected my parents' relationship with me

Nor do I know what scars were left in my parents' hearts. William's photo was always on display in our living room, his life and death acknowledged – perhaps his ghost would always be present, haunting their future.

There were no more children – I expect by design – and so I grew up 'only', which was more curse than blessing. I'm unsure whether my vaguely misanthropic introversion is simply in my nature or whether it was a product of that unsought, dark strand which forever stained the summer of 1955.

*

If you saw or heard an ambulance you had to clutch one of the lapels of your school blazer and not let go until you caught sight of a bird. What the consequences of non-compliance were we knew not: but we sure didn't want to risk finding out.

*

Mine was a privileged middle-class childhood of that period. My father, also William Hodge Dempster was beginning his career as a radiologist. My academically-gifted mother Helen (née Jackson) had studied modern languages at Glasgow University and taught briefly in a secondary school before, finding the classroom environment stressful, she switched to primary teaching. She was a gifted pianist and had 'letters after her name' both for music (at 'performers' standard') and elocution. In keeping with the prevailing custom she left work permanently immediately prior to my parents' wedding on 2 April 1951.

We had moved to Westerton, a pleasant 'garden suburb' to the west of Glasgow when I was two and there we stayed for eight years. For me it was the eternity of childhood.

Our semi on Maxwell Avenue where it slopes up to join Canniesburn Road was comfortable by the standards of the time. There was no double-glazing and no central heating: on cold winter mornings we'd sit warming ourselves with porridge listening to the news on the BBC Home Service, a feeble flame clinging to life among the kindling in the fireplace, the windows an explosion of Jack Frost's handiwork.

We had no fridge – although we acquired as a substitute a chest made of a white porous substance with a blue door called an 'Osocool', which allegedly had refrigerating properties, although its only fuel was water poured into the hollow on top. Nor had we TV or record-player – either because we couldn't afford them or more likely because my parents considered them to be, on religious grounds, 'worldly'.

*

In May 1962 just before my tenth birthday we relocated to Carluke, a small town in Lanarkshire perched above the luscious fields and fertile greenhouses of the Clyde Valley. My father had taken up a post at Law Hospital near Carluke and the move saved him a time-consuming commute through Glasgow before the city motorway system was built.

Just before we moved I sat in my bedroom, cut hundreds of little oblongs from the sheets of orangey paper used to protect X-ray film prior to use, and scrawled painstakingly on each of them 'The Dempsters are moving'.

I stuffed these in my school bag one morning and headed for the playground. The plan was to deposit them in strategic places where other kids would notice and pick them up. But having discovered that surreptitiously distributing my flyers was more daunting than I had imagined I shoved the remainder into a litter bin.

A few minutes later someone came up to me holding out the orange bundle which he had retrieved. 'Look what I found in the rubbish!' he said.

'That's weird,' I replied, feigning innocence.

Was my motive in preparing these notices of our departure self-promotion? I was coming to an end of a Primary 5 (at the new

Westerton Primary School which had opened in January 1961) in which I had endured both Mrs Harrod ('Horrid!' I called her, but not to her face) and a signally unempathic headteacher. Mr Thompson grilled me alone in his office when my parents complained about the lack of memory work in the school curriculum; belted me, refusing to accept that I had been wrongly accused of echoing in the Horrid's classroom the horn of a passing train; and mocked my (admittedly pitiful) attempt at drawing camels as a member of the Special Art Class to which I had been unaccountably admitted. Was I in announcing that 'The Dempsters are leaving' defiantly signalling that they had not broken me? I had survived.

Our house in Douglas Street, Carluke was a new-build, redolent of fresh paint and pristine carpet. It had double glazing and mum acquired the delicious luxury of a wooden paper-towel holder in the kitchen. I got to choose the wallpaper in my bedroom. Blue, with ducks.

*

I have a kaleidoscope of childhood memories at both Westerton and Carluke many of them positive which suggests that brightly-coloured threads predominated. The joy of Christmas, lying in my bed at number 13 listening to the Salvation Army Band playing at the corner of Monreith Avenue, knowing that Santa would come. The fulfilment of all my expectations the next morning. The Christmas-evening wistfulness: 364 days to go before we could do it all again.

My father, his breath condensing in the night air offering me a small peppermint ('whities' he called them) from the crumpled paper bag in his pocket. My father again, standing beside me as we pee together in the toilet, our respective streams of urine duelling: 'Streamies fighting!' I announce, gleefully. My father bare-chested, in khaki shorts working with wood, chicken wire and an old iron bed-frame making a rabbit run for our new family member Reggie. My father, not many months thereafter, paying a grief-stricken visit to the vet one evening and then sitting with Reggie beside the dying fire in our living-room and burying the small corpse in the rose bed before morning light. My father yet again, kneeling by my bedside before I start my new Primary School after moving to Carluke. It's still daylight outside. I can see the ducks paddling on the wallpaper, calm and comforting. 'It'll be OK,' dad says gently stroking my hair. I drop into deep, confident sleep in the peace he leaves behind him.

I have many good memories of my mother too. Mum, walking with me along Canniesburn Road as I scribble car registration numbers in cheap notepad. Mum tenderly dressing my wounds and stilling me after sharp wire in the grass across the road lanced my legs. Mum performing a crazy dance on the piano as my party kids and I played musical chairs. Mum inviting other children round after nursery, and me having such fun that I forgot to go to the toilet and wet myself. Mum buying me not just the *Dandy* and the *Beano* but the *Topper* and the *Beezer* too when I was ill in bed, together with a kids' letter-writing kit with patterned paper and matching envelopes with pretend stamps. Mum sitting across the table from me in the coffee shop at Esquire House in Anniesland where we'd gone for refreshments in the course of a morning expedition.

And there are all those holiday photos in which I'm smiling and I have no sense that the smile belies my true feelings. Here I am beside a model car crafted in sand by my father – I think it was a Sunday morning, and he was just about to leave mum and me on the beach in the sunshine while he went off to the morning meeting. Here I am perched in swimming trunks on a rock on the beach at Seamill Hydro: I loved creating water channels in wet sand and building sand-dams. ('Don't you think "Dempster's Dam" might be better?' mum suggested uneasily when she saw the imposing structure I had labelled, using small stones, 'Dam Dempster.')

I loved the Hydro – the lawns you could run around in the heat of water-pistol wars with other kids; the unforgettable echoeyness and the sandy-seaweedy aroma of the little gatehouse you clattered through to reach the steps to the beach, the sea sighing enticingly beyond. I loved Nardini's in Largs where you could savour ice-cream sundaes in tall glasses passing the sweet elixir between your lips with an elongated spoon as you sat at the wickerwork tables.

And here's a photo of all four of my grandparents visiting us at Seamill: John Dempster, retired headmaster after whom I was named; his wife Phemie; Archibald Jackson, foreman at Murray and Paterson's engineering works in Whifflet; his wife Jean.

*

There was always a soupçon of tension when we were together with both sets of grandparents. With the Dempsters, this was due simply to my parents' occasional lack of patience with the older generation which unfortunately I absorbed. With my mother's parents things were more complicated. I knew they were Not Christians, and had learned to look disdainfully as we drove past the football stadium to which Archie Jackson had recourse of a Saturday afternoon. I knew too that they had sold my mother's baby grand piano which had stood in the big front room of the Airdrie flat at the Tram Terminus from where I had watched the Queen driven up Motherwell Street early in her reign and often looked over to Snottery Annie's ice cream parlour from where grandpa was wont to purchase delectable pokey hats. They had sold the piano without my mother's consent before she had a house with a big enough room to admit it. As a substitute, my father bought mum an upright piano from Paterson, Sons and Co, Buchanan Street Glasgow for £88-0s-0d just before their marriage.

Mum was a dedicated student at Airdrie Academy, being Dux in June 1940, her sixth year. She strove for excellence in everything, but may have had the impression that her parents were hard to please – anything below 80% in an exam was deemed a failure. Her sister Jean on the other hand approached life in a much more relaxed way. My gran was an eccentric. Family lore has it that she was indisputably in charge at home. Each day after lunch she would retreat to bed for a nap after which she would rise and suitably attire herself to venture out for the day's shopping. A story places her at the front window of a Sunday evening watching the inhabitants of the Burgh promenading up to the Terminus and back as was their custom and muttering with snobbish derision 'There go the street walkers!' My mother too was prone to snobbishness and considered it 'a catch' to have married a medic.

Jean senior bore her own burdens. She was illegitimate, born six months before her parents' wedding and may have been wounded by attachment issues with her parents. She bore a still-born son between mum's birth in 1923 and Jean's a few year's later. Perhaps my mother felt pressured to take the place of the son her parents never had and sensed this was an impossible task. Perhaps mum's conversion to evangelical Christianity while a student drove a wedge between her and her parents as it certainly did between the two sisters. But hints of further darkness emerged toward the end of mum's life.

I was aware of little of this as a child but the relief was palpable on that middle Saturday of our holiday when the Vanguard, the Jacksons' car, headed out of the Seamill Hydro car park.

*

Apart from nine months of the Horrid, my primary school years were largely positive.

I went to a prefabricated building in Westerton for P1 and P2. Each classroom was heated by a stove surrounded by a protective guard over which you could dry damp coats. 'Good morning, boys and girls,' the wooden pointer spoke through Miss Paul's agency each morning, to which we dutifully replied 'Good morning, Mr Pointer!' I was off school for two protracted periods during P1 – having both appendix and tonsils removed but I can't say this held me back academically. I was frustrated that I learned faster than many of my peers and was given additional work to satiate my desire for learning.

My tendency to keep of the right side of authority showed itself early: when Miss Ramsay enquired about the whereabouts of a missing pupil one day after lunch, it was I who reported that he was last seen lurking in the toilets, I who was deputed to fetch him. I trotted back self-righteously with the poor boy following me, a turd making slow progress down the inside of his left leg beneath his short trousers.

'He was *dirty* wasn't he?' my class-mates hissed while cleaning operations were taking place in the staff-room. 'No,' I replied, obviously lying but I suppose seeking to show loyalty to my stricken peer.

For P3 and half of P4 we were bussed up to Bearsden before being among the first pupils at the new Westerton Primary School for the remainder of P4 and the regrettable P5.

The last six weeks of P5, and the following two years I learned at Carluke Primary School which I largely enjoyed apart from those six weeks when Maggie Cassells became obsessed with my cheerful smile, thinking entirely without reason that I was mocking her. I struggled to keep a straight face and was banished one afternoon to an adjacent empty classroom where I sat rather miserably on my own.

Our Primary 6 teacher was the redoubtable Miss Burns – of her teaching I remember next to nothing but I have an impression of lightness and laughter and joy. And yet in retrospect there was something peculiar and disturbing about her frequent belting of pupils of both sexes. On occasion she would line up the whole class and systematically belt each one of us. On my bedroom wall at home I pinned a 'Burnsie Belting Record' on graph paper, day by day meticulously recording the number of times Miss Burns drew her weapon. Her down-stroke was light and such was her democratisation of punishment that there was no shame. She told us that her leg was made of the strongest 'cahoochy', so that we 'couldn'a pull it' – I think she meant caoutchouc. This always slightly puzzled me, as you'd assume that an india-rubber leg would be more pliable than most.

By the time I reached Primary 7 where our teacher was Jeannie Angus I was at home with the traditional focus on memorisation so unlike what I had been used to at Westerton, and with the rote learning (which involved for example intoning 'Bar-ce-lon-a-and-Val-en-ci-a-and-the-Bal-e-ar-ic-is-lands' which taught me nothing about Spain). I was at home with the formal teaching of arithmetic and grammar. 'Grammar with a capital G is worse than the sting of a bumble bee,' I'd say on a Wednesday lunchtime when the dread lesson loomed ahead. I was at home with reading 'round the class,' though the cleverest kids would race ahead while some of our class-mates struggled falteringly. But in my own naïve, middle-class bubble I lacked awareness of the difficult lives some of them led and of the favouritism Miss Angus displayed.

*

I have positive memories of friendships in my primary years. At Westerton, I was closest to Douglas Anderson: more zealous in his approach to the school choir than was I, he had dutifully copied down the words of our songs which I failed to do. Douglas lent me his copy and my mother longsufferingly recorded them in blue ink in the black-covered notebook she bought me for the purpose. ('All in an April evening…' I loved the emotional charge of those words and music.)

Douglas and I went to one another's houses some Friday evenings. We watched *The Valiant Years* on his family's television, a serial history of World War II based on books by Winston Churchill. I loved the musical theme, the images of grey warships ploughing through even greyer seas, and the shot which concluded each episode of a black metal gate in an archway closing silently and seemingly automatically as the theme swelled and the credits rolled.

There was Isabel Rae in whose house I glimpsed with awe the very worldly *Black and White Minstrel Show*. I knew God would be very displeased with Isabel Rae and her family. And there was Hilary

Dunn, who taught me that it is easier for a girl to pee in public than it was for me, squatting decorously in long grass, her skirt around her knees, without attracting attention from passers-by.

There were friends at Carluke too – Colin Menzies, who registered my mother's openness to talk about William, and Paul Birrell with whom I walked home each day. Paul who deliciously shocked me by chanting 'Tarzan in the jungle, sitting on a gate, waiting for the toilet …[a well-timed pause, followed by as unspeakably rude a sound as he could possibly produce] Too late!' Paul who spelled out the name of comedian Tony Hancock syllable by syllable by pointing to parts of his own body; Paul who was somewhat aggrieved when after he sang 'Sluvsyah Yeah Yeah Yeah', I asked him what 'Sluvsyah' meant compelling him to acknowledge that he didn't know.

I was also close to the kids in our immediate neighbourhood who were slightly younger than me. Summer days in the cool of morning we'd make a great circular road with a toy bulldozer in the gravel behind Leslie and Norman Steel's building and spend the rest of the day propelling Dinky and Corgi vehicles round it, until sunset left behind it a still balmy evening.

Hearing *The Happy Wanderer*, we crowded round the Cappocci Man's ice-cream van when he pulled up outside Mrs Adamson's house at 6.15 in the evening. 'Could I have a noogah please' I said one evening, self-importantly using the pronunciation my mother had taught me. 'You mean nugget?' the Italian vendor replied equably. Somewhat deflated, I nodded.

*

'Wouldn't you like some roller-skates?' my parents asked kindly.

I guess they must have seen some kids skating and didn't want me to feel left out. But I was untroubled by any sense of need for wheels on my feet.

'Not really,' I said. 'I don't think I'd use them.'

But they persuaded me. Off we went to a sports shop at the bottom of Wishaw Main Street. We returned with my new gear. I strapped the skates to my feet and awkwardly staggered along the Douglas Street pavement. I held on to walls and railings, never quite brave enough to thrust myself forward, entrust myself to wheel-powered momentum, and thus break through the joy barrier.

Thereafter, the skates languished in a corner of the garage, gathering dust and cobwebs.

*

There were several moments of grace during those years, unforgettable instants when I was touched with a sense of wonder and peace. One evening, as a young boy, I was left with a child-sitter, mum's friend Marion Roberts to whom I always referred as 'Aunty'. When I wakened the next morning I saw in my blurry vision before I put on my spectacles a shape on top of the chest of drawers which had not been there the night before. Glasses on, I looked more closely – the shape was a cardboard box of sweets, a present from Marion constructed in three linked sections which folded together, decorated to resemble a house with a sloping roof. I was no stranger to presents to which I responded with various degrees of gratitude. But this – the surprise, the loveliness of it – was something different. It might have been pure gold – a wonderful thing, an expression of sheer love.

Two moments of transcendence involved a lamp post. One evening, I was standing half-way up the northern end of Stirling Avenue in Westerton with some other kids. I had been lent a watch to ensure that I was home at the required time. Twice already I had wound the hands back in the vain hope that my lateness could be blamed on a malfunctioning timepiece. The faces of the houses darkened as behind them the western sky blushed red. We were standing beneath a gas streetlamp (the very one I had run into on my bike years earlier before wandering home concussed and coming to in our neighbour

Mrs Dunlop's living room watching *Lassie* on TV – my parents were apparently out). The gas lamp was turned on automatically and began to glow, its brightness strengthening as the sun declined. The peace and wonder of this graced moment penetrated deep. Again I fumbled at my wrist and – another grace – there was no parental search party.

Again in Carluke in December 1962: I was walking home from school in the 4pm darkness after the Christmas party on the last day of term. There was a thin covering of snow on the ground; more flakes began falling silently. I'd said goodbye to Paul outside his house; I crossed the street, turned into Douglas Street. The grassy bank on the right hand side of the rising road was covered with snow over which an electric street lamp cast light and shadow. I looked up into the falling snowflakes as they freckled my face, and saw a myriad of swirling dots dancing in the heavens. I knew a warm kitchen awaited me and love, and holidays, and a Santa-sack. My spirit sang in expectation.

*

So you see it's simply not possible to argue that those years of childhood were overcast by the gloom which prompted my laughter the day the Christmas tree fell. In photos a smile can belie the pain behind bright eyes but can memories be false smiles?

Some bad stuff happened. Occasionally, I was punished for minor wrongdoing. It would be 'your trousers are coming down,' and my dear sweet father would administer the stinging slaps to my bare buttocks which he felt faith and duty required of him lest sparing the rod of his hand, he would thereby spoil the child.

There must have been some bullying, because one day kids were chucking stones at me outside Jamieson's shop on the corner of Maxwell Avenue. I picked up a pebble and retaliated, and witnesses claimed it was my projectile which broke the plate-glass window so that the cost of replacing it fell upon my father. But he was gentle and did not rebuke me.

At Carluke too there was bullying. My father Visited The School which I was pleased about, but also gave me some lessons in self-defence. These came to an abrupt end when my fist penetrated his defences and administered a black eye. Subsequently, Alec Lippiatt the policeman's son was aggressive towards me in the playground and I let fly, both arms pumping, landing fist after fist on his startled face. It felt so good to hear the shouts of the crowd gathering round us. 'Fight! Fight!' So good to win even though my glasses were broken.

But I did wonder why, at Westerton it was always me who pushed another two lads up Stirling Avenue in a buggy and then ran back downhill in their wake. Why, I mused, was I always the pusher and never the pushee? The injustice of it stung me with melancholy but I simply accepted my vassal role as destiny.

I was an anxious kid. Dad would be awash with sweat after my histrionics when taken for a routine vaccination. 'Is there no other way?' I howled dramatically on one occasion having somehow heard of an alternative vaccine delivery mechanism involving impregnated sugar lumps which sounded infinitely pleasanter.

If I was to go for some unwelcome appointment – say with the dentist (or at the dental hospital where I had treatment, suffering the indignity of having my name called out as JOAN) – I'd wrap my right hand round the comforting firmness of our back-room door handle and pronounce to myself 'The next time I touch this it will be OVER'. But inevitably, safe home once again, I would forget the second part of this safety ritual.

But I suspect a shadow was cast over my life because of attachment issues especially in my relationship with my mother. During pregnancy and the first two years of life a baby is influenced by the mum's biochemistry in ways which affect its future emotional life, ability to establish relationships, and level of self-esteem. I have no means of knowing how stressed my mother was during her pregnancy, nor whether her own early relationship with my grandmother affected her ability to impart to me as a young child security and confidence in managing my emotions. Details of those early months in my mother's care are irretrievably submerged in deep memory but some childhood recollections suggest that my future difficulties were caused at least in part by a poor attachment to mum.

As a child I felt a safety in my father's presence which, alone with mum I occasionally lacked. When dad was out at evening church one Sunday I stubbed my big toe on a toy fire-engine. Looking at my foot, I saw a small black discolouration on the toe and was convinced that I had stood on a pin which had penetrated so deeply that only the head was visible just beneath the skin. I didn't mention this to my mother but was tense and anxious until my father's return in itself brought reassurance.

On another occasion when I was ill in bed with a high temperature, a Wild West story I was reading, a tale of cowboys, Indians and locomotives with broad smoke stacks was whirling in my head in a fevered frenzy. I felt a restless anxiety when only mum and I were in the house, an anxiety which was relieved only when I heard a familiar voice in the kitchen below and knew that dad was home, and I could relax.

And I remember one day as a young child when there was a deflating balloon in the house following a birthday party. The crinkled, decaying texture of balloons 'going down' disturbed me: I hated touching them. But mum picked up this particular revolting piece of rubber and chased me with it. I ran out of the room, presumably screaming, and sat on the second bottom step of the staircase. For some reason I didn't flee upstairs but simply crouched there, frozen. My mother hunkered down in front of me and thrust the balloon towards my face even though I was indicating (and probably saying) that I wanted her to stop. As an adult I mentioned this to mum, but she simply swept my recollection aside. And indeed what parent has not inadvertently carried on with a game too long? I suppose she did not understand the depth of my revulsion. To me her action felt like an invasion of my being, an empathy failure by the person meant to be my primary source of protection.

*

In Pickering and Inglis, the Christian booksellers then situated in dusty premises far along Glasgow's St Vincent Street, my father picked up two slim volumes. Guides to sex education for boys, one targeted at eleven-year-olds, the second at mid-teens. He worked through the first of these with me – it didn't make much impression. I presume it was about body changes and wet dreams – but I found this tame, and begged him to let me see the second booklet. Of course he told me to wait until I was 15 which seemed an age away. Sadly, I didn't ever see that second book. My father and I never again spoke about sex. In that respect I was ill-prepared for puberty and adolescence.

There was a tragic story in the news of two kids, a boy and a girl taken into a wood and 'bludgeoned' to death. This excited my curiosity rather than fear or empathy. What did 'bludgeoned' mean? What was a bludgeon? And there was something else – a prurient excitement as I imagined myself sitting beside the girl, facing death together, reaching out to touch her hand even as the dark figure approached. This lurid sexual fascination surprised and haunted me.

A sunny day at the very end of our Primary 7 year. Miss Angus was out of the room as were most of the others. A small group of us including my friend Colin were standing close to the window, chatting. Caroline Muncie was in front of me. Teasingly, I pulled the zip at the back of her dress a short way down. I was unprepared for the negative reaction from the others. It seemed I had done something very wrong, and I couldn't understand why, but nobody enlightened me.

*

Earlier in our Primary 7 year, my class sat the 11+ exam which we termed the 'Qually' (P7 was known as 'the qualifying class'): it was the first time I'd faced a stapled exam book with the questions printed on it and space to record your answers. The results of this exam determined whether you'd proceed to the local four-year high school or to one of a number of so-called 'Senior Secondary Schools' in the area – which for most of us meant Wishaw High School.

There was discussion at home about the entry exam for the fee-paying Glasgow High School which my parents considered had a good academic record. The decision as to whether or not I should participate was left to me and I didn't feel under any pressure to agree. But one day I sat in a chilly, high-windowed hall at the school in central Glasgow taking two papers, and then had an interview with the head teacher. As a reward for my participation we subsequently proceeded to a toy shop where my parents bought me a brown plastic battery-powered cabin cruiser.

I was accepted for Glasgow High and given the choice by my parents of whether or not to go there. At this point the thought of a daily commute by train to Glasgow seemed overwhelming and I opted to go with the less scary of the two options and head with Colin Menzies to Wishaw High School. (Paul Birrell chose Dalziel High in Motherwell for family reasons.) I respect my parents for giving me a choice in this which I believe was genuine. This was one thread which I rejected through fear of the unknown, fear of adventure.

How many of the threads of colour running through my childhood, and indeed my life, did I choose with the same delicious sense of freedom as I experienced in reaching out for the wool in Miss Johnston's classroom? How many were thrust into my hand by my nature, or by life? And were my choices prompted by a desperate desire to match what I saw as the template of other people's expectations for the handwork of my life?

But I haven't been totally straight with you. There was another, dominant thread in my childhood. which thus far I've only mentioned in passing – the all-pervading influence of my parents' Christian faith.

TWO

THE NUMBER 13 BUS

I know exactly where to start this chapter.

The bus route running through Westerton was number 13. My mother repeatedly told me 'Remember! It's a number 13 you want to get back home. Never get on a bus with any other number.'

It must have been my first or second day in Miss Johnston's classroom at Bearsden Academy Primary School. The final bell went and we charged out of the playground to where a line of double-deckers waited by the kerbside to take us back to Westerton.

Except there was a problem.

There was a 6, an 8, one with the number indicator stuck half-way between 11 and 12, but no 13s. Backwards and forwards along the pavement I paced as my classmates piled on board. 'Of course they're the right buses. Come on John!' But they weren't 13s! I was still standing on the pavement as the buses drove off, engulfing me in a cloud of diesel exhaust fumes.

I walked home. It wasn't far – perhaps two or three miles. I went the back way, past the posh suburban houses with their neat hedges and long gardens fragrant with late-summer flowers. Eventually I walked down Maxwell Avenue and turned into our drive. Mum was watching out for me at the window with her friend Letty Anderson, Letty with the big, thick, round spectacles, a devotee of the Africa Inland Mission. Mum opened the front door. 'There were no 13s,' I sobbed as I hugged her.

I like that story. It symbolises my complete trust in what my parents told me; a willingness to assert my independence of my peers; a readiness to let the wild conviction that my parents were right, that my parents spoke for God, over-ride more rational considerations; a reluctance to make my own decisions. When it came to religious faith, I did not question what I was told at home or church.

*

While we were at Westerton my parents belonged to an Open Brethren (or simply 'Brethren') church – to be distinguished from the Exclusive Brethren. [1] The Open Brethren were less strict than the Exclusives and each 'Assembly' or 'Meeting' was managed by its own elders. Scottish society remained predominantly Christian in the 1950s yet I was conscious as a child of our 'difference', our superior grasp of truth.

We spent Sunday mornings attending the lengthy 'morning meeting' in Allander Hall, Milngavie. I sat beside my parents in the corrugated iron structure for the most part with patient resignation. The 'saints' (as people belonging to Brethren fellowships often described themselves) occupied benches around a simple table in the centre of the room, on which a globlet of wine and freshly-baked bread on a silver plate were concealed beneath a newly-laundered white tablecloth. The 'brethren' (never the 'sisters', for the church interpreted very literally St Paul's injunction that the women should keep silent) were free to pray; to 'give out' a hymn from the *Believer's Hymn Book* which the company would sing without musical accompaniment; to read a passage from

---

1. Which now calls itself confusingly the 'Plymouth Brethren Christian Church.' Even before the 1960s when Exclusivism became increasingly cult-like under the malign influence of Jim Taylor Jn, it had rigid rules of behaviour and practice.

the Bible, and share some thoughts. These brethren spoke as they felt 'moved' by God's Spirit. There was no plan or agenda except that towards the end of the time allocated someone would give thanks for the bread and the wine and then these 'elements' would be passed from hand to hand. Each person 'in fellowship' would eat, and drink.

This was the way things were; this I knew pleased God. At times however I was bored. I remember lying across my father's knee one morning kicking my legs furiously in the passageway; later my parents were sufficiently enlightened to let me take my own reading material to the meetings. I remember – it must have been towards the end of our time in Westerton – launching an imaginary rocket freighted with a cargo of gas, navigating it across the room through my telekinetic powers, and placing it into a perfect orbit round the head of Mr Phillips as he earnestly spoke, whereupon it released its payload. I hoped that this might dull his thinking and make him sit down more quickly than he had been anticipating, but sadly it proved ineffective.

In time I learned to laugh at the old Brethren jokes, such as the line of a hymn which became 'joyful, joyful Will, the meeting bee' and the reference to that other denizon of the Gospel Hall menagerie, 'Gladly, the cross-eyed bear'. There was also the first ice-cream parlour in the Bible, 'Walls of Jericho'.

I remember the summer 'Open Air' Meetings, when of a Sunday afternoon we would walk down into Milngavie town centre and congregate in the sunshine close to the Black Bull pub beside the purposefully flowing Allander Burn. There would be singing, a gospel solo, a 'testimony', a sermon, all broadcast through a crackly battery-powered speaker. I remember meals with welcoming families from across the social spectrum, a range of 'vaguely designated' aunts and uncles. Curiously I don't recall welcoming many of these aunts and uncles to eat at our house.

*

My father was one of the elders, a meticulous visitor and encourager of those who were ill and frail. Sunday by Sunday he made a careful mental note of who was missing from the morning meeting, and later contacted them to check how they were. This he did in a spirit of love and not of control. Occasionally he would participate in the morning meeting prompted by notes written in block capital letters, but he felt more comfortable ministering to individuals.

His parents were also members of the Brethren but when dad as born in 1922 my grandfather was headmaster at Wiston, a rural community in South Lanarkshire. The family attended the local Church of Scotland, and my father's two sisters Cathy and Margaret lie buried there. When grandpa moved to be headmaster of Greengairs Primary School near Airdrie, he joined the Kirk there (as befitted the headmaster, he probably thought) while my gran made her way to the local Gospel Hall. My father opted to accompany her and there he made a profession of faith. In July 1935 in neat handwriting he signed a 'My decision' card making the following commitment:

> *Knowing that I am a sinner and believing Jesus died instead of me I now take the Lord Jesus Christ as my sin-bearer and Saviour and I give myself – all I am and all I have – to him as my Lord.*

There was also a verse from Scripture printed on the card: 'I know Whom I have believed, and am persuaded that he is able to keep that which I have committed unto him.' (2 Timothy 1:12 AV) Later, my father was baptised by immersion.

My mother Helen Jackson's family belonged to Flowerhill Church of Scotland in Airdrie. She spoke of the quiet sense she had as a child of God's reality and love. As a student at Glasgow University in the 1940s she encountered evangelical Christians and underwent an evangelical conversion, which sadly affected her attitude to friends and family members who did not share her newly-found certainties.

My parents were not Sundays-only Christians. Each morning and evening my father would pray and read from *Daily Light* which contained compilations of Bible verses on various subjects, one for each day of the year. (The text was from the Authorised Version of the Bible, and I fondly remember the difficulty dad had getting his tongue around the word 'propitiation', and the embarrassment with which each year he scuttled self-consciously over the phrase 'bastards and not sons', as Hebrews 12:8 AV has it.) Before bedtime, in my early childhood my mum would take me through the Scripture Union *Honeycombs* booklets which gave thoughts and puzzles for young children based on daily Bible passages.

When we relocated to Carluke my parents decided we would attend the local (Martin Memorial) Baptist Church. I called it 'the church with the smiley minister', which is a tribute to the cheerfulness of the pastor George A. J. Balmer. Mum and dad appreciated his character, his faith and his preaching and my mother enjoyed being able to sharpen up her German by talking to Mrs Balmer who was Swiss by birth. Presumably my parents had checked out the local Gospel Hall and concluded either that it was too 'tight' (ie strict), or that the Baptist Church with more young people attending was a better environment for me. We went along twice each Sunday but I don't have much recollection of the services or sermons in the early years.

When first we moved to Carluke I was reluctant to become involved in the church's children's activities simply through shyness. To overcome this reluctance my parents walked me round to the outside door of the small hall where the Junior Christian Endeavour (CE) was meeting and all but pushed me into the room.

I think I quickly felt at home and rather enjoyed the CE – all I can remember of the weekly meetings is the singing of 'choruses' (short songs on a spiritual theme). They were mostly vigorous in style and rhythm, although some – such as *Climb, Climb up Sunshine Mountain*, *He Owns the Cattle on a Thousand Hills*, and (positively creepy in retrospect) *Echo, Echo, Echo, Echo is my name, I go wherever children go and always say the same* – were gentler and more reflective.

I particularly recall *Sailing home* (a heavenly harbour was in prospect) the singing of which involved crossing your arms and linking hands with the people sitting on either side of you on the bench, and rocking back and forward simulating a sailing motion while you sang. But small boys particularly enjoyed throwing themselves vigorously into the rocking process with the malign intent of making the child at the end of the row fall off.

*

I remember the sense of superiority I felt when we were reading one of the Psalms a verse at a time, and others in the group read out the word 'Selah' when it appeared, which I knew meant simply 'Pause' and should be left unspoken. I also remember 'dooking for apples' at the Halloween party – at this point, in that church at least, there were no evangelical concerns about celebrating the traditional joys of Halloween.

*

Paul Birrell tells me that he came along to CE with me once, at my invitation. 'You were trying to convert me,' he smiles. I had completely forgotten this. 'I've never tried to convert anyone in my life,' I reply. Did I issue this invitation because I felt completely at home with Christian faith? I think it's more likely I asked Paul because we'd been urged to bring someone along, and I felt pressure to conform.

*

I also attended Sunday School which was held in the main church after the morning service. Following a general time of singing each class met in its designated area of the pews, marked out with green curtains suspended from removable metal poles which slotted into the book-rests. The idea was to provide some privacy.

My first Sunday School teacher there was John Heron. I particularly enjoyed his invitation to write up stories of Jesus' encounters with people in the town of Capernaum as recorded in the gospels as though for a local newspaper, *The Capernaum Chronicle*. John promised to produce an actual edition of this, and I wrote a number of colourful pieces for him. I was rather disappointed when, perhaps due to lack of participation from the others, my articles were never seen again.

*

Back in the 1950s and early 1960s there was still a religious element in primary school education which I found enriching. I remember standing in the small room which led off from Miss Paul's classroom doing craft work with scissors and pastel paper The words of hymns were running through my head – perhaps there was singing in the classroom behind me.

Oh God of Bethel by whose hand
Thy people still are led

and

By cool Siloam's shady rill

I stood still amid the fragrance of glue and cardboard and the sound of a Blue Train's horn as it pulled out of Westerton station, ravished by the beauty of these syllables and their accompanying melodies.

In Primary 2 we learned John Bunyan's hymn, the robustness of its words inspiring even though imperfectly understood.

Who would true valour see
Let him come hither

These lines moved me in a way the songs we sang at Allander Hall did not. This may have been partly due to my over-familiarity with the content of the *Believer's Hymn Book*. But Brethren hymn-writers for the most part lacked the literary giftedness to clothe exalted concepts in subtle language and imagery.

*

Perhaps it's significant that I have no recollection of religious input in the more progressive classrooms at Bearsden and the new Westerton school. In contrast, at Carluke Primary 'progressive' was not on the agenda. Our 'reading book' included the sentimental story of *Jackanapes* by Juliana Horatia Ewing, published in 1884 by the Society for Promoting Christian Knowledge. This story glorifies death in battle on behalf of your country: the boy nicknamed 'Jackanapes' manages to save a fellow-soldier at the cost of his own life and the sermon at his funeral service is on Jesus' words 'Whosoever will save his life shall lose it; and whosoever will lose his life for my sake shall find it'. (Matthew 16:25 AV)

*

Miss Angus knew how to use story to captivate us. I have never forgotten her description of the death of one of the Scottish Covenanters, John Brown of Priesthill in Ayrshire during the 'killing times': it moved me more than anything else I experienced in any school classroom. The Covenanters refused to compromise on the values of Presbyterianism and the Scottish Reformation. John Brown apparently had taken no part in the Covenanters' military rising: it is said that his only crime lay in refusing to go to hear the local Episcopalian curate preach. He was shot at the front door of his cottage on 1 May 1685 by government dragoons led by John Graham of Claverhouse while his pregnant wife and young children watched.

The story has it that before John Brown's death he turned to his wife, reminded her that he had warned her when proposing marriage that the time might come when he would be killed for his faith. 'Are you willing to part with me?' 'Heartily willing,' she replied. 'This is all I desire,' he said. 'I have nothing more to do than to die.' He then kissed his children, and Claverhouse himself fired the fatal shot. I suspect this moved me so much because I identified with the courageous outcast, loyal to Christ, and saw myself standing there as the gun was raised.

I knew that those of us who met at Allander Hall and Martin Memorial Baptist Church were special, like John Brown's family. Once when I was eight or nine I stood in Westerton Church, just across the road from the school, with my mother. Perhaps there had been a school service. It seemed normal enough, but I knew something which my classmates did not – there was a deficiency in the hearts of those who worshipped there. God was not as delighted with them as he was with those of us who met round the table weekly. In fact he was perhaps not delighted with them at all.

This sense of ecclesiastical superiority was not something I was specifically taught but an assumption I made in the light of what I heard. Unhelpful in itself this attitude also served to distance me from my peers.

*

During most of my childhood I had no problems with what my parents, and our church, considered to be 'worldly'.

This thinking was based on Jesus' comment about his followers: 'They are not of the world, even as I am not of it.' (John 17:16) By 'the world', I suppose Jesus had in mind beliefs, philosophies, behaviours and systems which, he discerned, did not spring from an openness to God. He and (on their better days) his followers knew themselves at home in a different, spiritual environment, the kingdom of God.

The Christians I was surrounded with as a child sought to reflect this 'Christian difference' in their living. Human nature being what it is some Christians, perhaps those with little personal sense of oneness with God, sought to crystallize 'worldliness' in a list of practices which should be avoided – and then often used this list to pass judgement on others. In retrospect I can see that my parents were not particularly strict.

Christians didn't drink (we had a friend who gave up a secure post in a grocery firm because his conscience would not allow him to sell alcohol), or smoke, or use bad language, or go to football matches, the theatre or the cinema. In this area too, St Paul's instructions to women were taken very seriously: 'I also want the women to dress modestly, with decency and propriety, adorning themselves, not with elaborate hairstyles or gold or pearls or expensive clothes.' (1 Timothy 2:9) Makeup if used at all should be applied sparingly.

I had the impression that much on television was considered to be 'worldly': we didn't own a set during the Westerton years. Far from feeling deprived I sensed a smug-hearted superiority. We acquired our first TV shortly after moving to Carluke. The excuse was that it was for educational purposes, but soon I was sitting by the fireside at teatime watching cartoons as I ate.

I was allowed to attend a Halloween party in the corrugated iron community hall in Westerton. I recall us all thumping on the table with our fists, repeatedly chanting 'We want grub!' Running with the crowd I cast inhibitions to the wind and chanted more loudly than most; I recall bursting for a pee, and hanging on because I was afraid to slip from the table and scuttle along the dark corridor to find the loo.

I remember especially the costume my mother made for me. I was dressed as a wizard, my robe fashioned from an old pink curtain, my spectacular pointy hat made of black cardboard, and shiny tinfoil. In future years my mother was apologetic. 'I shouldn't have sent you as a wizard,' she fretted. 'I didn't realise at the time.' Clearly, thirty-five years before Harry Potter, wizards were less 'worldly' (or other-worldly!) than they became.

As for the other items on the list of proscribed activities, having no desire to do any of them, I felt not in the least deprived. I was allowed to engage freely in the things I most relished.

*

I loved reading. There was a small branch library in the Halloween party wizard hall but to feed my own and my mother's voracious hunger for books we regularly drove up the hill and along Canniesburn Road to Hillfoot Library. Each visit, I'd borrow the maximum quota of four volumes, come home and devour them, two or three a day – Enid Blyton, Franklin W. Dixon, Stephen Mogridge, Malcolm Saville.

At Carluke I borrowed from the cramped public library in the front room of the Rankin Memorial Town Hall, the children's section of which I mined with indiscriminate zest. On at least one occasion I had finished the books I'd borrowed in the morning before the time the library closed: it was only with difficulty that I persuaded the curmudgeonly librarian to let me use my cards more than once on the same day.

I remember sitting in bed one night, finishing a story and closing the book with an existential sense of loss – it was as if I were wistfully bidding forever farewell to a familiar country. I picked up the next title from my pile, opened it and found the early pages dry and uninspiring compared with the world I had just left. And yet I knew that as I persevered, this unexplored territory too would become a beloved landscape.

When I was 9, Mr Dunlop from next door lent me *Sink the Bismarck*. (It was not, I was pleased to see, a 'cadet' edition – I viewed with scorn the publishers' condescension in issuing for children these bowdlerised versions of popular works.) I read it avidly. But I remember Mr Dunlop turning up on the doorstep (perhaps sent round by Mrs D) to say to my parents that he hoped they were OK with my having the book. But even if they had objected, it was too late – I'd reached the final page.

*

There was no restriction on my listening to the homely Childrens' Hour on the BBC Home Service, the popular serials with titles like *The long journey*, *Joanna in jeopardy*, and the novel adaptation *Blast-off* at *Woomera*. I'd listen to its theme music from Stravinsky's *Firebird* with a shiver of anticipation. I remember a weekly voice intoning solemnly 'The Hobbit, by J. R. R Tolkien, read by David Davis', but at that point Middle Earth failed to capture my imagination.

I remember finding out about a new show on the radio called *Just Jazz*. In my innocence I imagined this probably featured a cute cuddly animal called 'Jazz', and I tuned in hopefully. When it began I knew immediately that I shouldn't be listening, even before I saw the disapproval on my mother's face. In this case, it may have been not so much that the show was 'worldly' as that it was, in my mother's ears, not 'good music' – which came to much the same thing. I did not question her judgement. Oddly though, I remember being allowed to listen to a music request show, and at least once wrote in and then listened in vain to hear my name mentioned.

When I was ill in bed, the radio was brought upstairs and placed on a chair by my bedside. I was able to listen to whatever I wanted. The songs and prayers on the *Morning Service* I found alien to my experience of worship; schools broadcasts such as *Music and Movement* bored me. *Mrs Dale's Diary* and *Afternoon Theatre* were more stimulating to my fever-clouded mind. I still remember that knife going into the teacher's back as he sat in a canvas chair during the school sports; and the story set on a farm which ended up with the words 'he smashed it with his little hammer', which left me, unable to take too much reality, with a sense of wistful melancholy.

*

I didn't hear much classical music in childhood, though I remember the thrill of listening to the *Hallelujah Chorus* for the first time: a 78rpm recording frenetically whirling on grandpa John's radiogram. The pile of classical music beside the piano which mum had inherited from her music teacher Chrissy Potts was largely untouched. On the music stand was a copy of the *Golden Bells* hymn book, and, ubiquitous in Scottish evangelical homes, the tartan-covered song book produced for evangelist Billy Graham's 1955 Kelvin Hall mission in Glasgow. I wonder if my mother had formed the impression that excellent though the classics might be, playing them professionally would somehow be 'worldly'.

By our early years in Carluke, I had concluded that pop music was not simply musically inferior to the classics, but considered 'worldly' by all true Christians. Hence, in listening to it you would both be indicating a lack of true spiritual commitment and exposing yourself to a baleful influence. (Although there wasn't too much concern about the kind of innocuous pop you heard at the barbers at the foot of Carluke High Street on a Saturday morning where the radio played *My Ol' Man's a Dustman*, *Puff the Magic Dragon* and similar songs. No one overthought what the 'magic dragon' in question might represent.)

My parents subscribed me to Arthur Mee's *Children's Newspaper*, then in its dying days. One week it featured an early picture of the Beatles, decently scrubbed-up, on the front page. By then Paul and I knew what 'Sluvsyah' meant. My father looked at the photograph. 'What very strange young men,' he pronounced.

*

'This is one for you,' said Leslie Steele's dad when *I believe* came on the car radio one Saturday. In that moment I hated being different. I was embarrassed both at this reference to my family's religious beliefs, and by the fact that *I believe* didn't seem to me to be sufficiently holy in style or content to win approval from *true* Christians.

*

But there were no parental objections to my attending when a theatre company came to Carluke Primary and set up what must have been a very simple stage at the end of the central hall, with curtains suspended from a metal framework. They gave a version of *Pinocchio*. I had never before seen a theatrical performance, and I was entranced by the story playing out a few feet away from my eager eyes, my wonder growing with each extension of the anti-hero's nose.

*

Different rules applied on Sundays: the first day of the week was special, to be set apart for God. In fact the day was so busy with God-stuff that there wasn't time for much else: off to Milngavie for the morning meeting; home for lunch; back for Sunday School; home for tea; then, when I was old enough there was yet another sortie to the Gospel Service in the early evening. Occasionally we were invited to spend the day at someone's house.

When I was at home it was understood that the radio was to be listened to very sparingly and that 'Sunday books' should be read. I had a rather off-putting edition of *Pilgrim's Progress*, which I received as a Sunday School prize. This pilgrim, finding nothing in its densely-packed pages to connect with reality as he knew it, made little progress. Other Sunday-School prizes were either Victorian moral children's books such as Amy le Feuvre's *Teddy's Button*, originally published in 1896, or various more contemporary attempts to express Christian faith in the context of an Enid Blyton-style storyline. I felt just a little embarrassed at the overt evangelicalism of such titles – reasonable stories spoiled by intrusive sermonizing.

*

These restrictions helped me define who I thought I was in comparison, for example, with those who attended Westerton Church and wouldn't have been told by their minister just how particular God was about your approach to life.

I recall sitting in the car with mum and dad at the age of about of 11, dumbfounded by my discovery that the library book I was reading expressed ideas and used language which would not have been out of place in a Sunday School prize book. It seemed to have been written by one of us! (It may, I think have been Patricia St John's *Treasures of the Snow*.) 'This story mentions Jesus!' I said in puzzlement. What was Jesus doing in a *library* book? What was a Christian story doing in 'the world'?

Yet I was zealous in policing my parents' behaviour: it's clear that my understanding of 'the rules' was much stricter than theirs.

When I was ten mum and dad told me early in December that there was to be a special treat round about Christmas. We walked to the Post Office one dark autumn afternoon just before tea and posted a letter which I was given to understand was in some way connected with the delight to come. One Saturday morning a couple of weeks later they told me the day had arrived and unveiled the mystery. 'We're going to the circus at the Kelvin Hall!' I remember the stomach-piercing stab of pain as, utterly confused, I slid off my chair on to the carpet, taking refuge beneath the table. 'But Christians don't go to the circus!' I protested. 'It's *worldly*.'

Had they been wiser, my parents could have replied along the lines of: 'We're so, so sorry if anything we've said or done has given you that impression, but it's wrong. God is really enthusiastic about circuses. So let's go along and see what it's like.' But in fact they took me to the shops instead and bought me a plastic Airfix station for my electric train set to make up for the disappointment of the treat which wasn't, and that afternoon there were three empty seats in the Kelvin Hall Arena. I glued my station together, a little sadly, but confirmed in my rectitude.

It was as though I had taught my parents a lesson. Perhaps they thought I was a difficult child, but from my perspective I was simply refusing to take the chance of stepping on the platform of any bus other than a number 13.

*

The weekly 'Gospel Service' at both Gospel Hall and Baptist Church featured an earnest sermon exhorting hearers to come to personal faith in Jesus Christ accompanied by songs from another venerable hymn book *Sankey's Sacred Songs and Solos*. This personal response to Christ was central to the evangelicalism my parents espoused,

I would have known about the death and resurrection of Jesus Christ and would have heard the call to personal faith. In my early years as far as I remember I believed, simply and unquestioningly. I don't recall feeling in any way pressurized while at Westerton to 'get saved' or to 'become a Christian.'

And yet I was always aware of the expectation, always sensed that the faith I had was inadequate. One evening I was sitting on mum's knee in front of a winter fire, my head on her shoulder, the light in the room switched off; I suspect it was a Sunday evening and dad was out at the Gospel Service. On that occasion I felt secure. Mum encouraged me to pray, and we said (or sang) the words of a chorus inviting Jesus to enter my heart and make it his home.

When the sound had died away, I admitted to myself, 'I don't feel any different! Nothing has happened!' But soon my puzzlement dissolved in sleepiness.

But this expectation that I would be 'saved' or 'converted' and the teaching that without this spiritual revolution there was no escape from judgement in hell weighed on me heavily at Carluke.

One Sunday when I was perhaps eleven or twelve we were in our Sunday-School class, about half-a-dozen boys in the corner beneath one of the tall windows at the back of the church. Our teacher had an exercise for us, he said, prompted no doubt by the American evangelical teaching manual which he and his colleagues used. At first he intended setting this task as homework, and I've often wondered if it would have made any difference to what followed had I had the opportunity of doing what was asked of me in a more reflective and less pressured way.

But he changed his mind. 'We'll do it now,' he said, handing out pencils and paper. 'I want you to write down for me when you became a Christian, and how.' I sat miserably, my blank sheet of paper on the hymn-book rest in front of me. Around me, the other children seemed to be scribbling furiously, but I felt I'd nothing to say. Eventually I wrote describing with perfect honesty matters as I understood them, 'I am not yet a Christian although I would like to be one'. I handed in my sheet of paper, feeling embarrassed and somehow humiliated, and the lesson was over.

I don't recall what I said to my parents; I do remember a knock on the back door a few days later. It was the Sunday School teacher. I lurked in the living room, refusing to see him, and after talking to my parents for a while he went away. Thereafter I was adamant that I wasn't going back to Sunday School (one of the few things I remember being stubborn about as a child). Perhaps because I was too reserved or ashamed to share what I was thinking, or because I feared my parents' reaction, I was never able to talk openly about this experience which for me was traumatic.

*

I didn't want to run with the crowd onto the waiting buses. I wanted to follow the way of life to which I believed my parents were called. I sought a way of validation through adherence to the rules, perhaps because I felt somehow unable to experience conversion. But the clouds were gathering as I hovered on the cusp of puberty. I was ill-prepared for adolescence, already struggling with the barriers I had erected between me and my peers, waiting for a number 13 bus which never came.

THREE

THE TUFTY CLUB AND THE BILLOWING GOWN

As I look back with compassion and some amusement at my Wishaw High School years I think the place to begin is with the Tufty Club. To my chagrin, I realized in my first few days at the school that I was eminently nicknamable. At Carluke Primary I'd been known for obvious orthodontic reasons as Bugs Bunny, but I seldom felt this was said maliciously. Indeed, the moniker 'Rabbit' dropped like a sweet benediction from one girl, Christine Odger's lips. But before I'd been at High School a week I had at least seven nicknames until the consensus settled on Tufty after the road-safety promoting squirrel. Whether I more resembled cartoon bunny or risk-averse rodent was immaterial: what mattered was the malice with which the word was sneered. 'Can we join the Tufty Club?' the mocking voices chorused. 'Certainly,' I replied equably, a passive defence.

There were small physical violences as well, unpredictable, so that you were constantly anxious, constantly over-alert. The hands grabbing your sides as you went upstairs in a file of boys, seizing your shirt and pulling it out of your trousers; the rough shove in the back when you stood at the foul urinal trying to relax enough to pee or worse when you were in mid-stream. I wonder if I'm exaggerating this bullying but recently, someone, a fellow-pupil at the time said, without prompting 'I don't know how you survived!'

It didn't occur to me to take any action against this. Perhaps I felt it was unavoidable given my personality, or worse that I deserved it. The psychological war of attrition seemed all-pervasive. The fisticuffs which tamed Alex Lippiatt would be futile against this hoard. There were no guidance staff in those days: to whom would I have gone? And of course, ashamed, I kept quiet at home.

*

I spent six years at Wishaw High, travelling by bus from Carluke. At lunchtime on my first day at the school, in August 1964, I escaped from the cacophonous dinner hall and found my way to Woolworths in Main Street where I bought a cheap plastic toy seeking a lost simplicity. Later, back home I sat in the security of the rocking chair beside the living room window. Looking across the quiet garden, I learned the verb conjugations on the first page of *Approach to Latin*. 'Amo, Amas, Amat…..'

The High School still had a Christian ethos: hymns were sung and prayers said at the regular assemblies in the octagonal hall; there were Christmas and Easter Services at the Old Parish Church; on that first morning our registration teacher, as new to the school as we were, gave us 1 Corinthians 13 in the then-standard Authorised version to learn over the next few days. Mr Annand made half-hearted attempts to continue these calls to Scripture memorisation but finally gave up due to the lack of compliance and perhaps a realisation that none of his colleagues did anything other than mark the register during the short period which began the day. I was surprised when a trainee teacher in the English department told us she didn't believe in God. It was the first time I'd knowingly encountered an atheist.

Of our teachers I have a mosaic of memories. Only one was outstanding, most were simply passable. Some were dubiously eccentric (take the technical drawing teacher who instructed the small boy guilty of some minor misdemeanor to stand in front of the class and pretend he was about to leap off a 100-foot ladder into a damp towel: when the victim had taken up position, he would be thwacked across the backside with a T-square). Some were incompetent (such was the history teacher who marched up and down his classroom year by weary year dictating unvarying notes relating to the Higher History curricululm, never encouraging discussion, further reading, or critical thinking).

The principal teacher of English George Brown, who had taught my parents at Airdrie Academy, managed in my case to make Higher English less than inspirational. In his teaching (though not in personal reading, for his classroom shelves were lined with editions of modern poets) English literature came to a halt around 1900. I appreciate I was very immature with little life experience and that therefore the fault possibly lay with me, but in his class I found allegedly great poems and plays irrelevant and uninspiring. Certainly he gave me scant guidance in preparing for the Certificate of Sixth Year Studies (CSYS) exam, in particular the creative writing element. I enthusiastically wrote long essays for him but received little constructive criticism other than his note at the end of an impassioned piece about attending a Scottish National Orchestra concert 'Write a little less and a little larger. Avoid polysyllabic words and phrases.' But perhaps I thought I knew all there was to know about writing – hadn't stories and poems appeared frequently for two years under my name in the *Glasgow Herald*'s Saturday Extra column?

Being published in the paper and paid for my work was almost the only thing which gave me some validation as a teenager. Occasionally I managed a powerful line as, when writing in *Jungle Rules OK* about gangland Glasgow (of which I had zero experience) I referred to 'the restless conscript of the night'. But the majority of my pieces were typical products of an angst-ridden teenager with literary pretensions: grim, judgemental texts, reflecting fears about Soviet aggression, nuclear holocaust, and extreme cynicism about human nature. There was in these pieces little beauty, joy or wonder.

I liked Maurice Kemp Bonner in the history department. He certainly inspired me, though I'm not sure of the wisdom of his permitting me one 'Dempsterism' per period in S1. 'Dempsterisms' were inane jokes such as my unhelpful translation of 'Magna Carta' as 'big cart'. If I exceeded the daily quota, I was belted. Mr Bonner also encouraged my writing. When I wrote a piece of doggerel about the 1966 General Election he typed it up and pinned it to the notice board in the open-to-the-elements corridor, where it fluttered in the wind for a few brief moments before the Rector's decisive hand removed it.

I'd meet Maurice on his way back to the staffroom from the canteen and show him my latest effusion. He enjoyed *Boadicea* an (extremely) sub-Shakespearian drama inspired by an early chapter in Churchill's *History of the English Speaking Peoples* – I didn't read any further. But 'Write about ordinary things!' Maurice encouraged me.

'I've done a poem about a television aerial,' I told him a few days later.

'Excellent,' he said.

I rather think he would have changed his mind when he scanned the first line – 'Wrought, not by aesthete's subtle style….'

I rather liked Robert Craig, head of classics, irascible, but kindly. In the Higher Latin prelim I scored 47%. Mr Craig relegated everyone who got less than me to a lower class but kept me in the A stream, and nurtured my Latin skills. I responded by regaling him with my translations of Virgil into English verse.

I was studying during a free period in Robert's classroom where two older girls were doing revision beneath the window. One of them went to a Brethren church and so I knew she must be a good Christian. She and her friend were discussing a magazine article of which the subject, I overheard, was 'sexercises'. I was both shocked and gleeful that such a word should fall from such holy lips.

When I went to say goodbye to Robert Craig at the end of S6 he wished me well. Then he opened his bookcase, withdrew a small volume from it and gave it to me as a momento. It was a 1920s edition of A. E. Housman's *A Shropshire Lad*, and I treasured it.

The outstanding teacher was Mr Mason in the English Department. He sat me up at the back left corner of the classroom, calling me 'Dempster' for he addressed all boys by their surname. At the diagonally opposite corner just in front of Mr Mason's desk sat Yvonne M. Davis, whom I rather fancied and for whom I wrote a poem about a snowy day beginning, uninspiringly 'It blizzarded; you gaped'. I thought fancying her was rather daring because her father, or so I gathered, kept a pub in Caledonian Road.

'Persevere with the opening pages,' Mr Mason insisted when he passed round rather nondescript copies of D. K. Broster's *Flight of the Heron*. 'I'm not interested in *birds*,' I thought scornfully. But I persevered, and enjoyed, and soon had read the whole trilogy.

One memorable afternoon in S3 Mr Mason played a recording of John Betjeman reading his own work. This was the poet speaking, the very man from whom the words had come. 'Miss Joan Hunter Dunn, Miss Joan Hunter Dunn.' For the very first time, I realised that poetry could be about ordinary experiences, and use ordinary words.

Betjeman would never be guilty of that 'aesthete's subtle style'.

I bought his collected poems, and his verse autobiography *Summoned by Bells*. I loved the lines 'An only child, deliciously apart, misunderstood and not like other boys'. (My mother was doubtful about this phrase when I read it to her – I could tell she interpreted the line as implying that Betjeman was gay. She clearly hadn't heard of Joan Hunter Dunn. But she said nothing, and nor did I.)

In S1, Mr Mason organised an evening's entertainment. Some of my schoolmates with thespian inclinations performed a few scenes from *Pygmalion*. I was one of another group who gave a presentation entitled *Songs and poems of the First World War*.

We sang a selection of wartime songs ('Brother Bertie went away to do his bit the other day....'). I remember Mr Mason mischievously pausing in dictating the words of *Mademoiselle from Armentiers* after 'Who was it tied his kilts with string, to stop him from doing...' We had a few seconds to reflect on possible salacious conclusions to the sentence before the voice continued prosaically '...the Highland Fling'. Between the songs, some of us read verse. I tackled Wilfred Owen's *Anthem for doomed youth*, fell in love with the War Poets and wrote about them in my CSYS Dissertation.

There were two occasions, vulnerable times, when I felt particularly wounded by teachers although their reactions were completely reasonable.

'Granny' Young, the history teacher who in the days before the guidance system was responsible for the general pastoral care of the girls (she was known to measure the distance from the hem of a skirt to the floor to ensure it adhered to regulations) organised a Christmas Fayre one December Saturday and was looking for helpers.

I was enthusiastic, yearning to be part of something. I volunteered and took the bus to Wishaw ridiculously early arriving at the school door at least an hour before anyone was there to open up.

Miss Young gave me basic training, and then put me behind a table of bric-a-brac with permission to accept offers lower than the stated price. The doors were opened to the public. I stood there nervously as adults streamed in to the school hall.

Someone offered me a low price on a piece of merchandise. 'Yes, yes,' I said too shy to haggle. 'Thank you.'

'Granny' Young remonstrated with me when she heard what I had let the object go for. If her words were followed by encouraging guidance for managing future transactions, I was deaf to them.

At the first opportunity I slipped out of the building and make for the bus stop.

One snowy day when I was in S6 I headed across the blaze pitch to a hutted classroom, early for a history lesson. The teacher was there, but when I tried the handle the door wouldn't open. I knocked, expecting he would unlock it and let me in as he had done on previous occasions. But he ignored the importunate senior on the top doorstep. By then I'd been spotted and relentlessly targetted snowballs were deluging. I gave one last futile rattle at the handle before turning and walking towards the main building, mentally distancing myself from reality as the missiles thudded vindictively into face and head and body.

The Tufty Club gatekeeper forever excluded.

*

But there's another revealing story besides that of my nickname – the one, both comic and sad, about the Billowing Gown.

One afternoon 1A2 were sitting in Room 3 awaiting the arrival of our Latin teacher, 'Goof' Lindsay, a gentle man with a stutter, no match for mischief. He didn't show, and the hubbub grew.

'I'm going to tell the Rector,' I said eventually.

'Oh come on,' my classmates rolled their eyes.

But I knew what was right and traipsed along the corridor to the Rector's office. At that point its occupant was the formidable, grey-haired, black-gowned war hero, Mr Neil McKellar.

I knocked, in my rectitude without fear.

Soon I was trotting along smugly behind the black gown as it billowed impressively in the direction of poor 'Goof's' classroom.

I re-took my seat in a glow of righteousness.

I had been brought up to Do the Right thing and to Stick by the Rules and spent my High School years seeking to follow those rules with legalistic determination while learning, though ever so hesitantly, that rules could actually be broken. The most binding rules were those I learned in a Christian context because of course those rules were God-given.

Though I still had no precise definition of the 'worldliness' I had been so aware of when younger and my parents and I never discussed the subject in detail, as a teenager I still believed that certain behaviours were acceptable in the life of the Christian and others not. Knowing to which category a particular action belonged was at times perplexing. My views were based on sermons and magazine articles and casual comments from parents and others.

But it remained absolutely clear to me that avoiding 'worldliness' was central to Christian living, at home, and especially in our daily contact with 'the world,' which in my case as a teenager centred on Wishaw High School. My worldliness antenna was in overdrive and I sought refuge behind the billowing gown of conformity. Was this legalism a way of proving (to myself as much as to others) that I conformed to my church's expectations despite knowing nothing of the emotional uplift of belief? I did not realise I was suppressing the 'me' who struggled to show his face. I sought to be who I was expected to be while also taking refuge in in oddity and difference, in an eccentric persona. I was the boy who, according to my mockers swallowed dictionaries for breakfast. And when I did have opportunities to break free, I scarcely knew how.

*

Dancing, I knew, was to be avoided as 'the vertical expression of horizontal desire,' although I never heard this from my parents. With a self-righteousness which legitimised my fear of involvement in social events I insisted that I be excused from the dancing practices to which PE periods were devoted in the weeks before Christmas. And of course I shunned the annual school dances. Rather than gently challenging this extreme view my parents supported me. They may have considered they were charitably allowing me to make my own decisions but I viewed their support as an indication of agreement with me.

The PE teacher Jock Bonomy looked at me and shook his head with a wry grin as the boys in my class arrived for dance practice. He handed me paper and pencil and set me to work sitting in the locker room as the *Gay Gordons* wafted through from the sports hall, writing an essay explaining my non-involvement.

I poured out my justification for avoiding vertical expressions in order to protect myself from horizontal desires using very florid phraseology which no doubt provoked gales of laughter in the staff room.

It was some consolation to me that I suspected one other girl, a Brethren lass was sitting out the dance-practice in the mirror-image locker room beyond the sinning dancers.

I have never subsequently learned to dance, lacking freedom to abandon myself to the rhythm.

*

I didn't know how to play cards which I considered dubious if not downright evil; I didn't smoke; I looked with horror at a stretched-out palm offering me a purple heart; I was uncomfortable with bulletins recounting Saturday night encounters in the back row of the local fleapit.

But my legalism had its limits. When Geordie Barr gleefully pointed to a salacious paragraph in his well-thumbed copy of *Fanny Hill* in the boy's lines, I sanctimoniously averted my gaze, but not before quickly (not too quickly, though) scanning the awakening secrets on the page.

'Why don't you ask your father what Durex is?' my mockers suggested.

'Oh, it's paint, isn't it?' I replied with false brightness.

*

Attending the cinema was definitely 'out' – I don't think either of my parents had ever known the pleasure of sitting in the darkness watching an alternative world unfold on the screen.

It wasn't simply that our Christian faith and our moral integrity might be undermined by what we saw. We might be strong enough to keep standing despite the worst excesses of MGM. Miss Taylor, after all, may have provoked shock, but there was also a quiet admiration among the saints at Allander Hall when she took herself off to see *Ben Hur*. But giving ourselves permission to go to the cinema might encourage others who lacked our spiritual strength or perceptiveness to follow in our wake: for any consequences in their lives the argument went, we would be held responsible by God.

But (oh joy!) I discovered that visits to the cinema were permissible if they were educationally justifiable and I joined a group of fellow-pupils watching Christopher Plummer in *Oedipus Rex* in the Cosmo cinema just off Glasgow's Sauchiehall Street sometime in 1968. I confess that Sophocles's noble lines went over my head. But we stayed for the B picture which was a spy thriller called *Charade* starring Cary Grant and Audrey Hepburn. I watched this, the first mass-market film I had ever seen, with unalloyed delight.

But theatres, associated in my mind with hedonism and loose-living were be shunned. When I was in S6 a teacher arranged a class visit to see Nyrée Dawn Porter (what a delicious, sensuous name, I thought) in Shaw's *St Joan* at the King's Theatre in Glasgow. Could I go I asked, no longer so rigid in my convictions but still, even at 17 thirled to my parents' wishes.

'You can go this time, John,' mum said. 'But don't let it give you *a taste for the theatre.*'

*

Wishaw High was invited to send delegates to an inter-school Burns' Supper and a few of us from the Debating Society agreed to go. Someone had to speak, and I composed a very poor parody of *Tam O'Shanter* for the occasion, beginning 'Oor Tam wiz in the Railway Inn'.

I told my parents about this, and my attendance was forbidden – presumably there were concerns about alcohol, though I doubt if any would have been served at the event.

Weakly, I had no thought of rebellion but I agonised over admitting this set-back at school.

I copped out, said nothing, and on the day pretended to be sick and unable to go.

Yvonne M. Davis read my poem for me.

It was well-received, she said later.

*

The concept of worldliness also affected my attitude to friendships. I had friends at school – Colin Menzies and Gregor Anderson who reached out to me almost from my first day at Wishaw High and a number of others – but always aware of a barrier between us I felt unable to draw really close to them, or to be open with them. I was more at home with George Cringles whom I knew was a Christian, but even with him I was not particularly open. Not knowing myself I had nothing genuine to share. Not liking myself, I imagined that others would see me as I saw myself. 'But we liked you, John!' Colin told me recently.

Behind my reserve lay shyness, a sense of being (not so 'deliciously') apart, and introversion, but it was also my belief that it was the Christian's duty not to get too close to people who because they did not share faith as my church interpreted it were deemed to be 'in the world' and hence might have sidetracked me into 'worldliness'. How arrogantly I assumed that these friends had no beliefs worth considering!

As a consequence of this attitude I have very few memories of encounters with others through which I felt encouraged and nurtured.

I took part in a public speaking competition organised by the Motherwell Gavel Club when I was in S4 at which I lectured on the grim theme 'Wolves in society'. I didn't win: a younger boy from another local school was more eloquent, cogent and confident than me. (I think the same boy won the year before, when I had spoken on 'The Nagging Ennui'.) But there was a senior Wishaw High School pupil from Carluke at the event and we got the bus home together. I was surprised and a little embarrassed by his supportiveness – he got off the bus at my stop and walked with me as I went home. As far as I know he had no motive other than to encourage me in my sadness at not coming first. I sensed a blessing in his presence and was grateful for that though I can't recall our ever speaking again.

At around the same time, I was often joined on my early bus to Wishaw by three siblings – Arthur, Marion and Linda Parker. I realise looking back how at home and affirmed I felt in their company, particularly with Linda who was a year younger than me and with whom I walked from the bus stop to the school building. In retrospect, I can see I had something very special in that friendship.

*

When it came to girls, there was an additional challenge on top of all the others holding me back from forming close relationships. It was the understanding that I should only go out with Christian girls, and that the one girl whom God had chosen to be my wife would definitely be a believer.

The first time I was conscious of sexual awakening was on holiday in Northumbria where I saw a group of schoolgirls about my own age in gingham dresses standing in the sunshine outside Alnwick Castle. As we walked past, I noted with interest how my eyes were drawn to them and I felt a strange restlessness. Then there was the rather forward girl

I met when my parents and I were at the Windsor Hotel in Nairn and she was also a guest. She taught me chopsticks on the piano in the guests' lounge. One night when I went to bed I found it had been apple pie'd – the bottom sheet folded up so that I couldn't get my legs to the foot of the bed without remaking it. She must have slipped in through the unlocked door earlier in the day. Deeply sad on the morning her family and mine were leaving I asked her for her address and wrote it on the back page of one of the paperbacks I was loading into the car – she came from Burnley. But I knew even as I wrote that I would never contact her. I wasn't brave enough and besides, she was probably not a believer.

As we drove down to Fort William where we were staying for a night on the way home, I pined for this lost, unacknowledged love. Not for the first time, I reached across the car seat to the empty side, and fantasised that a sister was sitting there behind my father. I was confused as to the object of my longing.

For a while Bairds Department store in Wishaw Main Street had a display of grey school skirts just outside the restaurant entrance. (I went there for most of my school career to have a more tranquil lunch in the restaurant than the school could offer.) Passing the skirts, I hesitated, my eyes resting on them, my hand almost reaching out. I fantasized about buying one and taking it home.

No one had ever told me about masturbation and when I tried it instinctively on top of my bed with a pillow and a toilet roll tube my surprise and consternation as I came outweighed any sense of pleasure. I leapt up when I realized what was happening, and spilled the semen on the carpet. I tried to clean up the evidence with a hair brush liberally sprinkling aftershave to mask the strange new odour. I cringed fearfully when my mother came in to kiss me good-night, feigning normality while afraid her eyes would be drawn to the damp patch beneath her feet. I was more circumspect in future, but the guilt troubled me.

I was attracted other girls in my class besides Yvonne M. Davis – notably, Alice C. R. Wright (I loved those initials and the dated feel to the names they represented) who sat across the aisle from me in history. I was drawn to the curve of the petite breasts beneath her pale blue shirt. She wrote in her jotter in ink with fastidious neatness. I began mimicking her italic script. One year, I sent her a Valentine card anonymously, dropping it with trembling hand into the pillar box beside the flats in the Main Street. Its origin must have been obvious – I received a card in return. The poem inside began 'Don't make love in the cornfield' which embarrassed me. I had no thought of making love anywhere. That was the end of my tentative flirting. Except that I've never since then used joined-up writing.

Alice was a fellow-member of the Debating Society committee and we were good friends on a fairly superficial level. Some of S6 went to a Scottish National Orchestra prom in Glasgow – nervous about getting caught short on the bus, I didn't go. But when I heard later that Alice had sat on the floor in the prom area back to back with Gregor Anderson, shoulder against shoulder with only thin linen shirts between his skin and hers I was profoundly, yearningly jealous.

And then there was Helen Arbuckle from Hutchison's Grammar School in Glasgow, whom I knew was a believer. Our families were attending the annual Scottish Christian Medical Fellowship weekend conference at Crieff Hydro which took place each November. We young people mucked around the hotel while our folks were at the conference sessions which took place in the Hydro's massive lounge equipped with a pipe organ. I was jealous of the easy friendship of these kids from different medical families despite their willingness to let me run with the pack.

Helen was lovely, and droll and probably like every other boy she ever met I liked her a lot. For some reason on the Sunday afternoon while the conference was winding up in the lounge on the other side of the great windows, she and I stood side by side on the open balcony, looking out towards the hills and forests of Perthshire. I said nothing and did nothing and the moment of stillness quickly passed. I sat in the back seat of the car on the way home, words and lust writhing in my head. When we arrived in our cold, sad house, I grabbed a piece of paper and wrote a poem beginning *Myself, and Her, and Silence Eloquent*, lines of febrile longing which imposed on the brief co-incidence of our standing together a deeper meaning which was altogether in my imagination. It was published in the *Glasgow Herald* and earned me 10s 6d and I wondered if she had read it. Once again, I had lacked courage. That silence was mine to break.

'Oh yes, I have a girl-friend,' I'd sometimes say at school. 'She's called Helen and she lives in Glasgow.' I found this fable relieved the pressure I felt to engage romantically with girls at school – or gave me an excuse not to?

But there was a younger girl from a Carluke church whom I increasingly came to notice. She was quiet and gentle and I liked it when she was close to me in the bus queue. I wrote a poem for her but I didn't show it to her and I said nothing. Not even that afternoon when going home from an event in Motherwell at the end of the school day I got off the bus and waited at the stop outside the Old Parish Church in Wishaw just so that I would be there when she came out of school.

All these longings fed into the best of my writing for Saturday Extra My hand was Jimmy's hand as he encountered Lesley's warm fingers in the bag of peppermints they shared in *First and Last True Love*. And I know who I was thinking of when I had the Nadia-obsessed narrator in *Finding the Secret of Eternal Life* tell us that he stood at the organ, 'touched the stops that she had touched, and ran my fingers over the keys, and envied them'.

*

My memories of schooldays are coloured by unacknowledged anxiety, introversion and struggles with worldliness. So tenaciously did I project the bombastic persona that I sometimes believed it was my true self. In my later years at school, I loved the Debating Society of which I became President. It gave me a front for the persona allowing me to display my verbal pyrotechnics: it provided a role, a platform, an audience, affirmation, a hope of future significance.

*

At the start of S6, Sid Laird in the music department indicated that he was planning putting on another Gilbert and Sullivan show in June 1970.

I was involved in all the conversations and talked at home about the plans to perform *HMS Pinafore*. Daringly I didn't ask for permission to participate but in time it became obvious to my parents that I was committed to the show. I sang in the chorus line – and in one performance led the whole ensemble disastrously astray through a loudly-voiced mis-timing. I also understudied the romantic lead's part: to my great relief my friend James McGonigle was able to continue playing Ralph Rackstraw even though his leg was in plaster after he broke it a few days before the show took to the stage.

I think mum and dad were a little uneasy but I assured them that Barbara Kirkland from a good Brethren family was taking a starring role as Little Buttercup, so it must be acceptable. My parents came along to one of the performances at Coltness Primary School as did my grandparents John and Phemie Dempster. Their presence, both of them Brethren stalwarts by that time, somehow validated my involvement. It was OK. It really was OK.

I didn't go to the final night party – too worldly, I felt, too wild, a rebellion I didn't even want to make – and as I took off my costume and makeup for the last time I felt that though I had been up there on the stage with the others, somehow I was detached, not really part of the proceedings.

*

'Can I join the Tufty Club? There's an irony in my peers addressing me as if I were a gatekeeper, for I wanted nothing more than a club to belong to, a confident billowing black gown to follow, a secure community of fellowship and positive regard. I did not find what I was looking for at school, and when in another world I prayed 'Can I join the Jesus Club?' that there was only silence.

The practice of Christianity was central to my life during my school years but as far as I can remember it was forever a burden and a reproach, and never a consolation.

FOUR

'I'VE GOT AN AGATHA CHRISTIE!'

I remember standing in a newsagents at Seahouses in Northumbria during one summer holiday in the mid-60s (was it the year of the girls in gingham at Alnwick?) I was asking my mother if it would be acceptable for me to purchase a detective story by Agatha Christie. Or was that, I wondered to myself, simply too 'worldly' to contemplate?

She said yes!

I bounded along the pavement back to our hotel clutching my new paperback, and chanting to myself in naïve delight 'I've got an Agatha Christie! I've got an Agatha Christie!'

It's unclear why this should have been such an issue at a time when I was regularly borrowing both fiction and non-fiction from Carluke Library.

*

I was about 15 and my mother was washing my hair in the bathroom sink. That she did this was a reflection both of her love and supportiveness, and her reluctance to encourage my independence.

That I let her do it showed a reluctance, or fearfulness to be my own man. There was concert on the radio which I'd positioned on the floor – some rather advanced piece was playing.

'You don't like that, do you?' mum said, referring to the music, as she vigorously towelled my hair.

'No,' I replied hesitantly.

Which was true. But I knew I would have appreciated being given the freedom to like it had I wished to. But I said nothing.

The struggle to detect worldliness, and to separate my parents' tastes from their religious principles took place in the safety of home as much as in the world of everyday life.

*

We watched television frequently but judiciously – news, children's programming, quiz shows. I enjoyed watching Sherlock Holmes dramatisations, which were permissible as they were 'classics', and the *Last Night of the Proms*. I sat through Verdi's *Aida* on BBC2 immersed in music and story.

But I sensed that to watch *The Man from Uncle* which folk were raving about at school would be a step too far.

And I found it difficult as a teenager to watch TV with my parents in case something appeared on the screen which they found unacceptable. *This Man Craig* was a drama series screened in 1966-67 in which Scottish actor John Cairney starred as Ian Craig a physics teacher in the fictional Scottish town of Strathaird. Together my parents and I had watched several episodes of this innocuous show without mishap but on one occasion the plot involved some teenagers attempting to persuade a mate to share some alcohol with them in a dark lane. This was enough for my father. He rose to his feet, and turned the television off, even as my mother was protesting 'But he's not going to drink it!' I found this cringe-worthy.

In this atmosphere the legalism which had rebuked my parents for planning a circus trip was still in play when I was a young teenager. One Christmas my father saw there was a film on TV set in Rangoon where he had been during his National Service, and sat down to watch it. I glimpsed the black-and-white images on the screen. 'But it's a *feature film*, dad, not a documentary. It's a story. You shouldn't be watching that.' Meekly, without comment and without using my wholly inappropriate intervention as a teaching opportunity my father turned off the television.

*

But mum and dad continued to encourage me in the three things closest to my heart – reading, classical music, and creative writing.

I was still pillaging the library shelves, reading biographies of writers, composers and engineers. I also read fiction, including many of Thomas Hardy's works. I was, I guess, reading in hope: these books were classics; such books were by some mysterious process of osmosis supposed to enrich you. But in time I came to realise that while I enjoyed a good story I didn't at that stage normally find my understanding deepened and my humanity enriched through reading fiction. One book however – John Buchan's *Witch Wood* which I read in an old, re-bound edition – touched me in some indefinable way as no other book did. I can only assume that I felt at home in its pages because of the spirit of sane Christian grace which coloured much of Buchan's writing.

*

Classical music, at least of the more serious kind, was not 'worldly' and was my second source of joy as a teenager. My parents signed up to the World Record Club, and bought a number of discs on a monthly basis. This was my introduction to classics such as Mendelssohn's

Midsummer Night's Dream and Beethoven's Sixth Symphony. My musical tastes were expanded by the Music For Pleasure range sold in Bairds store in Wishaw for 12s 6d. I bought Schubert's Great C Major Symphony, and Rachmaninov's Second, and Holst's *Planets*. (Walking back to school prominently clutching one of these albums enabled me to cultivate my eccentric persona – but one day when I had an album of piano concertos played by the pianist Solomon it drew the attention of another pupil, and that's how I met George Cringles who would be a long-term friend.) I discovered the annual Proms season broadcast nightly from London on Radio 3 and listened to many of them each summer, swaying back and forwards gently in the rocking chair in time to the rhythm. My thinking was stimulated by the grandeur of the music and to some extent I daydreamed along to it. Its beauty moved and transported me, and brought an inner touch of coherence and wholeness.

I realise now that I missed out through largely ignoring 'worldly' pop and rock music which would not have been welcome in the house. But classical music was definitely 'my music' not simply by choice but by disposition.

As I teenager I judged and never tired of telling people that Wagner's *Tannhauser* overture was 'the greatest piece of music ever written'. I was moved by the nobility of the Pilgrim theme but what truly thrilled me was the moment when very near the end, out of a chaos of orchestral texture the theme returns, swelling with increasing confidence and power until it blazes out triumphantly. Order from disorder. It was for exactly the same reason that I was thrilled by Britten's *Young Person's Guide to the Orchestra*: again the seeming chaos of the fugue births a triumphal return of the main theme. All is well with the world. This was anything but sophisticated musical analysis but I knew what I liked.

I bought, and read avidly Michael Kennedy's 1968 volume *Portrait of Elgar* and walked through Elgar's life with him sharing his moments of triumph and despair, particularly moved by the scene in which, emotionally exhausted after completing a major work the composer turned to experimenting in his chemistry lab. I resonated with this description of the satisfied exhausted joy which lets you, in your tiredness, do fun stuff because of your confidence in the worth of something you have created.

The most poignant Elgar piece of all was the *Cello Concerto* (1919) – I had Jacqueline du Pré's recording shortly after it appeared. I read the work (perhaps wrongly) as a creative swansong, the last time Elgar was able to pluck music from the air, a mournful resigned farewell to a lost pre-war society. There would be no return of the grand theme, only silence.

*

My mother had given me to understand that she wasn't comfortable with music on Roman Catholic themes.

Late one December, I went to Glasgow to spend my Christmas gift tokens.

I returned on the train with a boxed set of Verdi's *Requiem*.

Back home, defiant, I played the *Dies Irae*, very loudly, and with only a soupçon of guilt.

*

My parents, while encouraging, may at times have found my writing embarrassing. 'You won't be writing about this, will you?' they said pointedly after I'd attended a Free Church Communion Service and been given a communion token allowing me to participate. I think they suspected I might have somehow made fun of this procedure, and I was little hurt that they made this assumption. But they would have been horrified by the last Saturday Extra piece I published in the *Glasgow Herald* just before I began my university course, a truly embarrassing diatribe arguing against pretension and elitism in music. Its valid point was undermined by snide remarks. I sneered at 'Schoenberg's little 12-note thing,' dismissed parts of Beethoven's Seventh Symphony as 'sophisticated Royal Academy fairground music' and coined this florid aphorism – 'music is a balm to sooth anguish, not a catalyst to provoke it'.

More defiance!

*

Avoiding 'the world' made it more difficult for me to interact with those I deemed to be 'in the world'. The phone rang at home. It was for me. A journalist from the *Glasgow Herald*, phoning young people to ascertain their views on the government's decision to give the vote to over-18s. Frankly, having no well-formed thoughts about politics (and no thoughts at all about politics other than a visceral passion for the Scottish National Party) I had little to say to him. I got a passing mention in the finished article. What I do remember is my mother standing at the door, listening.

'Remember you're a Christian,' she whispered.

Her presence within earshot made me even more tongue-tied than I might otherwise have been.

*

Eschewing worldliness also meant that Sundays remained different in my teenage years. It was a day for avoiding the secular, avoiding school work. In the afternoon we'd sit in the living room. My parents read Christian magazines and missionary biographies. Even classical music was forbidden, unless it was a setting of religious words. I would sit with them listening to our three-LP set of Handel's *Messiah*. Every Sunday, from the first note to the last – it just about filled the time between clearing away the lunch dishes and sitting down to tea. I loved Handel, and although in retrospect I can see sadness in those long, friendless afternoons at the time I was content.

*

I remember my mother occasionally putting her hands around my father's waist in the living room as we were sitting of an evening and saying 'Choo Choo! Let's be a train!' And she and dad would shuffle round the house making appropriate locomotive noises while I looked on with horror. Perhaps they were showing me that life didn't have to be serious; perhaps they were teasing me in my puritanical gloominess. Perhaps they were simply having fun. And I remember the teenage revulsion I felt when my mother placed her palm on dad's knee as they sat together. As my embarrassment grew, it crept inexorably towards the crotch, though never quite reached its destination.

*

The concept of 'aleatoric' music – fragments of musical score played in the order determined by throwing a die – intrigued me, although the resulting avant-garde dissonances were less appealing. Occasionally I took an 'aleatoric walk' where the direction my steps took whenever there were options was selected by tossing a coin. I suspect I wished I could thus navigate my way through life without taking personal control of my future. A billowing gown. Someone reaching from the sky and passing over the next threads in the handwork project.

*

No doubt I was a difficult teenager, but when it came to defining 'worldliness' mum and dad gave me mixed and confusing messages about what this entailed. Yet my most nurturing memory from the 1960s involves my father.

I was having difficulty sleeping. It was close to midsummer.

For a few successive evenings dad took me out for a walk before bed. In the stillness of evening, the air enduringly balmy although the sun had set we'd go to the end of Douglas Street, follow Clyde Street to Carluke Cross and then come home via Mount Stewart Street.

He walked calmly beside me talking gently I suppose of positive unthreatening things.

What I remember most was a deep sense one particular night at one particular spot just opposite the top of School Lane where the sweetie shop used to be, of the healing peace of his presence.

There were deeper joys than reading Agatha Christie.

FIVE

TICKET TO BRIGHTON

I was still having problems with the lyrics of Beatles songs. When I was part of a Scripture Union (SU) camp in the spring of 1965 I was conscious of a blur of boys bellowing out the Fab Four's latest number. 'She's got a ticket to Brighton!' was what I heard, somewhat puzzled as to why the lady in question had a pressing need to travel to the south of England.

Throughout my time at Wishaw High I was loosely part of the poorly-attended boy's Scripture Union group. (SU was, and is, an evangelical organisation committed to introducing children and young people to Christian faith through Bible reading, in-school groups, holidays and other activities.) I suppose we had the usual Bible studies and talks, quizzes and visiting speakers but I wasn't in any way helped or encouraged by any of this. My sharpest memory is of the occasion when a boy a year ahead of me mercilessly and repeatedly stuck a pin in my thigh during the proceedings. Attending because it was expected of me I felt on the periphery.

In S1 at the school, I went to the Easter camp along with Colin Menzies. It was held at Belmont campsite at Meigle in Perthshire where the accommodation was in barrack-like wooden dormitories named after areas in the locality – I was in Eassie.

I recall little about the camp. There were outside games and indoor activities. There was a short religious service after breakfast each day, and time spent in small groups with a leader reading and discussing a Bible passage. None of this made much impression on me. But daily we sang a hymn which was new to me – *Thine be the glory* to Handel's stately tune Judas Maccabeus. I loved the grandeur of the music and the richness of the words. 'Risen, conquering king.' I didn't for a moment doubt the truth of a resurrected Jesus.

I was impressed by the camp Commandant (SU camps still in those days used military terminology) who seemed very old and kind and Gandalf-like wise – he was an SU stalwart, the Rev J. W. Meiklejohn ('Boss'). When the quiz team I was part of came first in a competition by somewhat devious means I felt shame when the prizes were handed out. Mine was *Some want it tough* by Everest mountaineer and Christian Len Moules, neatly inscribed by 'Boss.'

My parents were keen that I should enjoy the camp, and perhaps make what they would have called 'spiritual progress' in the course of the week. It was a touching expression of my mother's love, but highly embarrassing for me, that every morning my name was called to go up in front of the whole camp and receive post which had arrived for me – each day a different comic wrapped in brown paper.

'Maybe you'll make friends with some other Christian boys,' mum and dad had said hopefully. But whenever it came to initiating conversations I felt awkward and tongue-tied. I don't think I ever did speak to the Heavenor boy, son of a dentist whom my parents knew was also at the camp and thought might be a good friend for me. And I suspect that going home, new friendships unmade, I felt some guilt.

Reluctant to engage with others, I sought comfort as ever in hiding behind an ebullient persona. Acts were sought from each dorm for a 'camp concert'. Someone suggested I should compose a 'camp alphabet' and this I did with some help from one of the leaders.

The Commandant's side-kick, known as the Adjutant, abbreviated to 'Adgie', visited the dorms morning by morning to check that each bed, each locker was immaculate. Hence my alphabet began 'A is for Adgie, his head is so bust that he's always looking for small bits of dust'.

I recited this poetic masterwork gleefully, particularly relishing 'V is for Vomit which means the same as spew, and after you've heard this is that what you'll do?'

We didn't tackle Len Moules's Everest but we did all traipse to the summit of a local hill. Mostly I walked alone and pushed ahead to reach the summit first.

'The little boy who always does things with all his might,' someone said about me when I was little.

The evening before we returned home the dorm leaders told with relish a ghoulish story about a ghost reputedly haunting Eassie dorm which was said to appear on the very last night of camp. I lay long awake after the lights were put out, too frightened by the thought of spectral encounters to risk venturing to the toilets.

The bus journey back to Glasgow. I was reading Alan Burgess's book *The Small Woman*, about missionary Gladys Aylward's time in China, and sucking at a stick of rock. Saliva and molten sugar dripped like candle-wax over my irritatingly sticky fingers.

Back home I took to bed for a few days, utterly washed out. Concerned, my father took me to see his physician colleague Robert Walker who hooked me up to an ECG machine, pronounced my heart healthy, and suggested I take up tennis.

I was just not one of those who 'like it tough'.

*

At church too I felt on the outside looking in. Throughout most of my time at secondary school I obediently attended Carluke Baptist Church twice each Sunday with my parents. I graduated from Junior to Senior Christian Endeavour.

I remember 'chain prayer' (where you were supposed to pray audibly one after another in no particular order, but with no gaps in the 'chain'). My prayers were dutiful – I knew what to say – but as I realized even at the time, of questionable sincerity. At the very end of each meeting, we'd repeat the 'Mizpah Benediction' – I found these two words in themselves had an inherent, healing tranquillity. 'The Lord watch between me and thee, when we are absent one from another.' (Genesis 31:49 AV)

Once a month was 'consecration', a ritual which had no doubt been very meaningful to those who developed the Christian Endeavour model, but I suspect for many of us (and certainly for me) it was simply a routine. The intention was that each Christian Endeavour member would publicly renew their commitment and dedication to God. You'd select a verse from the Bible which was an expression of devotedness and read it as an indication that you were making the words your own. For me, what I said had little significance.

And yet I still believed. Some of the poems I wrote expressed a Christian faith – one described a baptism ceremony displaying understanding of what it signified; another expressed confidence that the God who never forgets the individual held the key to my future; yet another anticipated a joyful re-union in heaven with my brother William.

At home each night I tried with fluctuating degrees of conscientiousness to have a 'quiet time' and read the prescribed passages from the Bible and accompanying comments in Scripture Union's quarterly *Key Notes* for teenagers. But I found it hard to connect, and rarely if ever discerned any spiritual nourishment issuing from this. I believed but at times I was puzzled by the lack of that inner joy which I thought was the Christian norm and at times unsurprised, for how, I reasoned could God bless me when I was somehow incapable of taking the one step expected of me?

In early 1966, still involved in the church's Christian Education programme, I sat a 'Young Teen Achievement Test' covering studies in John's Gospel, and came first in the church, with 83%, hardly a spectacular score.

In a section of theological questions, I had ticked all the right boxes. Yes, only 'a personal faith in the Lord Jesus' could 'really satisfy a person's heart'. Yes, the way for a person to be happiest is 'to think little about himself and live for Jesus' (I don't know what the girls made of this sexist language, and it seems such a self-diminishing teaching, offering no encouragement to a hesitant child with little self-esteem.) 'What sanctifies a believer, or makes him holy?' was another question. Without hesitating, I chose 'Reading and obeying God's Word'. 'Why does every person need to be born again?' No doubts about the answer to that one: 'Everyone is a sinner by birth.'

That was the issue, the step I had not taken. I still had not been 'born again'. My understanding of what this entailed was based on stories from the Bible and on the 'testimonies' I listened to in church when people would share their own stories of coming to faith. Typically these accounts began with the person describing life before they were 'born again', their dissatisfaction, their attempts to find fulfilment by routes other than coming to God. Next they would talk about hearing the Christian gospel perhaps for the first time, or as if for the first time. Perhaps there was a struggle as they felt torn between what they formerly were and the new, Christ-born self which beckoned, but in the end Christ would win out. They would kneel in repentance. There would be an in-flooding of joy. And the testimony would conclude with an account of their living the changed life which began that day: new priorities, a new love for God and for others.

I had known nothing like this and I heard nothing in these testimonies to affirm the flickering candle of my own faith.

The call to be born again, to accept Jesus as Saviour was preached Sunday by Sunday. The consequence of failure to connect with Christ in this way was as I knew eternal and desperately severe.

It was clear to me that it was not enough simply to believe in God. 'The devils also believe, and tremble,' James had written in his New Testament epistle. (James 2:19 AV) You had to have that experience of conversion and you had to be sure to believe the right things.

*

In the mid-60s my parents and I visited Peterhead where the Baptist minister was their friend Harry Seawright formerly of Shotts Baptist Church.

As we sat round the table in his dining room, Harry expressed disquiet about a new book by the Methodist theologian Leslie D. Weatherhead entitled *The Christian Agnostic*. Weatherhead describes a 'Christian agnostic' as:

> *[A] person who is immensely attracted by Christ and who seeks to show his spirit, to meet the challenges, hardships and sorrows of life in the light of that spirit, but who, though he is sure of many Christian truths, feels that he cannot honestly and conscientiously 'sign on the dotted line' that he believes certain theological ideas about which some branches of the church dogmatize...His intellectual integrity makes him say about many things, 'It may be so. I do not know'.*

To Harry Seawright and I suppose my parents this was heresy.

'There's no such thing as a Christian agnostic,' Harry proclaimed with finality.

I believed him.

*

Occasionally, on a Saturday night, the church would show one of the films produced by the Billy Graham Evangelistic Association, dramatizing a typical conversion story in the context of one of the evangelist's stadium Crusades (as they were termed) in the USA.

There was a frisson of excitement as we entered the church where a screen hung in front of the platform and a Bell and Howell projector was propped up in the back pew. It clattered away in the darkness as the story unspooled before us. We knew what was coming: a family situation where most of the members were staunch believers, but one was resisting faith and exploring life without God. The development of this storyline was mildly interesting especially to someone with limited experience of television drama and cinema, but we knew the trope with which it would end.

A third of the way through the second reel, the much-prayed-for person having resisted attempts to persuade them to come to the stadium would nevertheless slip in unobtrusively. We'd hear what seemed like half an hour (but was probably only 10 minutes) of Billy Graham preaching and then appealing for people in his audience to respond to Jesus Christ. The camera would focus on the black sheep's face as they agonised over the challenge Graham presented and would then track them as they hesitantly stood up and made their way to join the crowds in front of the platform. The film would end with joy, tears, reconciliation. After the lights came on our minister would very often prolong the agony, making his own appeal.

Thus, it seemed, the whole culture by which the church defined itself underlined the inadequacy of outsiders and summoned us to rebirth.

*

My parents and I were walking home one dark evening in the early 1960s from Carluke Town Hall where an Irish Evangelist, Hedley Murphy was leading a gospel mission. The format was similar to those Billy Graham Crusades. That evening, Murphy spoke of his own coming to faith in a sermon entitled *Death by Proxy* which focussed on Christ's substitutionary self-sacrifice. Earlier, as we waited for the event to begin, the polished wood on the auditorium ceiling troubled me. It's texture and sheen screamed out the dread of coffins in undertakers' parlours

At the top of Mount Stewart Street my mother turned to me, her face silver in the lamplight.

'One of these days John's going to tell us he's become a Christian.'

I kept my silence, but in fact there was nothing I wanted more than to find the way in.

Occasionally I'd come home from church having heard a particularly alarming sermon and throw myself on my knees at the foot of my bed.

'Save me God, please save me.'

But there was no sense of having been heard, no unmistakable transformation, no reorientated life, no flood of joy.

I was knocking at the door as best I knew how, yet it wasn't being opened.

There were no tears other than tears of frustration.

The fault, I assumed, was all mine.

The message of wrath was overwhelming the parallel message which surely, surely must have been present, of grace, love and a Father's heart.

I went downstairs, put on a smile. My bedtime coffee and toast was no sacrament.

I don't know why I held silence rather than pouring out my pain to my parents. Perhaps I felt there was no real channel of communication between us and feared I would not be heard.

*

On Sunday evenings, I often attended Youth Fellowship at the Baptist Manse, generally a light-hearted affair. I particularly recall Billy McCulloch singing very loudly one evening the 1968 Scaffold hit *Lily the Pink* about the salvific effects of the eponymous heroine's potions.

Charles Simpson the minister (by then George Balmer had moved on) and his wife roared with laughter but my parents were mildly shocked when I told them. Knowing they would be I brought the story home like a choice morsel of gossip which I was maliciously eager to share.

*

My anxiety over feeling 'on the outside' was deepened by another of the church's teachings – on the 'Rapture of the Saints'.

It was believed, according to the Dispensationalist teaching which originated in the 19th century, that at a particular point in history Jesus would return, not to the earth but to the 'air'. He would call to himself those who were truly his, while the rest of humanity would be 'left behind' to face the anguish of what was known as 'the Great Tribulation'. At a later date Christ would again return with his people, this time in judgement.

In the 1960s, there was a sense in those evangelical circles where this theology was espoused that the coming of the Lord was particularly close. Hal Lindsey's book *The Late Great Planet Earth*, published in 1970 expounded these beliefs in the context of contemporary world affairs. The creation of the state of Israel in 1948 was seen as a fulfilment of Biblical prophecy which intensified expectations that the end was near, and during the Arab-Israeli war of 1967 many Christians believed that God must soon intervene on behalf of the Jewish people.

The purpose of the sermons on 'the Rapture' which I heard as a child was to encourage listeners to prepare themselves for Christ's reintervention in history by embracing the faith thus ensuring that they would not be 'left behind', but in me they induced a mentally paralysing terror.

When the preacher announced the Bible reading, and it included Jesus' words about some being taken and some being left, or St Paul's certainty that 'the dead in Christ will rise first. After that, we who are still alive and are left will be caught up together with them in the clouds to meet the Lord in the air. And so we will be with the Lord forever.' (1 Thessalonians 4:16-17) I would desperately attempt to distract my mind from the rest of the sermon, mentally building increasingly intricate structures with imaginary Lego.

But I could never fully divert my attention from the terrible words coming from the pulpit. I'd imagine myself waking up one morning to find my parents gone, raptured by Christ, leaving me hideously alone to face a maelstrom of personal and social trauma with the prospect of a 'lost eternity' stretching ahead.

*

Having developed an interest in Unidentified Flying Objects (as you did), I borrowed *The Warminster Mystery* from the library with enthusiastic anticipation, shortly after it was released in 1968. Naively I didn't question the truth of what I read, which combined pseudo-science and mysticism.

It was written by journalist Arthur Shuttlewood, and reported on the series of alleged sightings of UFOs in and around Warminster in Wiltshire which began at Christmas 1964. The blurb claimed that 'The Warminster Mystery is a dramatic unfolding of these sightings, with eyewitness accounts of strange "things" seen by day and night; of bewildering mushrooms of smoke, crescents of fire, weird and disturbing sounds and even accounts of conversations with those from outer space.'

I found Shuttlewood's reference to alien encounters disturbing and I was particularly shocked to come across a sentence to the effect that the UFO activity over Warminster was an indication that the return of Jesus Christ was imminent and specifying the year in which it would happen. I suspect Shuttlewood (who is said to have claimed to have been visited by Jesus Christ) had in mind the then-popular theory that 'God is an astronaut', and that religions are explained by encounters with an alien race. However, I read his words in the context of the Christian teaching about the Rapture and the second coming of Christ with which I was so familiar. As the specified time approached, I was deeply, deeply anxious.

*

One day I sat on the stairs in the mid-1960s hugging our King Charles Cavalier Spaniel Prince and looking anxiously through the landing window. It was a Saturday afternoon, about three.

My parents had gone shopping to Glasgow.

I'd expected them home by now.

Supposing…..

Little comforted by my companion, I sat out the long minutes until the familiar car came into view.

*

On some occasions when my parents had been delayed I'd lift the phone and dial the number of someone in our church and then put the receiver down as soon as I heard their voice answering. In those pre-1471 days they would have been unable to detect the identity of the caller.

It was enough that I'd heard the familiar voice.

The Lord had not come. Yet.

But tonight? Or tomorrow?

*

Very occasionally, people asked me if I'd been 'saved' yet. One evening, the questioner was a young woman not much older than I was whom my mother had befriended.

We were standing in our living room – I recall the scene vividly even down to the title of my library book lying on the coffee table.

Tessa asked the question: 'Have you been saved yet?

For some unaccountable reason, perhaps simply to get her off my back, I replied 'Yes'. Or did that 'Yes' spring from the deep desire within me for it to be so?

When had it happened, she asked. I simply referred to the most recent occasion when a sermon had troubled me, and I cried out to God with no discernible response. It was when we'd attended the Free Church evening service during our holiday in Nairn when spiritual angst commingled with another, unfamiliar yearning as the girl from Burnley bewitched me

My parents did not as I recall show any particular joy at the news Tessa had extracted from me. Perhaps they were hurt that I had not told them at the time, personally. But their expectation had been fulfilled, their prayers answered. The time had come.

*

Once told, the lie as I saw it was perpetuated.

The following year, when I was 16, I typed the form applying for baptism and membership of Carluke Baptist Church each keystroke underlining my hypocrisy. This was the next step expected of me. In the Baptist tradition, baptism by immersion is a sign of personal coming to faith, a symbolic identification with the death and resurrection of Christ.

'You'll need to do it sometime, so why not now?' my parents told me when the minister, Charles Simpson announced a forthcoming baptismal service.

Had Charles been just a little more sensitive as he talked me through the significance of what I was about to do at the one-to-one baptismal classes, had he questioned me with a compassionate probing, had he conveyed to me that it was safe to be real, he must surely have uncovered my confused mix of hypocrisy and yearning, for I think I would have welcomed the opportunity to come clean. Or was conforming to my parents' and the minister's expectations more important to me than being real? As it was he made assumptions without questioning and I gave the expected answers, continuing to play my game.

The date for the baptism of myself and a few others was fixed for Sunday 1st September 1968, over a year after my supposed conversion. All summer, I was filled with dread at the prospect. I suspected God's wrath at my falseness would be unleashed as I stepped down into the water, or subsequently as I took for the first time the bread and wine at communion having been accepted into membership of the church. Didn't the New Testament say 'For he that eateth and drinketh unworthily, eateth and drinketh damnation to himself'? (1 Corinthians 11:29 AV)

There was to be a Sunday concert in the Royal Albert Hall Proms season on the appointed night – a concert performance conducted by Colin Davis of Berlioz's opera *The Trojans*. I thought, fancifully, that this wonderful music would be in the airwaves all around me when I descended into the waters of God's wrath.

The evening arrived. Those of us who were to be baptised sat at the front of the church, the guys in short-sleeved shirts and casual trousers, the girls wearing long purple robes, weighted with lumps of lead to prevent them floating up revealingly at the crucial moment. My father sat beside me.

When the time came I went forward, walked up on to the platform, and down the steps into warm water in the old, tile-lined cistern. I clasped my hands together in front of my chest, and Charles Simpson put his left hand over them. His right hand he placed on my shoulders. 'On your confession of faith in Jesus Christ, I baptise you in the name of the Father and of the Son and of the Holy Spirit,' he declared and then pushed me back down into the water before returning me to a standing position.

Later he told me it had been hard to get me under. 'It was as though you were resisting me,' he said.

Dripping copiously, I walked out of the tank and through to the room at the back where I dried myself and put on a change of clothes. My father passed me a towel and I thought I saw tears in his eyes. 'Little does he know,' I said to myself sadly.

Back in church the bread and wine were handed from person to person symbolising the death of Christ for his people. For the first time I took one of the tiny, melt-on-your tongue cubes of white bread and drank from the individual glass cup filled with a sweet cordial and I didn't die. Not that Sunday.

But each week thereafter as I morosely toyed with the bacon and egg my mother made for breakfast as a Sunday treat I couldn't forget that once again I would be eating bread and drinking wine unworthily. Would this be the Sunday judgement was unleashed?

The next day at school the Scripture Union pin-in-my-thigh boy came up to me. 'I hear you were done last night,' he said.

*

A new, additional pressure I felt now that I was allegedly a Christian was the expectation that I would 'witness' – that is share my faith with others in the hope that they too would come to believe in Jesus. I found this impossible because of my personality, my lack of true engagement with others, and especially, the hollowness of my faith. I felt I had to live the lie even in 'the world' of Wishaw High School and my failure to speak of Christ further burdened me with guilt.

I was a member of the editorial committee for the school magazine, *The Octagon* during my last year at school and made my mark in fairly trivial ways, such as insisting we needed a title page and pretentiously printing as a motto a quote from Shelley – 'Rarely, rarely comest thou, spirit of delight' (words with which I knew Edward Elgar had prefaced the score of his Second Symphony).

I felt I should be ensuring we ran something on a faith theme. But I lacked the courage to suggest this to the other committee members directly or to ask for a contribution from someone sharing a Christian outlook. And so I wrote a piece (I think it was a faith story) which I placed anonymously in the box we'd put in the school's admin corridor to receive contributions.

The piece was briefly discussed at an editorial committee meeting. I spoke half-heartedly in its favour but no-one else had any interest in seeing it in print so we discarded it.

Though the others said nothing I suspect they saw through this cowardly subterfuge.

*

In early 1970 my parents and I stopped attending Carluke Baptist Church – which they had served loyally – and joined the Brethren assembly at Carluke Gospel Hall. I suspect the assembly was not significantly less 'tight' than it had been eight years previously. The decision was my parents', though I happily concurred.

My recollection is that the issue was not so much to do with theology as it was relational – I think there had been friction between my mother and some others in the congregation. For me, it meant leaving a church where there were young people of my age for a much smaller group where there were none. But as almost always I was happy for my parents' decision to be my decision.

The only interview for membership was a group session with the three of us and some of the elders. There were no awkward questions about faith and conversion.

I was excited about the change.

I phoned my grandfather John Dempster, by then staying in Lanark:

'We're coming home,' I said. 'The sheep are returning to the fold.'

My parents bought me my own copy of the *Believers' Hymn Book*.

*

I had longed to have that ticket to ride, but the booking office seemed perpetually closed. In desperation, I had forged my own but I had no confidence that it would get me where I wanted to go.

*

Unsurprisingly my anxieties grew as the years passed. The Monday Neil Armstrong stepped down into moondust I woke up at Faillie Mains in Daviot near Inverness where I was staying with family friends Margaret and Norman McGrail formerly of Carluke. Slightly younger than my parents they were warmly loving people of a deep if slightly austere spirituality. They had kept in touch after moving north subsequent to Norman taking up a post with the Highlands and Islands Development Board and each month I received in the post from them a copy of the (very conservative) Free Church youth magazine, *The Instructor*. Margaret and Norman were active in the Inverness Christian scene and led a youth group which met regularly at Faillie.

After our family holiday that year, my parents dropped me off at Daviot on the Saturday for a week, and went to stay in Strathpeffer. Sunday morning, the McGrails took me to the nearby Farr Free Church, where it was communion, and Norman ensured that I was given a 'communion token' so that I could take the bread and wine.

The church sat in a field and there were no visible toilets. I was anxious that I would need to go before the end of the interminable service.

That night we watched on black and white television as the lunar landing module made its descent. I got the impression at the time (though Norman later denied it) that turning on the TV on the Sabbath day was a concession to history or perhaps to my presence.

Worries over toilets and the remoteness of Faillie Mains and an unfamiliar room with wooden floorboards somehow worked a strange toxic curse. By the Monday morning I was overcome by anxiety.

My parents were called for; they collected me and took me north to Strathpeffer where there was a single room available at their hotel, Holly Lodge.

The local GP wrote me a prescription.

I walked through the gardens beside the Strathpeffer Pavilion at peace. Never had toast and butter and ginger marmalade and black coffee tasted as lovely as it did those Holly Lodge mornings.

It was my first experience of Valium.

I didn't get to watch live Neil Armstrong's descent to the lunar surface.

*

I believe that the anxiety which has been an unwelcome thread running through most of my life made it difficult for me to connect with faith in a way which I found enriching and then tortured me both through what I was taught at church and through the consequences of my deception. And this very failure to be genuinely Christian as I defined it served only to ramp up my anxiety in a vicious circle of mental pain. All the teaching I had as child and teenager was given by good-hearted people – lacking perhaps in imagination and empathy – who were acting as their beliefs told them was in my best interests. And yet it was abuse.

For many years I believed that the root cause of my anxiety was purely genetic, especially since I came to understand that my mother's emotional life was similar to mine. But more recently I have learned that infant attachment issues in her case and in mine may well have triggered the anxiety, and 'switched on' the genetic component of this condition. Childhood attachment issues make it hard to 'connect' emotionally with parents and also in a religious sense with God. If however unintentionally a loving unconditional acceptance of a child has been poorly modelled by parents this can have two opposite effects: one person may find it hard to connect with the lovingkindness of God; another throws themselves into the arms of God in their quest for deep affirmation. I discern these contrasting reactions in my own questing disposition and in my mother's glad-hearted embrace of the evangelical Father.

*

I must have been a difficult teenager to parent. But my mother never discussed her issues and in turn I did not find home a place where deep confidences could be shared.

By the time I left Wishaw High I was a strange mixture of arrogance and extreme vulnerability, lacking confidence to see my future as anything other than fulfilling parental expectations.

I completed my schooling at the end of July 1970 with 8 'O' Levels, a ragbag of Highers and English CSYS at C grade. I had applied to various universities, but my acceptance depended on the Higher results due in mid-July.

There were a few wild antics on the last day of term – someone had managed to suspend a bra from the very centre of the hall roof where it hung high above the scuffed floorboards. I thought this was rather daring.

My school-leaving was low-key. I simply walked out of the building onto Dryburgh Road, turned left and kept walking, never once looking back.

SIX

A PHONE CALL, AND EMBASSY TIPPED

Two stories from my time at Law Hospital's General Store where I had a holiday job during my years at Glasgow University.

One afternoon in August 1970 the boss called me into his office.

'It's your father,' he said, handing me the telephone.

The Higher results had been released a few days earlier and concerned that the meagre fruit of my six years at Wishaw High might be inadequate to ensure my acceptance at Glasgow University, dad had phoned the Admissions Office.

His call brought the good news that I was 'in' and would be matriculating at the Gilmorehill campus that September. I listened numbly and said 'Thank-you'. I had not made a positive choice to go to uni, nor had I a specific goal in attending. It was simply the next step expected of me as I'd realized ever since commenting on that picture outside Miss Johnston's classroom.

I had applied to other universities as well. I know I would have found living away from home challenging: independence would either have grown me in self-knowledge and maturity or else broken me. I reached out gratefully for the safer option.

The fact that my father negotiated with Glasgow University on my behalf is indicative both of his love for me and of a somewhat controlling over-protectiveness which may have been a reaction to my lack of self-confidence but had the consequence of deepening it.

*

The second story. The boss at the General Store was a grey-haired gentleman, rather elderly, who spent most of his time in a smoke-filled office.

One afternoon, summoning me from the Store, he handed me a grubby pound note, and asked me to go to the canteen to buy him a packet of cigarettes.

I baulked at this and must have said something presumptuous like 'I don't believe in smoking.'

'I respect your beliefs,' he told me 'and you need to respect mine.'

Meekly I went and bought him his Embassy Tipped. I learned something that day about living and letting live.

*

Almost all my peers would have handled any interactions with universities and colleges themselves. Similarly, they'd have made their own arrangements for summer jobs.

But my five weeks at the General Store each summer from 1970-1972 were arranged by dad. He sat on the hospital's Board of Management and seems to have arranged for the post to be created simply for my benefit. My former school-mates employed at the hospital were there for the whole vacation, doing *real* jobs like labouring in the flower-beds dotted around the site. My post, in contrast, was a 'cushy number' limited to five weeks each summer because dad reckoned I would benefit from a family holiday and time to prepare for the start of the university term.

I'm frustrated both with him – nepotism, financial inefficiency and a reluctance to kick me out of the nest, and with myself – meekly following a pre-ordained scheme without a hint of teenage rebellion or even of appreciation of how privileged I was.

But in fact I enjoyed my time in the General Store.

Law Hospital had grown from a World War II POW camp. It had four main blocks, labelled A to D, each a long corridor from which Florence Nightingale-style wards projected on either side. The Nurses' Home and staff Sick Bay were in a similar block the corridor of which, extending beyond a door, gave access to shadowy wards – a relic of the wartime camp – in the eeriness of which sections of beds, cabinets and screens lurked in musty darkness.

The Store itself occupied a pre-fabricated building close to the centre of the extensive site. Its role was to supply wards with cleaning materials, toilet rolls, cutlery, beds and much else besides. Radio 1 played constantly – one July was the summer of *Puppy Love* when Donny Osmond's single topped the charts for several weeks. Just inside the door there were some saucy seaside postcards (I was in equal measure shocked and fascinated by the drawing of 'Rawfanny Nudist Camp') and a whisky bottle full of what I was assured was cold tea. Knowing my religious background hospital staff teased me gently about anything they thought might give rise to puritanical ire and I played along with this

My colleagues were both from Law Village – Willie Flanaghan, and John Orr (whose brother, Paterson Orr wore a suit and had a more senior role in hospital administration). Willie and John made mention of evenings spent at the Old Store and I was full of admiration for their work ethic until I realised they were referring to a pub in the Village.

Our days were spent making deliveries to wards using motorised trolleys. There was a wooden framework with cubby holes on either side which were covered by rubber screens – the whole contraption could be loaded on a trolley. We'd fill the compartments with cloths and bleach and toilet brushes, cleaning materials and scrubbers, and then progress slowly down the corridors, stopping at each ward entrance. The ward staff responsible for cleaning would besiege our trolley: the trick was to supply their stated requirements, record what had been provided and watch eagle-eyed for their inevitable attempts to whip the rubber screen aside and purloin unobserved.

Sometimes, we made deliveries to the room where about ten women sat at sewing machines, superintended by one who assured me that her name was Maria Theresa Donoghue (plus a few other random middle names) Johnstone. I, still wearing my zany High School persona would perform songs for them, such as Gounod's *We were not born with true love to trifle*.

On wet days, we'd stay in the store, sending out hearing aid batteries in response to requests from pensioners, or stamping A, B, C or D on knives, forks and spoons to denote which Block they were being supplied to. I had lunch at the staff canteen where you could get wonderful hot curries made, it was said, to authentic Indian recipes which Asian medical staff had shared. My vocabulary was expanded. For example when Willie went to the toilet he would announce: 'I'm going to wet my boots.'

Sometimes we'd be asked to deliver a bed to a ward for a newly-admitted patient – this required locating a set of cast-iron bed parts which actually fitted together (some sharp hammer blows might be required to achieve this) and loading them on a trolley. I never heard of bed shortages – there were always more and space was always made for them.

The hospital was dad's territory, a microcosm of society, and there I felt safe in benign paternalism. At the end of each day I would clock out, then make my way across the site to my father's room in C X-Ray. Though it had its own loo en-suite (a consultants' status symbol) it was a small room: a desk, two chairs, a small table with a viewing box for examining X-Ray films and a poster on the wall of a beautiful rural scene with the words 'Slow me down, Lord'.

Clearly I thought I was working on my terms, not the hospital's.

'I've got some overtime for you,' the boss said one afternoon.

It had been decided to collect all the old pianos, languishing unplayed and untuned for many years at the far end of each ward in the day room, and feed them to a bonfire of musical vanities on waste ground behind the POW buildings.

These instruments were uplifted in the vehicle called by staff, with black humour, the 'meat wagon' because it was used to take bodies of deceased patients to the mortuary. There was consternation in some wards when it transpired that what was being collected was dead pianos.

The conflagration was scheduled for a Saturday, and the boss naturally thought I would welcome the opportunity to earn some extra money.

I was *not* enthusiastic when he asked me.

'What, work on a Saturday as well?' I said to myself. 'No way!'

'But I thought you'd like some overtime?' the boss said when he got the message.

I don't know if my response was even as polite as 'Thanks, but no thanks'.

*

Each year, on the Friday at the end of my five weeks, I left the General Store for the last time. My father's car swept me past the other students still labouring in the rosebeds.

SEVEN

SCATOLOGY:
ESCHATOLOGY

I have a vivid memory of standing waiting for the train beside the iron stairway across the line at Carluke Station. It had occurred to me that it would be smart to write a poem about misunderstandings arising from two words which sound similar, but which have radically different meanings – scatological, and eschatological (a theological term referring to the 'last things').

Nothing came of the idea before the rails sprang to life, signalling the approach of the train. In any case, while I knew more than most about the latter term, my knowledge of what 'scatology' embraced was limited.

But that story symbolizes my struggles to negotiate a relationship between myself and the world, the sacred and the secular. It was more difficult in the University than it had been in the General Store.

*

Each day during my three years at uni, I travelled from Carluke to the city by train: many Glasgow University students from Lanarkshire also travelled daily. My father – another indication of his commitment to me – kindly dropped me off at the station in the mornings.

Because many of the trains had no corridors and no toilet, my bladder anxiety drove me into the foul gents' toilet at Carluke Station each morning despite my having peed immediately before leaving home. A few globules of urine fell in the leaf-scattered concrete trough. And then I'd stand with the crowds on the 'up' platform neck craned southwards. Thirty minutes to Glasgow, barring delays. And I knew which of the intermediate stops had unlocked loos.

Often I'd travel with friends – Colin Menzies, James McGonigle, Gregor Anderson, Alice C. R. Wright. Always, Mr Galbraith from Carluke Gospel Hall would be on the train often in the same compartment, his nose in a book about Conservative Party history.

We'd pile out at Glasgow Central station, run across the concourse and under the glass canopy in Gordon Street. We'd dodge buses and taxis in Hope Street and wait on the far pavement for the 59 bus (still the same number as in my parents' day) which took us to University Avenue via a Charing Cross newly bisected by works for the cross-city motorway.

But on days when I had major exams dad would give me a lift right into the city – a 90-minute round trip for him – to ensure I reached my destination calm and unfraught.

*

With unconscious arrogance I assumed that the University was an environment hostile to faith and that many academics were ungodly people seeking to pervert the truth. I believed that what we were studying was 'worldly', and while in some respects alluring, at odds with the values of the invisible kingdom to which I aspired to belong. The spiritual dimension present in the texts I studied was invisible to me because it was not expressed in the conventional religious language I was familiar with.

In my French classes, while I tried to understand Sartre, Gide and Cocteau reading their work in English translation, I regarded them as 'the enemy' and lacked the intellectual curiosity to truly engage with them. Surprisingly enough despite (or because of) cheating by not reading the texts in the original, I did well enough in my essays to win an exemption from the literature element of the final exam.

At that time Moral Philosophy was a compulsory subject. I struggled with Hobbes, sadly didn't connect with Plato's eloquent vision of the shadows in the cave, and found even the Professor, Robin Downie's own textbook *Roles and Values* difficult to comprehend. I wrote an essay for my Moral Philosophy tutor, a wizened begowned eagle who seemed incredibly aged and perched in a room at the very top of a tall, echoing staircase. He was a kindly man and I made bold in my essay to postulate an 'X Factor' representing God.

*

There was no way I was taking Moral Philosophy beyond my first year. Professor Downie called me into his study.

'Would you not consider taking this forward?' he said. 'We often find people like you do well.'

I suppose the eagle had told him about my 'X Factor', and that the 'people' he was referring to were those with religious belief.

My answer remained 'No'.

Who needed Moral Philosophy when you had God I thought, superciliously. Philosophy was a vastly inferior, substitute religion.

*

I regarded the student population with suspicion. Coming from a right-wing anti-socialist family, I felt diffident even setting foot in the Student Representative Council building. In my French course there were some lectures on contemporary France – this was just two years after the May 1968 protests in which students played a significant role. The lecturer outlined these events and showed us stirring images with an excitement which was entirely alien to me. I regarded the protestors, instinctively and without any thought, as dangerous opponents of establishment securities.

On the first stage of my journey back to Carluke each afternoon the bus swept past the Men's Union at the bottom of University Avenue, an intimidating space permeated with the stale smell of alcohol from the Beer Bar; a building I entered only infrequently, full of noisy students who I had no doubt held outrageous political, religious and moral views.

As a child I'd enjoyed the University charities day, an annual Saturday when a walk along Sauchiehall Street was a series of pleasant confrontations with extravagantly costumed students shaking collecting cans in your face. But now I was there myself the annual campaigns, with slogans such as 'Kramacanfu!' or 'Butchercashin!' (the latter accompanied by a picture of a cheerful meat-vendor in traditional gear) seemed alien.

Yet I saw no radicalism at the university: I simply lacked the desire, or courage, or self-confidence to engage with my fellow-students and learn from them. I felt at times like a child thrust unwittingly into an adult environment while lacking the skills to cope.

I attended the occasional Christian Union (CU) meeting, but these made no impression on me, and I felt a disconnect between myself and the CU leaders whose zeal troubled me. These gatherings were every bit as alien to me as that liquor-smelling Men's Union in which they were held.

I hadn't taken to heart the lesson I'd learned in the General Store that afternoon of the Embassy Tipped: to live unthreatened by different views people hold, respecting them and anticipating respect in turn.

*

'You need a friend John, you need a nice Christian friend.' I wonder if I thought that since God would order my life, submitting to my parents' wishes in some way counted as submitting to the divine programme?

I did spend some time with a fellow-student called Jack. He had a church connection, but I don't believe faith was particularly meaningful to him – which meant that from my perspective he was unthreatening. Jack responded to my disclosures about lack of faith – why was I able to discuss this with him when in other settings I found it impossible to articulate – with a sardonic humour which I found difficult to interpret. But I was able to mention him to my parents as evidence that I was trying to find that friend.

One Saturday my father lent me his green Austin 18, and I drove to Kilmarnock to spend the day with Jack. I read him a 6000-word story I'd written called *Dross* – its contents I fear, were as dispiriting as its title.

My parents invited Jack to attend the Northern Convention (a Christian event) with us that September. He promised to come and a room with two single beds was booked for us at the Holly Lodge Hotel in Strathpeffer. But Jack pulled out, and my grandfather Archie Jackson (by then a widower) accompanied us instead. I think I always suspected the plan would fall through. It was my parents' plan and Jack was not the uncomplicated evangelical I had led them to think. Once again I lacked the courage to make my own way.

*

In the Higher Ordinary English class I was in the same tutorial group as Max Donald who always seemed confident in his black leather jacket, the son as I was vaguely aware of a Baptist Minister in the city.

Our English tutor was William Brooks who frequently made inappropriate comments to women in the tutorial group in the context of erotic passages in the set books. When he invited us as a group to his flat for an evening event. I was apprehensive but up for going. My parents knew nothing of his reputation, but having driven past his flat they opined that it was not in a reputable area and so I should not attend. End of story.

Max was going. 'You can go with me and then stay over at mine,' he offered. But I declined this invitation – going against my parents' wishes and staying with someone I barely knew was beyond me. I was 19! Did I allow myself no freedom?

Later in life I came to know Max very well. His invitation was a thread which I rejected. But could it have been any other way?

*

Classical music still spoke to me, and from time to time I'd meet up with Gregor Anderson and James McGonigle simply to listen. Yet even as we sat together I was conscious of the abyss between us and of what God expected of me in terms of faithful witness: I was glad of the music as it left no space for words. George Cringles and I also met to explore classical music and with him I felt more at home. As we sat there in the house just along the road from the Waterloo crossroads accompanied by George's enormous Alsatian dog we ate jammy pancakes his sister Mary had brought up from the kitchen. I learned a great deal about pipe organs and organ music and perhaps George learned a little about Elgar.

I still loved Elgar's music, both the brash and brassy and the profound. The First Symphony moved me: again there was a triumphal return of the main theme at the end of the work and the third, slow movement must surely be one of the loveliest episodes in all music, the strings reaching up and up and up as it were into clear blue sky. I bought a Penguin book on *The Symphony*. I didn't ever read it (just as I never really read Donald Tovey's *Essays in Musical Analysis* which I also purchased, somehow thinking to establish thereby my credentials as a serious classical music enthusiast). But *The Symphony* included musical examples, one of them of the main theme of Elgar's 1st. This I played over and over on the piano, impressing my mother who thought I was performing by ear.

I loved *The Dream of Gerontius* although there would be a time later when this troubled me due to my disagreement with aspects of the work's theology. Could something untrue be so beautiful I wondered? Or did the beauty vouch for the truth of the words? Or in reality, as I came to see, is beauty reflecting something true beyond all words, beyond all theological formulations? 'How still it is! I hear no more the busy beat of time.'

*

Each day at University I attended lecturers and tutorials which often had generous gaps between them. Some were in the draughty eyries of the main 19th century building; others in slightly decaying former town houses in University Gardens; others still in the new Modern Languages Building. In between, I sometimes visited the library or the circular reading room. Occasionally I encountered friends in lectures or in the refectory but for the most part I was on my own. I often went for long melancholy walks through Kelvingrove Park – where the University's façade towered above me as it did in that schooldays painting – or past the Kelvin Hall and the soot-black Western Infirmary, or round the shops in Byres Road.

At the end of the day, I'd catch the 59 back to the city centre where I'd visit bookshops before the train was due – John Smiths in St Vincent Street, the Grant Educational in Union Street. My father was most generous. Because of his pay grade I received the minimum student grant of £50 per annum. Dad didn't want me to have less cash in hand than friends who received more generous grants and therefore, ignoring the fact that they would have to contribute to their parents' household expenses, he gave me a monthly allowance. I used it chiefly to purchase books – literature, poetry, history – many of which I did not read in any depth.

I had a subconscious sense, or hope, that by the mere fact of buying a book (for example the Donald Tovey volume) I was connecting myself to the author and to the scholarly community and that by some process of osmosis I would acquire wisdom, recognition and status.

And then in the station, I'd stand watching the elevated glass-fronted office with one big pane assigned to each platform. In these windows the staff laboriously mounted boards indicating which train was departing from where, and listing the stations each would call at. At least in the matter of train travel I knew my destination if not my precise departure point. Eventually the board for the 17.07 or the 17.35 went up and there was a ripple in the busy concourse as people surged to the announced plaform.

*

My *modus operandi* at lectures was identical to my approach in the history classroom at school where lessons were a taking-down of dictation from the teacher. I would try to capture what the lecturer was saying, whatever the subject and was so busy writing it down that I seldom engaged with it intellectually. Often, sitting in the reading room or at my desk at home, I would laboriously re-write the lecture more legibly and with more detail. These notes I would then memorise and regurgitate as appropriate in exams.

In Scottish Literature, for example, I was stimulated by Alexander Scott's lecture on James Thomson's poem *The City of Dreadful Night*. I memorised my notes of what he had said and poured his thoughts enthusiastically back to him in the exam – and yet I did not trouble myself to read the poem. But my work generally was sufficient to win me the class prize in Scottish Literature.

We were no doubt intended to read the titles on the book lists, but I made only a desultory attempt at this. There was no encouragement to read widely or think critically other than in Higher Ordinary History: my tutor inspired me to explore the consequences in the UK of the Depression in the 1920s and 30s. I found this recent history easier to engage with, although my understanding of human nature was still shallow and innocent.

In English Literature I couldn't progress beyond the first page of Henry James's *The Golden Bowl*, and all I recall of the lectures on the work is the lecturer taking the anti-obscenity protestor Mary Whithouse's name as an illustration of the fact that people's names sometimes reflect their characters. *Middlemarch* was a plodding storyline to me with no instinctive recognition of the protagonists from my own experience. Not having learned to read beyond the literal I found Spenser's *Fairy Queen* turgid and unyielding. I achieved a disastrous mark in an open-book exam on a Shakespeare play – I bought and read the critics, but at that stage Shakespeare's language and characters did not reach my heart. Philip Hobsbaum's lectures on the poetry and life of Sylvia Plath and his account of her suicide troubled me. Not at that point understanding mental illness I feared it and shrank from Plath's writing. I found Edwin Muir's *Autobiography* similarly disturbing, as my fear of inner darkness drew life from the darkness in others.

I saw my courses as presenting a series of hoops to jump through rather than challenges to learn and grow. I had no motivation other than making it to the finishing line.

*

Some literature did connect with me. I loved the concept and language of Hugh MacDiarmid's poem *The Bonnie Broukit Bairn*, and was mesmerized by the poetry and rhythms of Lewis Grassic Gibbon: I tried to reproduce 'the speak o' the Mearns' in my own writing to the point of pastiche. Two authors I loved almost from the moment I encountered them because of their power of expression and their struggles with world and Spirit. One was John Donne. The imagery of his erotic poems both aroused and captivated me:

> Licence my roving hands and let them go
> Before, behind, between, above, below.
> O my America! My new-found-land.

And the holy sonnets reflected my own longing for God –

> Teach mee how to repent; for that's as good
> As if thou'hadst seal'd my pardon with thy blood.

– and for decisive divine intervention in the doubt-fortified citadel of my mind:

> Batter my heart, three person'd God…..
> Take mee to you, imprison me, for I
> Except you'entrall mee, never shall be free,
> Nor ever chaste, except you ravish me.

I longed to be able to say of God and more to hear God declare of me: 'O my America! My new-found-land'.

*

The other writer with whom I felt an almost immediate connection was Gerard Manley Hopkins who at one point considered writing poetry to be 'worldly' and not an appropriate occupation for a Jesuit priest. Two of his poems touched me particularly. We studied *The Wreck of the Deutschland* in which Hopkins draws parallels between a recent shipwreck and the courage and faith demonstrated by a group of nuns who were on board, and his own experience of trauma-tested faith.

He speaks of God the Creator who 'hast bound bones and veins in me, fastened me flesh' and who subsequently subjected the poet to an experience so severe that he was 'almost unmade'. And he says, in breath-bated joy: 'dost though touch me afresh? Over again I feel thy finger and find thee.' I knew something of this sense of being 'unmade', and I longed to be reached by that questing finger. 'Over again I feel thy finger and find thee' – that line, with its beauty of rhythm and alliteration expressed the experience I longed for most, and somehow through its agency the Creator's finger brushed against mine across the abyss.

The second Hopkins poem which brought me close to tears was *To R.B.* in which he sadly expresses his sense of desertion by the creative flame. He longs for 'the one rapture of an inspiration,' and gives its absence as the reason why his friend Robert Bridges to whom the poem was addressed may have missed 'in these lagging lines….. the roll, the rise, the carol, the creation'. These words are all the more poignant to those of us who also seek the same touch of rapture since despite (or perhaps even because of) Hopkins' pain and sense of failure, he was still able to write divinely.

*

Despite my judgmental rejection of the world and most of the ethos of university study I longed for what people like Alexander Scott and Philip Hobsbaum had. I wanted success; I wanted to be a writer. Perhaps I felt this was the only achievement within my reach. I hero-worshipped Scott and wrote a poem about him talking us through the works of Hugh MacDiarmid. I left this on his desk anonymously but confessed when he questioned its authorship. He was a little flattered, more than a little amused, but the fact he didn't ask to see more of my work or encourage me in my writing suggested that the quality of my offering was in his opinion, poor.

Not having found a solid place to stand, not knowing myself, I had nothing of substance to say and my dream of taking a place in the Scottish literary pantheon evaporated.

*

I was still aware of mum and dad's expectation that somewhere along the line I would meet and marry the 'right' girl, the person God intended for me, whose 'rightness' for me I would recognise with absolute clarity.

I reasoned that due to my utter hypocrisy and distance from God I could not expect any such intervention, and so must do for myself what true Christians left to their heavenly Father.

There was a sweet girl from Dumbarton who sat near me in English in my first year at university, and with whom I chatted about Lewis Grassic Gibbon's *Sunset Song*. I was drawn to her but kept my distance. She was a Roman Catholic: to me that was an impenetrable barrier, and so I drew back.

It's ironic that Gerard Hughes, author of *God of Surprises*, a man whose writings would prove so helpful to me worked in the Roman Catholic Chaplaincy at Glasgow University from 1967-75. How often I walked past the building as a student! If only I had met him, I later thought. But of course I was not at that time in a place where his love and wisdom could ever have reached me. It would be 45 years before I was ready to hear his words.

*

And then there was my disturbing behaviour towards a German girl in my English Language class. Her name was Hannelore and I became somewhat obsessed with her, or with her name (itself a poem in four syllables), despite never having engaged her in a proper conversation. I wrote Hannelore a bizarre poem in which my lines were interspersed with quotations from Lieder – I had purchased a translation to guide me in this.

'Hallelore, Hannelore,' if began, followed by one of the quotations from German love songs. The poem concluded

You are my entowered Rapunzel
and your hair a chain to me
You sit, spinning at your wheel
spinning love's eternity.

I left this weird piece of writing for her to read. She ran her eyes down it and laughed, but I didn't speak further to her, or even particularly want to. Was I making a dramatic play for the unreachable to mask my inadequacy in forming real relationships?

The elderly lecturer in that class – Leslie Blakely, author of *Teach Yourself Old English* – was delightfully eccentric. You would hear him panting as he climbed the stairs, and then he would burst into the room with a wicker basket under his gowned arm from which he'd take lecture notes and a large alarm clock primed to go off at the end of the hour. At some point during his lecture he would briefly leave the lecture theatre and someone would take advantage of his absence, nip to the lectern and re-set the clock. Dr Blakely would then return and recommence his lecture which would shortly be interrupted by a strident cacophony of sound and vibration long before the sixty minutes had elapsed. Whereupon he would sweep notes and clock into his basket before bumbling out of the room.

*

Regularly over the winter months, Missionary Conferences were held at the WEC (then called Worldwide Evangelisation Crusade) training college in Glasgow's Prince Albert Road, consisting of sermons and reports from missionaries home on 'furlough'. My parents frequently attended and I dutifully accompanied them.

On one occasion, they also took Tessa with us – Tessa whose question had prompted my great lie.

I remember the journey back to Carluke, this young woman

and me in the back seat. My parents sat in grey-faced, stony silence. Apprehensively I sensed a storm was gathering.

It broke when the three of us were back in the house.

'You put your arm round her,' they said, accusingly.

'I did not!' I protested.

I had no recollection whatsoever of the action which had offended them so much.

'I may have inadvertently had my hand on the back of her chair when I was leaning forward to speak to someone, but I did *not* have my arm round her.'

Nothing I could say was enough to convince them and I retreated to my bedroom, wounded and confused.

I had spoken truth, and had not been believed. And in any case why was an arm on someone's shoulder so offensive? I was crushed: my parents' reaction drove a wedge between us. How could I entrust my parents with any of my thoughts about girls when they had been so incomprehensibly indignant, allowing no opportunity for discussion?

*

Emily, he girl I'd been drawn to during S6, came to Glasgow University in the autumn of 1971. Morning by morning I saw her on the train, agonised over expressing my feelings for her and chronicled my angst in an red-covered looseleaf notebook.

Eventually, I concluded histrionically that 'the anguish of not knowing is deeper than the anguish of knowing the worst' and one morning, somewhere between Cambuslang and Glasgow Central I declared my love.

She responded positively to my great joy, with old-fashioned candour.

'Yes, I care for you, John.'

I remember sitting in our dining room at Douglas Street that evening, flushed with the warmth of the story I bore, spooning oxtail soup into my mouth while anxiously wondering how to tell my parents.

Of the two challenging conversations that day, the second required the more courage.

Emily and I prolonged those morning trips to Gilmorehill – we'd walk from Central Station to the Underground in St Enoch Square and catch the shoogly Clockwork Orange up to Byres Road. At least once, we stayed on the train all the way round the circle before getting off. Emily was studying French – I bought a copy of *Old Goriot* in English so I could read it with her.

We discovered that my postcode ended 'BJ' – 'beloved John'; hers 'EB' – 'Emily beloved.'

Her parents and sister made me welcome in their house and treated me as one of the family. I recall the huge, traditional steak pie for family lunch on New Year's Day.

I remember those prolonged goodbyes in her tiny kitchen; sweet and chaste. And then powering along dark pavements back to Douglas Street, hard, full of joy and expectation.

My own parents welcomed Emily, but not with great warmth. They hoped our relationship was a passing infatuation opining that Emily and I were not suited. But this relationship was real. It was the first truly important thing I had done on my own initiative.

We went to a Scottish National Orchestra prom at the Kelvin Hall in June 1972, Emily and I. My parents, as always anxious, were unhappy at the thought of us travelling back to Carluke by train late at night and insisted on driving to Glasgow to collect us. They'd wait along University Avenue at around the time the concert might be expected to end they said.

The final piece was Holst's *Planets*. Somewhere close to its conclusion the auditorium lights failed. The music stumbled to silence in cacophonous collapse as some of the band gamely tried to keep going before realising the effort was futile.

Emily and I could have left but decided to stay. The power was restored in twenty minutes. We heard the rest of the music through to its ethereal conclusion.

When the final notes had died, we joined the crowds heading for the exit.

Grim faces awaited us along University Avenue. Why were we so late?

Not a word was spoken as, Carluke bound, we headed for the M8.

*

That summer my parents tried to persuade me to break up with Emily. I was mildly irritated with her over some minor issue but I suspect it was nothing that could not have been resolved.

My parents and I stayed at the Falls of Lora hotel at Connell in Argyll for our August holiday and even there the pressure to bring our relationship to an end continued.

I remember the letters Emily and I sent one another, the red post box in Connell village I walked to in the healing sunshine, the guilty sense of relief as the cream envelope dropped out of sight.

Possibly, given my personality and circumstances it was inevitable, perhaps it was indeed for the best, but what I did to Emily and how I did it was the cruellest thing I have ever done to anyone in my life. Emily was my first love.

She parcelled up in brown paper the things of mine she still had, and posted them to me: some books, and a piano reduction of the *Enigma Variations*.

*

I made it through my three-year course, never failing an end-of-session exam and graduated in MA (Ordinary) in July 1973. I had expected to progress to an Honours course in English Language and Literature: my lack of maturity and life experience meant, I knew, that I was unable to engage many of the literary texts we studied with sufficient understanding and empathy and my essay results were correspondingly disappointing.

I hired a gown; my parents arranged for a photo to be taken on the morning of the event by their friend Nisbet Reid who was a photographer at Annans' studio in Glasgow. I posed for him as best as I could, struggling with worry about the day ahead and the uncomfortable shirt I was wearing.

Later, up the familiar staircase into the Bute Hall at the University for the interminable ceremony holding myself tense, fraught with bladder anxiety. I felt no sense of joy, no sense of achievement. I had simply down the next thing.

Widor's *Toccata* rang out triumphantly from the organ as I left the hall to join my parents in the quadrangle. Someone took our photo; we went for lunch in the refectory – a special, graduation menu of smoked salmon. My parents thought that was what I'd want, and I hadn't told them otherwise.

They must have been disappointed by my attitude but at that stage surviving was all I could do. Much of my nervous energy was expended in combatting the religious fears which were taking me to the brink.

EIGHT

GUNSQUAD AT THE GOSPEL HALL

I imagined armed Soviet militia bursting into the church and rounding up the worshippers. Such things I had heard happened behind the Iron Curtain.

'If you're not a Christian, you're free to go,' someone barked. I knew this was my opportunity to escape, for I was not a believer. But I was afraid. What would life be like without the group of people who more than any other had given me security and identity? I remained standing with the rest,

An order was given. Machine-gun fire raked the room mercilessly.

*

I wrote a story about a fisherman's wife in an East Coast village. Her husband was at sea, battling a raging storm. As wind and waves lashed the gable of her cottage, she prayed for God's mercy, prayed that the storm would abate, that the men of the village might survive. But especially she prayed for her man.

As a sullen dawn broke her neighbours bore his body homewards, up from the shore-line.

Her faith died with him.

Ironically my sense of faith's absence was itself an expression of faith.

*

The knot of anxiety was tightened by two deaths in the family.

My grandfather, John Cumming Dempster was gravely ill in Law Hospital with cancer. His signature on the copy of John Donne's *Poems* which I bought with the money he gave me for my 20th birthday was shaky and weak.

Each day that summer of 1972, I visited him in Sick Bay. He was propped up in bed, grey-faced, angry fluid draining into a plastic container suspended from the bed frame.

We said little of significance. He told me he detested the name of the new Hillman car model, the Avenger. 'It's not a good name for a car,' he said. 'It suggests aggression, vengeance.' He pointed repeatedly at a plant on the table. It was beginning to wilt. He speculated that his destiny and the flower's were inextricably linked. I told him about Emily.

I wish I had been able to relate to him man-to-man.

My father was admitted to the same hospital for a non-urgent operation, confident nothing would happen to grandpa until he was on his feet again.

One evening, my mother and I had a call from Sick Bay. Grandpa did not have long to live. I left at once and drove to the hospital. Strangely my mother did not accompany me.

I reached his room. Through the small, square inspection window in the door I saw the familiar face, ashen and lifeless. No one who loved him was with him at the end.

I hesitated. A nurse came, and blocked the window with a purpose-made wooden panel. She didn't offer me time with him. I saw my grandfather no more.

While recording his death at the Registry Office in Carluke High Street I discovered he had been born in Brownlie, just down the hill. His middle name was the same as Emily's. I wondered if they were distantly related.

The funeral, on a sunny day early in September was held at Wiston Church in the lea of Tinto Hill where John had been headteacher in the 1920s and where his and Phemie's girls lay buried. I remembered the story of him blundering through the graveyard in pitch-black night on his way back from the manse to the schoolhouse.

During the service in the church a cat nonchalantly padded down the blue-carpeted aisle.

Phemie lived on alone in the bottom flat in Brierybank Avenue, Lanark: gentle, apparently serene, perpetually humming, stone-deaf. Her neighbour, delivering the paper, found her dead on the kitchen floor one morning in March 1973. She had been making her breakfast. She had not suffered.

Once again the grave at Wiston was opened.

*

These two deaths, coming as they did so close, filled me with fear of dying. I read every symptom in my body as a dire portent. Following my gran's funeral I typed a reflection, over-written and heavily derivative of the thinking and writing of Lewis Grassic Gibbon. Behind its humanist posturing, I see a young man reaching for a Scottish family to belong to, for a form of immortality without the complications of the Christ.

But in that purifying fresh springlight, with the high-voiced funeral incantations shrilling in you, you felt immortal and not downcast but with a strange triumph. Here where you stood generations had stood and would stand to mark a passing. Generations before Christ and after wept for an individual but rejoiced for a race and life had gone on. And from that soil at my feet, from the very mould of dead flesh sprang the life and the spring that give continuance to man, and continuance to my family, and gave me my breath and my being. And I knew the soil was mine, and the earth was mine.

*

I was still attending Carluke Gospel Hall with my parents. Each Sunday I took bread and wine and wondered if this was the morning when divine wrath would strike. Occasionally however I would stand up into the great silence and share some thoughts. I taught a Sunday-School class, a group of 8-year-old girls whom I collected from the Crawforddyke housing scheme in those pre-child-protection days, squeezing them into my mother's Ford Anglia. I wrote plays for the Girls' Class about *The Sunshine Gang* a cheerful, evangelical equivalent of Enid Blyton's Secret Seven.

I helped my father lead the youth group, accompanying songs on the harmonium. One evening a girl called Gail prayed the prayer and became a Christian and as dad and I drove home in the Austin 18 and garaged it in the darkness I felt numb, distressed again that others could do what I failed to achieve.

There were lavish Sunday-evening suppers in other people's houses, sitting eating salmon sandwiches and cake in the warm radiance of a coal fire, for the moment secure though the world beyond the windows and the Monday morning which lay ahead were dark and unpredictable. There were the Hogmanay gatherings, a wholesome alternative to other ways of spending the year's last evening. Singing, prayers; hugs and chocolate after the bells.

And speculation. 'I wonder if this will be the year he comes?'

I stood with the others, goat among the sheep, as the machine-gun barrels were raised.

'The Lord must come soon!' Andrew Weir said one Sunday in the autumn of 1973. That was what I feared most, the time when I would be left – in the terrible Greek words of St Paul – *Anathema Maranatha*, which I understood to mean 'cursed at the coming of the Lord'.

The syllables gyrated in my mind.
Anathema Maranatha!
Anathema Maranatha!
Maranathema!

*

Everything would be resolved if I simply had courage to admit I was a hypocrite and that my story of conversion was a sham. If I could only verbalise this hypocrisy, I reasoned, somebody surely would help me.

One Saturday night in tears of dread at what lay ahead the following morning, I blurted out my terrible confession to my parents and relaxed into the certainty that the worse was over.

'Of course you're a Christian,' my father said, ruffling my hair tenderly. 'That's the devil trying to get at you! It wouldn't be right to stop going to the meetings. Have faith!'

And my mother said more tersely 'And if you're not a Christian you know what to do.'

This next morning as we sat round the communion table my hands still trembled, but beneath the quotidian anxiety there now lay a further deep stratum of anger and despair.

On the Monday I was sent to the doctors and left the surgery with a prescription for Valium. What I in fact needed was empathic listening, an acceptance of my story.

*

This belief in the devil's involvement in human lives was standard among evangelicals.

In the summer of 1973 my mother gave me a book to read, *His Name Was Tom* the biography of Tom Rees, an evangelical preacher. 'That'll show you a thing or two,' she said.

One passage from the book shook me:

Before he was a Christian, he did not believe in the devil, but never doubted the existence of God; after his conversion, there had been the occasional question: 'Is there a God?' but he never doubted again the existence of his old master. 'Do I believe in the devil?' he would say. 'Of course. I used to work for him.'

I viewed my inner turmoil as a battle with the devil. But attempts to dampen down the soundless thought-voices in my head – let alone to defeat them – served only to increase their stridency.

I sought to describe this interior confusion in another overwritten, troubled piece very derivative of C.S. Lewis in concept if not in execution.

I am much assailed by my attendant personal devils who have greatly intensified their assaults of late. They are all vaguely of the genus Snatchsoul – indeed, in some strange way, they all seem to be related to a particularly nauseating and sickening devil, Mr Dempster Snatchsoul by name.

I mentioned other equally nefarious members of Clan Snatchsoul, including Archdeacon Snatchsoul who:

reminded me of the time as a boy when I took Christ's name in vain, and he told me I was damned for a certainty. If I am of the elect, then why bother fighting? I'll be the victor anyway? If I'm not of the elect, well, I'm damned already. And verses of Scripture on damnation, and weird sequences from requiem masses, and the terrible throb of the Dies Irae [thank you very much, Verdi] all hurled through my mind, and Archdeacon Snatchsoul laughed.

Eventually, I continued, the demonic campaign flagged somewhat and

I found myself again, very inadequately, able to talk to God, and He gave me some assurance, and the strength to read Christian

books, in which I found great solace, and moreover I read the Bible
in which I found the ammunition to fight the Snatchsouls' missiles.

*

My parents were accurate in their analysis if not in their response to me. Only a believer, and someone who totally bought in to the great story could write these words. I was not a hypocrite but a struggling believer, enmeshed in negativism and obsessed by the conviction that until I had the one experience I sought moving forward was impossible.

This 'particularly nauseating and sickening Mr Dempster Snatchsoul' was, of course my cruel image of myself. I was not yet in touch with the deep self who observes my doings and thoughts in an attitude of grace and patience, who injects hope into the narrative, who insists 'You are loved! Choose joy!'

I wrote some verses, published in the Brethren magazine *The Witness* in March 1973 expressing a longing for God. 'Lord I believe; please help my unbelief.'

Lord, take my hand, and lead me to the place where
Your blood and sweat poured forth that I might live
O, for the faith to look upon that face there
And murmur, softly, 'Jesus, Lord, forgive.'

This, too, was an expression of faith.

I came across an old, crackly recording of the tenor Walter Widdop singing an aria from Mendelssohn's *Elijah* which sets two passages from the Bible. The central section in an anguished minor key resonated with my experiences. 'Oh that I knew where I might find him that I might truly come unto his temple.' But then the music drops back to the major and Widdop continues full of vigour and triumph: 'if with all your heart you truly seek me, ye shall surely truly find me, thus saith our God.' I found, momentarily, a sweetness in these words.

I was encouraged by C. S. Lewis's response to someone who asked 'If it is true that one has only to want God enough in order to find Him, how can I make myself want Him enough to enable myself to find Him?' Replied Lewis:

If you don't want God, why are you so anxious to want to want Him? I think that in reality the want is a real one, and I should say that this person has in fact found God, although it may not be fully recognised yet. We are not always aware of things at the time they happen. At any rate, what is more important is that God has found this person, and that is the main thing.

I read a reissue, from the Reformed publisher Banner of Truth Trus,t of Hugh Martin's 19th century book on *Simon Peter*. I felt inclined to cry to God with Peter 'Depart from me; for I am a sinful man , O Lord' (Luke 5:8 AV) and longed to hear with Peter the Lord's reply 'Fear not!', and his words in another context 'Simon, Simon, behold, Satan hath desired to have you, that he may sift you as wheat: but I have prayed for thee, that thy faith fail not.' (Luke 22:31-32 AV)

I wrote shortly afterwards: 'Had Jesus *prayed* for *me*? Satan had certainly desired to have me, but had Jesus actually *prayed* for me?' The wonder of it filled me.

But I failed to identify these experiences as tender shoots of faith. Still seeking a conversion story similar to those which been modelled to me I felt desperate.

*

I had confessed, and had not been believed. What must I do to persuade them I needed help?

I wrote a letter to my friend Gregor, outlining my hypocrisy and frustration. I can't recall what I said but I know there were several

BLOODYs in large, emphatic, catharthic capitals. I placed this on the ledge in front of him at a lecture we were both attending.

Gregor opened and read my letter before replacing it in the envelope and returning it to me. It was too much for him to process.

I wrote a short play called *Possess it merely* – from the *Hamlet* quote, 'Things rank and gross in nature possess it merely'. It centred on a girl from a Christian family who has pretended to be a true convert, feels anguish at her hypocrisy and confesses to her parents but is not believed. In her despair, she becomes pregnant (quite how this comes about is not discussed), believing that her openness to pre-marital sex will be the evidence which will clinch the case, proving that she is truly an unbeliever. To her astonishment and despair her mother and father forgive her and do not see her actions as a sign of faith's absence. One stormy night, she walks down Glasgow's Jamaica Street, and flings herself over the bridge parapet into the Clyde's dark swirling waters.

*

In the summer of 1973 I went on holiday with my parents (our last family vacation together) at Thornton-le-Dale in Yorkshire. Torn between faith and its rejection I refused to go to the nearest Gospel Hall in Scarborough. Instead we attended a service at the local Methodist Church which listening through my parents' ears I judged uninspiring and felt guilty at having dragged them there.

We were staying in a hotel, an old building in the grounds of which peacocks strutted in the clawprints of five centuries of ancestors. I was burdened by lethargy and by a sense that I was viewing reality through dark glasses. Twice in bed during that holiday I had an experience of peace. 'A strange feeling crept over me,' I wrote, continuing 'It was a feeling of immense joy and peace and rest, and it hovered in me very briefly, then was gone. It was almost as if God were speaking to me, and saying "This is the joy, the peace, the comfort, the love." In the stillness, I found myself longing to be a Christian, to know Christ and His peace.'

And then on another occasion: 'For a few seconds I had a free sample of the peace of God, and then, like a mirage, it vanished and I was empty.'

There were two other bedroom experiences at Thornton. One night I woke in deep fear as though a dark being had brushed past my bed as I slept – a ghost, another troubled presence. And one morning when a young woman about my own age brought me morning tea while I was still in bed I felt delicious arousal stirring beneath the covers as she handed the tray to me, her blue skirt inches from my fingers.

*

That autumn I began to read Christian books with more seriousness, tried to pay more attention to daily Bible reading, and vowed that in future I would only write religious pieces.

Looking back a year later it seemed to me that God in the language of Donne's poem was besieging my citadel of self. I became increasingly gripped by the fear that Christ would return soon and I would be left behind, with no hope. The screw was tightened by the Middle East War of 1973 as it had been during the previous war six years before. In line with the theology of books such as Hal Lindsey's which I unquestioningly read as truth, I believed God was not about to let the State of Israel, miraculously re-established in 1948 after centuries, be crushed to extinction by its neighbours. God would surely intervene. Christ must surely come!

Anathema Maranatha!

The screw was tightened further by the political crisis in the UK that autumn when emergency measures to conserve fuel supplied in the face of industrial action by miners led as I noted

> *to a dimming of lights and a sombre curtailment of brightness. The gloom closed in around us; television transmissions stopped earlier than usual in the evenings; the shops were cold; the great neon signs were lifeless; everywhere there was chill and dread of the future.*

Finally there was the Prime Minister [Edward Heath] on the television, justifying his introduction of the three-day week, and warning the nation to take full benefit of the relaxation of power restrictions around Christmas.

He could promise only continuing crisis after the New Year. 'I could hardly bear to listen to him: his words brought the world outside so forcefully in that I couldn't ignore it.'

*

That autumn I was working as a Trainee in Carluke Library. I daren't watch the news but surreptitiously glanced at the newspapers sticking out of readers' shopping bags scanning the headlines to reassure myself that, for the moment at least, things were no worse if no better. Evening by evening, I walked home in the darkness deeply afraid that the house would be empty, my parents taken by the Lord. It was small relief when my mother opened the door, as the dread of tomorrow remained.

A year later I might see my anguish as a sign that a well-intentioned God was battering my heart into submission, but in fact any battering there was came from my anxious, neurotic spirit. My issues that autumn were much less spiritual problems than they were mental health issues. I had been wounded not by machines guns, for the Soviets never came but by the very teaching in which it seemed other people found freedom.

Sunday, December 16th 1973. Evening. I was at the Gospel Service. John McEwan was preaching. John was known to everyone in Carluke – he worked in the town centre, pushing two bins on a wheeled carriage, brushing up litter.

He read Jesus' parable about the rich man and Lazarus in Luke 16. The rich man, and Lazarus both die. The rich man finds himself in hell, Lazarus in 'Abraham's bosom'. The man in hell is concerned that his brothers might also end up there unless they are warned. Could Lazarus be restored to life so that he can warn them. No, says Abraham. 'They have Moses and the prophets; let them hear them.' (Luke 16:29 AV)

And those words came alive within me. Here was I, wanting some miracle from God to bring me to faith – and yet I had not just the Old Testament but the whole Bible.

As John read the passage I scanned ahead. The rich man, convinced that the miracle of Lazarus's resurrection would be enough to bring his brothers to repentance repeats his request. But Abraham replies 'If they hear not Moses and the prophets, neither will they be persuaded, though one rose from the dead.' (Luke 16:31 AV)

That verse was transformational. I recognised that I not only had the Bible but the reality of a risen Jesus – what more did I expect God to do to persuade me? And in addition there was a movement of inner response, a saying 'Yes' to God.

After the service doubts still swirled in my head, but at home I came across quite by chance a section in a Bible study book which acknowledged that someone might be uncertain whether a previous commitment to Jesus had been sincere. It advised 'Tell the Lord that you are not sure if you were ever saved before, but you want to be saved right now' and gave words to use as a prayer.

And I prayed the prayer and knew in fulness the joy and peace of which I had had a brief inkling while in Yorkshire. I sat on the edge of my bed in spiritual elation, sobbing silently.

In that moment I was given what I longed for. It's hard to see that this could have been manufactured by my own psyche – otherwise why had it not taken place long before? I see it as a gift from God, the perfect gift I needed at that time, the gift which gave me both the self-confidence and God-confidence to move forward. This experience marked the beginning of my journey towards knowing, and loving myself.

I went through to my parents' bedroom. I told them I'd become a Christian, and how joyful I felt.

My mother looked up, surprised.

'But we've been telling you that for years!' she said.

I felt that I had proudly brought them something very precious, a diamond of great value and it had been dashed from my hands.

*

Why was my story, brought with such joy, rejected? Possibly my mother, struggling with her own mental health issues found it hard to accept anything which didn't correspond to her image of the son she wanted me to be. It seemed at the time – and I know I was narcissistically over-dramatising – that I had no-one, no parent, no friend, no church leader to try to understand and help me.

But nevertheless after this Sunday there was a new stirring of life in me. Doubts and fears remained, but something had indubitably changed.

And if the militia had burst into the church, raising their weapons, I would have taken my place with the others believing that though I was incorrigibly messed-up, I belonged.

PART 2

PART 2

NINE

INTIMIDATING
PERSPECTIVES

I watched through the glass door as the Senior Library Assistant whose name I knew was Karen crossed between the book shelves on her way to let me in. In the spring of 1974, towards the end of my year as a Trainee Librarian with Lanarkshire County Libraries I'd been asked to temporarily manage two branch libraries, one of them in Shotts.

'How tall she us!' I thought, feeling daunted. Having introduced myself I followed Karen downstairs to the staff room.

*

I had been offered the trainee post following an interview with Willie Scobbie, the Chief Librarian – it was, in fact more of a friendly chat than an interview, for Willie, a leading figure in the Airdrie community, was known to my parents and I suspect the job, probably created for me, was mine before I'd opened my mouth.

I joined the staff at my local library, Carluke immediately after leaving university and over the next seven months learned basic library routines. I knew everyone who worked there, having been one of their regular customers. On my first shift I was apprehensive about meeting Noreen: some years before she had admonished me, in a very courteous and professional way, upon finding in books I had returned on my mother's behalf some products of the Victory Tract Club which mum had secreted between random pages. But Noreen smiled, seemingly warm, no doubt every bit as uncomfortable as I was.

Despite the spiritual angst, there was much to enjoy during those months at Carluke – I had no responsibilities, a clear role and a familiar workplace. And I loved the building. It was an architecturally progressive structure opened less than a decade before with glass walls beneath a striking, hyperbolic parabaloidal roof sprung between two brick buttresses.

*

In early 1974 I was reassigned to one of the Council's mobile libraries, based at Library HQ in Hamilton's Auchingramont Road. It was driven by Fred Reynolds, a gruff, taciturn man who had seen librarians come and go and thought (accurately) that he knew his readers' tastes far better than I did.

'No one will read it!', he said, shaking his head and tutting, as he brandished a copy of a biography of Soviet leader Leonid Brezhnev which I, now with a budget and responsibility for choosing stock, had optimistically selected.

I watched the volume, surreptitiously. It remained obstinately on the shelf, rebuking me.

But we did have some thoughtful readers of eclectic tastes – I remember one enthusing passionately about E. F. Schumacher's *Small is Beautiful: a study of economics as if people mattered.* In my conservatism, its theme and the customer who requested it seemed suspect and radical.

Each day, I'd travel to Hamilton by bus, and meet Fred and the mobile library in Auchingramont Road. I first heard Abba's *Waterloo* on the radio in a double-decker speeding downhill past Motherwell's Dalziel High School, confused that a pop group should address a historical theme.

Fred and I spent most of each week visiting rather bleak east Lanarkshire communities – Allanton, a small former mining village on the road to Shotts and along the M8 corridor towards Edinburgh, Harthill and Salsburgh. On Tuesdays we were in more scenic territory in south Lanarkshire, with one stop beside the castle Walter Scott had made famous under the name of Tillietudlem.

Fred often had the radio on in the mobile library, mostly tuned to Radio Clyde. I'll forever associate a street in Allanton where we stopped at tea-time on Monday nights with *Sugar Baby Love* by the Rubettes; one artist was *Down in the strawberry patch with Sally*, although as far as I could gather what they were doing there was left to the imagination; while another had just 'called to say how much I love you'.

My relationship with Fred was not particularly warm. Insecure in myself I lacked the confidence to relax in his presence, especially since I suspected he questioned my competence. A major concern was my anxiety when toilets weren't immediately available and there were no convenient trees to slip unobtrusively behind. I would drink as little as possible when I was working, and my days became increasingly worry-filled. When I was scheduled to begin work in the afternoon, my mornings too were dread-stricken. Eventually, I found I simply couldn't face going in to work and someone, presumably Willie Scobbie transferred me to the Auchingramont Road HQ until something else could be found for me.

Spending my days in a warm, comfortable environment with toilets just along the corridor was a blessed therapy, particularly when I stood at an upper window each day and watched the mobiles driving off from the car-park to visit their first customers knowing I didn't have to go with them.

*

Not long afterwards, I was asked to look after Shotts and Newmains Libraries and met Karen of the Daunting Stature

Mum kindly lent me her old Ford Anglia to solve my transport problems. (I wanted to plaster enormous adhesive JESUS SAVES roundels on either side of this car but my mother, fearing vandalism, demurred. I can't recall if my desire to do this was an expression of faith, or an attempt to define myself in my own eyes and in the eyes of the church and the world as a member of the security-imparting Christian clan.)

I coped well in this role but my insecurity showed in one incident. Late on a Friday afternoon, Mr Walker, who was Willie Scobbie's deputy phoned me at Newmains asking me to do the evening shift at nearby Newarthill Library. This should not have been a problem – it would merely have meant delaying my return home and grabbing a sandwich for tea.

However, I'd heard that there were occasional problems at Newarthill with teenagers making life difficult for library staff and I was very anxious at the prospect of working there. 'I'm not going,' I told the boss without, I think, helping him understand my reasons. Despite his attempts to get me to change my mind, I refused and eventually he rang off, a very unhappy man. I drove home, sobbing profusely.

I had planned to phone the long-suffering Willie Scobbie on the Monday morning to explain my insubordination. But before I made contact with him, he came on the line, far kinder to me than I was entitled to expect. 'I believe the man upstairs has been giving you some grief?'

'Yes,' I replied.

Nothing more was said.

That year I was shown more kindness and patience than I probably deserved. Though willing and eager to please I was anxious and lacking in initiative, and found it hard to 'manage' other people, being too willing to accede to their wishes. But then, I had received no practical training. I lacked any sense of 'ownership' of the job just as I had no sense of 'calling' to librarianship as a career. It was simply a question of doing the next thing which came along. And so I spent academic year 1974-75 in Strathclyde University's Livingstone Tower securing a post-graduate diploma in librarianship (which was awarded with Distinction).

*

I looked at Karen as we were taking our leave after my last shift at Shotts Library. It struck me that she seemed smaller, no longer intimidating. What had changed was not Karen's height, but my perspective. By then more secure and confident in my work with the Shotts team I saw things in a truer light.

I smiled, shook hands with Karen and walked along to road to where I had parked the Anglia with care, so as not to annoy the grumpy resident who once complained about it being left all day at the roadside in front of his house.

'Where have you been?' he said sharply when he accosted me.

'In the library,' I replied mildly.

'In the *library*?' he exclaimed in a derisory tone which implied the utter incomprehensibility of my answer.

*

I enjoyed the post-graduate course, once again travelling daily to Glasgow. The subjects I studied included cataloguing and classification, public library management, bibliography, and 'analytical and descriptive bibliography and textual criticism'. The staff at that time were not visionaries – computers were already beginning to transform library procedures and yet the new technology scarcely featured in their teaching.

I loved the bibliography class which imparted the skills necessary to make a formal listing of an author's output. We were required to demonstrate our learning by producing a practice bibliography: I prepared a fairly comprehensive listing of the works of George MacKay Brown in books, pamphlets and periodicals.

Historical bibliography fascinated me – the lecturer was the professor, W.E. Tyler. We looked at the history of bookmaking, printing and publishing and the techniques of differentiating between editions of early works. Printing history was full of colourful characters: on account of his name alone there was always a ripple of laughter in the classroom whenever there was mention of Caxton's contemporary Wynkyn de Worde.

A job involving the custodianship of older books was appealing. I wondered if I would be able to transition from the Public Library track I had set out on.

*

I attended the Christian Union at Strathclyde, and was welcomed. I found that since most of the members were younger than me and had already made friendships I wasn't particularly close to any of them; however I frequently joined a group of CU members for lunch in the canteen.

But here as at Glasgow I found the CU committee members offputtingly holy. I remember a few of them discussing meeting George Verwer the charismatic founder of Operation Mobilisation, an organisation committed to Christian mission. They repeated in awe his story about going the length of a train during a journey speaking to everyone on board about Jesus. I cringed. What was wrong with me? I felt again the heavy burden of the superego telling me what I thought I ought to be.

*

Travelling home in the train one evening after CU. I was with three contemporaries from Carluke who happened to be on the same train, two young women and another bloke.

We were chatting away, and the guy suddenly interjected à propos of nothing, a rather agonised 'Oh, I'm feeling *randy*'.

I was astonished. Does he mean what I think he means? And is that the sort of thing you can say, in public, on a train, with *girls* present?

*

As usual, my parents were keen for me to make Christian friends and in particular a special girl. To please them or to get them off my back I asked a guy whom I met at the CU to the house for a few days but it was someone I felt more comfortable in relating to because he was shyer than I was, socially awkward, and perhaps a little needy. But I was on edge the whole time he was in the house.

'What did God say in your quiet time today?' he asked on the Saturday morning.

I recoiled. I had read the Bible that day but God had been silent.

I invented things heaven might have said had heaven spoken, putting words in God's mouth as it were.

Perhaps we were both playing games.

*

That interest in publishing had been piqued prior to my course. At Carluke Library I particularly loved the book trade 'organ' (as it called itself), *The Bookseller*. This weekly publication didn't simply contain details of new and forthcoming books (and with a young man's wide-eyed optimism I simply equated 'the new' with 'the best'), but also articles on book-trade history which, I discovered fascinated me. And a reader at Newmains Library had requested a copy of John Sutherland's

1974 study *Thackeray at Work*: I found the book beneath the counter and was fascinated by its insights into 19th century author/publisher relations and the processes of literary composition and publishing.

As I was leaving the Livingstone Tower for the last time after completing the course, Professor Tyler said to me 'If ever you'd like to do further research in the department, just get in touch with us.'

I smiled to myself, thinking how unlikely it was that I would take him up on this. The prospect of academic research was more daunting than Karen had ever been, and I couldn't imagine time making it seem any more achievable.

TEN

IMAGINARY YACHTS

I could have sworn there were yachts heading placidly downstream and I could have sworn that the sentences describing them must have formed a significant section in Mary McDermott Schidler's *Creed for a Christian Sceptic*.

One day I was browsing in Pickering and Inglis bookshop in Bothwell Street before catching my train home and came across Shideler's book. I was surprised that P&I, a bastion of theological conservatism would stock such a title but then I noticed it had a forward by F. F. Bruce, an academic theologian and member of the Brethren, and must therefore be 'safe'. Instinctively drawn to the book, I bought it. Shideler's work is thoughtful exercise in apologetics informed by the works of Charles Williams and C. S. Lewis, an exploration of the Apostles' Creed. But on my first reading, little resonated with me.

Except for the river and the yachts. But when I re-read the book years later I completely missed the passage which had been of such significance to me, so brief was it. And when I eventually found it I realized there was just a river and some ramblers. No yachts.

Here's what Shideler wrote:

While the way of Christian life may be narrow, it is more likely to twist and bend like a river than to run straight like a Roman road, and we who follow it down-stream to the sea may be temporarily heading west around one curve while our companions are heading east around another curve, yet both may be travelling in the same current to the same end.

I saw this river in my mind's eye when first I read the book, sinuously making its way to the great ocean. I am standing on the flood-plain and all I can see of my yachts is their masts. As the river curves some of these move from right to left, others from left to right so that they seem to be heading in opposite directions. But in fact each yacht is on the same river, borne by the same current towards the same sea. That is the image which consoled me and made me value *Creed* even if at that point I did not fully understand the nature of its consolation.

*

What did I expect to feel the day after that significant Sunday in December 1973. Overwhelming joy? My recollection is that life continued much as before. A year later I wrote a detailed account of my 'conversion' interpreted in the theological language I was familiar with as a victory of Christ over diabolic oppression. *The Lord, the devil and me* was written close to the events but I do not always recognise the past it describes and as an account it should be treated with considerable caution. It is protective of everyone but myself. 'Neither Christian home nor [the Brethren] kept me from God, as the devil would have it. I was kept from God solely because of a duplicity in my character. The fault was mine, and mine entirely.'

I recorded that

for the first week after that December Sunday my brain was a turmoil of oaths and curses as I tried to sleep at night, and that

I saw these signs of obsessiveness as arrows catapulted into my consciousness by the devil himself.

'Lord, I'm yours. Tell him to go away,' I groaned.

I quoted scriptural texts at the devil. 'Verily, verily, I say unto you, he that heareth my word, and believeth on him that sent me, hath everlasting life, and shall not come into condemnation; but is passed from death unto life.' (John 5:24 AV)

And I expressed in my account gratitude that over the years 'I was kept from wandering off from God by the longsuffering love of a genuine Christian home.' There was no recognition of my own uniqueness and loveliness as a person; no acknowledgement of the harm done to me albeit unwittingly by the church, and by my parents. I was writing what I felt was expected of me, unaware that I had any further options.

I also described continuing fears that Bible prophecies were being fulfilled, that the apocalyptic clock was ticking towards midnight, that the Lord would come and I would be left. I agonised over whether having messed up baptism I should seek to be re-baptised, 'this time in full knowledge of the faith'.

I described a period of depression. I wrote of loving the 'unconsciousness' of sleep and of the feeling of heaviness, numbness and lack of purpose which greeted me when I woke. I described myself as being 'God's, yet with no sensation of being his; God's, yet feeling he can't hear me as I pray for joy and purpose'. I felt 'out of touch with God forever,' and yet concluded with apparent resolution that 'he's my God and he *must* hear me'.

And I drew an analogy from contemporary lunar exploration referring a space craft on the far side of the moon, out of touch with Mission Control, yet set on a pre-determined course. 'On earth they've got it down to the last second when communication will be resumed.

And God knows when I'll come into his sunlight again, for he's set me on the course I'm travelling.'

I now realise that this continuing angst was the fruit not, as I believed of my spiritual failure or of diabolical intervention but of my troubled mental health. My nerves had been screwed to breaking-point by years of fear and pressure and stirring beneath my consciousness there was also a volcano of legitimate anger.

*

And yet as I also recorded in my fraught typescript, there had been an authentic change in me. The tectonic plates had shifted; a well deep within had been uncovered. I drew comfort from lines allegedly by Martin Luther:

> *Feelings come and feelings go*
> *And feelings are deceiving;*
> *My warrant is the Word of God –*
> *Naught else is worth believing.*

Words from Proverbs 3:5 sustained me: 'Trust in the Lord with all thine heart; and lean not unto thine own understanding.' (AV) And I was inspired by C. S. Lewis – 'Obedience is the key to all doors: *feelings* come (or don't come) and go as God pleases'; and 'The moment one asks oneself "Do I believe?" all belief seems to go. I think it is because one is trying to turn round and look *at* something which is there to be used and worked *from*.'

I wrote of experiencing 'great faith and happiness'; I described coming to feel an intermittent but sincere 'deep love for fellow-Christians' discerning the 'true love of Christ' beneath the legalistic approach of some of the Brethren. With a fearful determination I did what my parents had been urging me to do for years, and signed up as a volunteer on a Scripture Union summer mission team. I even noted that I regarded that Sunday-School class I taught as 'a gift from God and a trust from God' which is considerably at variance with my later recollection (accurate I'm sure) of sitting ill-prepared on that bench seat facing thirteen small girls, bribing them to come with Polo Mints while failing to communicate in language they could understand.

An inner prompting – an idea accompanied by an empowering surge of 'Yes!' – took me to Pickering and Inglis bookshop in Glasgow to buy a hardbacked Revised Standard Version of the Bible. As I stood there turning to the first page I sensed that here was a new, unexplored country, terra incognita. I purchased it, covered it with a sheet of the famous orange paper from dad's X-ray department and read it, a lot.

*

One afternoon while at Strathclyde University I attended dutifully rather than with enthusiasm a Christian Union prayer meeting in the Livingstone Tower. I'd felt depressed during the first few weeks of term, finding it difficult to transition back to an academic environment. Between lectures I often wandered aimlessly in the city centre. The student leading the meeting read a praise-filled Psalm. Later, I wrote 'suddenly, there in the stillness of a room five floors above the streets of Glasgow, I heard God speaking to me. I had emerged from behind the moon into His sunlight.' God seemed to say, I wrote, 'you should be praising me for what I've done for you instead of moaning about what you *think* I *haven't* done for you.' And that experience released a river of praise.

When I wrote of God 'speaking' I was referring, I think to a further surge of creative energy which brought a joy and freedom. It was as though the water from the inner spring welled up in my consciousness and flowed from me: an experience which I regarded as a gift of divine self-giving.

*

One September evening in the mid-1970s, I was at the bookstall in the foyer of Strathpeffer Church of Scotland in Ross-shire. For some reason I was attracted to a well-produced blue-jacketed volume of sermons on a section of St Paul's Epistle to the Ephesians by Dr Martyn Lloyd Jones, which he had preached during his time at London's Westminster Chapel in the 1950s and '60s.

'What are you buying?' my mother asked. We were attending the Northern Convention

'It's called *Life in the Spirit in Marriage, Home and Work.*'

'Not that I'm thinking of getting married,' I added nervously, judging it expedient to stifle my longing.

But I think it was another yearning which prompted that purchase – a yearning for whatever was meant by 'life in the Spirit'. For I believed there was still something more.

I don't particularly recall reading that book but I found the succeeding volume *Christian Warfare* unforgettable. The sermons it contains deal in great detail with part of chapter six of Ephesians, discussing both the reality of a personal devil who attempts to bring chaos where God has created life and joy and the reality of the victory over this persistent opponent in which Christians participate by virtue of Christ's ultimate victory. I read chapter after chapter of this book with an increasing sense of joy and a liberating lightness of spirit.

It felt as though my eyes were opened to the source of the smog of doubt which at that point hemmed me in. It was dispelled I believed by the breath of the Spirit and I saw more clearly than ever before the sun shining brightly. I experienced a similar sense of freedom a decade later when I read Michael Green's book on the same subject, *I Believe in Satan's Downfall.*

I formed the habit of reading one of Lloyd-Jones's published sermons on St Paul's letters in bed each evening just before going to sleep and thus evening by evening expanded my education in the Reformed, Calvinist school of theology. I understood for the first time what it meant to be 'justified' – I was accepted by God not because of my own merits, and despite my own demerits, by virtue of the death of Christ on my behalf.

The reason Lloyd-Jones preached so many sermons in the process of unpacking St Paul's writing was his desire to explore every nuance of the work in the light of the Bible's overarching theme. Hence his exposition ranged over the biblical text as a whole and as I read on I gained an overview of the entire Bible and discerned God's continuing strategy to reconcile with its Creator an alienated cosmos.

Often as I read I was conscious of being somehow released, conscious of a welling up of praise and thanksgiving. This is where I was blessed – not sitting in church aware of my body pressing into the hard seat, unable to reach beyond the material because I was distracted by the crowds around me and by the noise of hymn-singing and the thought of the journey home, but here lying in bed able to let go of my surroundings and lose myself in the Doctor's exposition.

In my evangelical formation Lloyd-Jones was the key guide.

And yet I also remember my dejection as I sat in bed reading a book by another author entitled *Prayer – the Christian's Vital Breath*. I suspect my reaction to any book on prayer would have been similar but I felt unable to connect with what was described and this inability puzzled me.

*

When I wrote *The Lord, the Devil and Me* I was certain God had given me the talent to write (though I over-estimated my abilities) and that I should be 'using [this gift] for God'. But I was unsure what to write. 'I embarked on a series of tortuously-worded apologetic articles, called *Faith and the Meaning of Life*.' And I wrote a very wordy account of my year as a trainee librarian with a title which did not exactly reflect the professionalism of the career I found myself in – *Stamping Away the Days of my Years*. I reasoned that if James Herriot could write with winsome humour about veterinary practice in Yorkshire I could describe from a Christian perspective the realities of librarianship in South Lanarkshire. I prayed sincerely if rather pretentiously:

> So Lord, my talent is here. Please use it when you want to, and as often as you want to, and Lord, just make my heart ready, so that it will know your will, and know when and what you want me to write.

Perhaps in time that prayer was answered.

As I sought more of the inner freedom I had begun to experience writing seemed a way of asserting the self I hoped I was becoming. In fact it was only as I took further steps on the journey of self-discovery that I found myself with something to say and the words to say it.

*

I published an article, *Christian Love and Action* in the March 1977 issue of *The Witness*, a Brethren periodical. In it, I argued that the love Christians are called to involves action rather than emotion. And I noted in conclusion that God's love also involves divine action.

> It's much more marvellous when we can say 'God is love', and really grasp that it doesn't just mean that he has nice feelings about us, or even that he sent his son to die, but that now, in this very moment, he is actively loving us, and working for our good in every situation. Jesus promised this: '…he who loves me will be loved by my Father, and I will love him and manifest myself to him'.

There was faith in me as I typed these words but it was a faith accompanied by confusion and doubt. Even as I emphasised that what mattered was action, not feelings, so I longed for a greater experience of loving and being loved. It took years before I knew with any consistency that the Father was 'actively loving' me and the rest of my life to enter even superficially into the implications of what I wrote with such apparent confidence in that article.

Yes, I had experienced glimpses of love and joy but they often faded as soon as saw them, leaving only an afterglow. I felt somehow I didn't deserve these glimpses and I longed for what I assumed was the Christian norm – that perpetual sense of divine presence. I felt I was not as others were. Which is why I found the image of the yachts on the river so powerful. Many going east perhaps, while one went west; many going west, while one went east. It was OK. The one river was bearing us all forward, lovingly.

ELEVEN

THE SIGH OF THE RISING TIDE

When the barbeque at the Maiden Rock was over, three of us – myself, Charlie Young and another team member wandered along the shoreline away from the town. I walked a few steps in front of the others who were deep in conversation. It was completely dark by now, silent except for the sigh of the rising tide fingering its way between the rocks at the water's edge. I shivered slightly in the wind's chill, and yet felt completely at home. It struck me that the cold, isolated shoreline would in many circumstances have been a fear-inducing environment, but because I was there with others, and especially because of the joy and peace within me, I saw and sensed the beauty of it. It was another reminder of the extent to which my perception of external circumstances depended on my state of mind.

And there's another powerful memory from my years on a Scripture Union summer mission team at St Andrews (1974-78) At the parents' night in Martyrs' Church Hall a couple of fellow team-members dressed entirely in black mimed the Bible story which describes Jacob wrestling with God all night 'until the breaking of the day'. His hip is put out of joint by the deity, and yet he refuses to let go of God. 'I will not let thee go except thou bless me.' (Genesis 32:24, 26 AV) I saw myself in that dark, limping figure wrestling importunately with the Almighty.

*

'It's not like this every-day!' Mike Woodward said to me as we sat on the grass.

My first time at St Andrews, I was there for the second half of the fortnight as a 'taster', and so arrived at lunchtime on the middle Saturday. In bright sunshine, we spent the afternoon relaxing at Craigtoun Park and it was there that Mike spoke.

I nodded, secretly embarrassed that he'd imagine for a moment that I thought I'd signed up for a week of relaxation.

Later that afternoon, Colin Taylor a teenage member of the twenty-strong team and I picked our way slowly along the rocks between St Andrews Castle and the harbour. Colin introduced me to the new world of rock pools, and we discussed our respective travels in Narnia, a country we discovered we both loved. And already, despite my fears, I felt an unwonted joy.

Mum and dad had dropped me off outside the Martyrs' Church in North Street with my camp bed and gear. I was so nervous that we had to stop twice on the way from Carluke to let me pee copiously, barely out of sight of the road.

The mission leaders, Hugh and Margaret McWhinnie welcomed me warmly, and my anxiety receded. My parents had supportively decided to have their own holiday in the St Andrews area that summer. They visited Martyrs' Church several times in the course of the week, bringing copious gifts of fruit, and a supply of sulphaguanidine tablets when we were smitten with the runs.

Our aim at St Andrews (one of a number of missions held in the summer around Scotland by Scripture Union) was to contact both local children, and children on holiday. We organised games and activities and encouraged the young people to read the Bible, and pray listening out for God.

Weekday mornings were spent at a caravan park – after games we divided into small groups each led by a team member in which we read and reflected on a Bible story. In the afternoons, we held a beach service on the East Sands with singing, team competitions, and a story-with-a-lesson. I remember once playing the part of the Ethiopian eunuch who, as is recorded in the book of Acts in the Bible was converted to Christianity through the ministry of the Apostle Philip. I wore a stripy dressing-gown for the part, and blacked my face with coal dust showing a racial insensitivity I was unaware of at the time. It so happened that the well-known evangelical theologian Jim Packer was holidaying in St Andrews at the time. He saw me dressed for action and commented apparently without the slightest trace of irony that I was the most convincing Ethiopian he had ever seen.

In the evenings we arranged crafts for children at the church, and games followed by a youth café for teenagers where I struggled to communicate effectively. In everything, the intention was that we model Christian love and grace.

On the evening of the final Friday night of the mission each year we had a barbeque at the base of the Maiden Rock, a solitary outcrop of sandstone springing from the rocky end of the beach in the East Bay. Our routine those Fridays was even more manic than normal. There was food to collect, and firewood, and then after tea we'd drive to the bottom of the Kinkell Braes caravan site and carry all we needed down the steep path to the beach. There, in the last hour before twilight, the kids we'd been working with and some of their parents gathered round the bonfire we kindled and we presented a programme of serious and fun items. I remember leading a spirited rendition of *Little Peter Rabbit had a fly upon his nose*.

We'd sing some of the spiritual songs we'd learned over the fortnight, and then someone would give a brief talk on a Christian theme. It was there that I heard Hugh McWhinnie telling the unforgettable story of a strange, mythical, hybrid creature to highlight the blessings of contentment both with what God has made us to be, and with the gifts God has given us. The story was about a camel, who envied the elephant's trunk, wished that he had one, and saw his wish granted, thus becoming a camelephant. Still, however, he was not content; nor was he after subsequent wishes also were granted and he acquired characteristics of antelope, pelican and canary, so that the story ended with a miserably discontented camelephantelopelicanary.

I felt happier than I had been for years. When the sun had set, and the sausages and burgers had been eaten, the fun over, the 'goodbyes' said, we tidied the beach and carried our stuff back up the path.

*

Each evening of the mission, late, we would be on our own as a team in the church hall, and someone would read and pray, and we'd sing, perhaps accompanied by Charles Young's earnest guitar playing. I remember him singing, passionately what I recall was his favourite hymn, Charles Wesley's *O for a Thousand Tongues to Sing*.

> *He breaks the power of cancelled sin,*
> *He sets the prisoner free.*
> *His blood can make the foulest clean;*
> *His blood avails for me.*

But my soul was neither praying along, nor singing along. I lacked the confidence which the others seemed to have that God heard and answered and Wesley's words, though I was theologically comfortable with their language, did not resonate personally for me. I felt, if not on the outside, then certainly on the edge.

Eventually, we'd drift off to bed. We guys slept on camp beds on the church hall floor, just a few feet from the pavement, listening to the sound of voices passing outside, and the throaty roar of motorbikes racing along North Street. The girls' dorm was at the other end of the corridor. Each evening we'd be awake until just after midnight, and as we lay drowsily in our sleeping bags, I'd sometimes amuse my companions by singing silly songs, or rather by singing serious songs sillily, as in the sewing room at Law Hospital: *We were not born with true love to trifle....*

At midnight Hugh, after closing Solzhenitsyn's *Gulag Archapelago* turned on the BBC news, and we listened to the headlines, which in 1974 centred on the unfolding revelations surrounding Richard Nixon's Presidential re-election campaign, before finally going to sleep.

*

I was blessed incalculably through that week at St Andrews and my fortnights there in the following four years (when I drove there in my first car – a blue Mini which I called The Blue Bug.) It was a hugely significant milestone. For the very first time I was living in community, sharing breakfast with folk who medicated their early-morning scowls with black coffee in mugs bearing the legend 'I am not a morning person'. For the very first time I felt a sense of unconditional acceptance from people my own age; I appreciated the friendly respect I was shown by younger folk on the team; I learned a little more about relating naturally to girls.

I welcomed the freedom to discuss theological issues which were never raised in my home church. One year the Christian magazine *Crusade* had published a controversial article on the theology of childhood. This reflected on whether the correct approach to Christian education was to teach children that they were on the outside, requiring to be 'born again' before they could find God, or to emphasise that God loved them deeply, and that every day brought many opportunities of choosing either to act in a way which pleased God, or to be driven by God-ignoring, self-focussed thinking. The fact that this debate – so central to what we were doing at St Andrews, and so central to my questions about my own experience – was possible encouraged me.

I was, I think, very gentle with the kids I worked with, speaking of response to the love of God rather than putting any pressure on them to be 'born again'. However, blaming myself for my earlier struggles, I hadn't yet realised that the language and emotional charge of those calls to conversion which had troubled me as a teenager were inappropriate.

I appreciated being with intelligent, creative Christians who shared my cultural tastes. I remember attending an organ recital at Holy Trinity Church one Sunday evening with Mike Woodward; I recall Pam Williams playing the second movement of Beethoven's *Moonlight* sonata from memory on the piano in the hall at Martyrs' Church, blonde hair cascading over her dancing fingers; I remember Fiona McLachlan thanking me for being like a brother to her; I recall Charles Young's disapproval, signified by a shake of his head accompanied by a grin when he saw some of us on a Sunday afternoon eating ice cream we had just bought from Janetta's in South Street despite the fact that it was the Christian Sabbath.

As with all Scripture Union activities, a creative zaniness ran through the program alongside the serious stuff – there was plenty of room for laughter and fun. In that context, I was able as usual to mask deep insecurities with a flamboyant nuttiness. The McWhinnies put up a roll of paper on which you could write down amusing things team members said, and I featured on this list with my coinage 'supermarvellous', sometimes extended to 'supermarvellous hyper-brilliant' to denote something about which I was especially enthusiastic. Eventually, some of the comments on the list became rather risqué and the roll disappeared.

There were many times at St Andrews when I had a sense of seeking God's help with the tasks for which I was responsible. Every morning I'd get up before everyone else at about 6am, and go into the main church where there was a still calmness, and the musty ecclesiastical smell of kneelers and varnished pews. There was little traffic in North

Street. I'd read the Bible passage for the day and the accompanying note in Scripture Union's *Daily Notes*; I often sensed my prayers for help were heard as I prepared what I had to do in the day ahead, and was somehow conscious that God was with me, seeding my mind with creative insights.

*

Anne was one of the group of us who worked with the kids at the Kinkell Brae site one year. She was, she told me, the cousin of one of the Bay City Rollers.

The team was relaxing in someone's house at Strathkinness on a Sunday afternoon. The patio door was open, and there was a pond in the sunny garden. And it came to pass that Anne threw one of my socks into the water.

She had long black hair, and wore a dark blue smock. I think it was when we were parked in my car in South Street one morning before returning to Martyrs', eating ice-cream, Anne's free hand resting contentedly in her lap, that I realised how much I loved her.

Throughout the rest of the fortnight, I agonised to find words and opportunity to express this.

As we walked past the Cathedral ruins in a group one evening after dark, for a moment Anne's face was transfigured in street-light. I glimpsed this vision, and ached for her.

Before the mission ended I did find courage to ask her if I could see her again.

She said no.

I tried, one more time, a few months later, in Stirling, sitting with others on Hugh and Margaret's living-room carpet.

The answer was the same.

*

At 11pm on the final Friday of mission we'd walk, the whole team, to the end of North Street and down to the harbour by the path which skirts the Cathedral graveyard ('Is that a shadowy ghost on St Rule's Tower?') and along the harbour wall's uneven stones – made world-famous by graduating students in their red gowns – until we reached the beacon at the end. We stood huddled together both for warmth and in order to read by torchlight the hymn books we had taken with us, and sang. I surveyed the bay, watching the moonlight reflecting on the water, and the regular pulse of lighthouses on the horizon, and the brooding shadow of the Maiden Rock merging into the deeper darkness, and I felt profound contentment.

Running through my mind was the peaceful evening hymn *The Day thou Gavest Lord has Ended*, its serenity at one with my mood. Not long before, I had been tortured by the thought of hearing this tune in a very different context. I imagined that the Lord had come, and the saints had been taken, and I was left to fend for myself as clouds of chaos darkened the sky and night had fallen on the Day of Grace, and in my anguish I heard celestial voices singing *The Day thou Gavest Lord has Ended*, its sweetness a mockery, and there was no hope. Now I felt only the joy of inclusion, and I wished the day would never end.

*

But I was not completely free from fear. One Friday evening the team had been out very late, and some of them, including Hugh McWhinnie got into conversation with a very intoxicated fisherman whom we met beside the harbour with his equipment. I came back to the church hall with many of the others, and went to bed. Time passed, and those who had stayed with the fisherman had not returned. By 3am, I was still surrounded by empty camp beds, and I began to be afraid. For there was a subset of the doctrine of the 'rapture' which speaks of a 'partial rapture'.

Those who promulgated this view held, on the grounds of what shaky biblical exposition I know not, that while faithful believers would be taken by the returning Lord, unfaithful Christians would be left behind to pass through the 'Great Tribulation'. And as I lay there in Martyrs' Church Hall while the others who had returned with me slept securely, I saw faintly illuminated in the soft light from street lamps those other sleeping bags still rolled-up and I fought the terrible fear that the Lord had come, and that I was among those who had been left behind. Eventually there were footsteps in the hallway, and whispers about how the drunk fisherman had had to be escorted back home to Cupar and I was greatly relieved. 'I thought it was the partial rapture,' I muttered to Hugh. He looked at me blankly.

Many years later, having described to another member of the St Andrew's team my anxieties and my occasional sense of being on the edge I was moved to hear her unprompted comment: 'My main memory is how brilliant you were with the children. You seemed to me fully formed and comfortable in yourself and a lovely person to have as part of the team. You never talked down to us as young teenagers but came across as friendly and kind.'

*

My last year at St Andrews was 1978, Hugh and Margaret were not leading the team. I remember it as a difficult summer, a fortnight of mists on the Kinkell Braes, and thick haar on the East Sands where small groups of kids shivered in their anoraks at the Beach Service. I felt a sense of responsibility for ensuring things went as well as possible given the circumstances, and I supported the leaders as best I could. I remember one morning towards the end of the fortnight when we were in the middle of a game of rounders at the Cairnsmill Caravan site seeing Hugh and Margaret and their young daughters arrive to check out how we were getting on. I felt huge relief as I watched them emerge from their car. I remember thinking this must be the way the kids in an

Enid Blyton novel felt – they'd be deep in an adventure, mired in crisis, unsure what to do next, and then their parents would arrive, and there would be enormous relief at handing over responsibility for resolving the situation to people mature enough to make wise decisions.

*

As I said a final 'good-bye' at the church door that first year, and walked across the pavement to where my parents were waiting in the car it struck me, and it was a saddening thought, that I was about to 'resume the mantle of my former self'.

*

One of the team at St Andrews, a lawyer called Fraser, asked me if I'd ever listened to any stories by Gerard Hoffnung, the artist, musician and humourist. He particularly enjoyed the 'bricklayers' story' part of a speech Hoffnung gave to the Oxford Union in 1958.

Shortly after I'd returned home, I noticed that the speech was due to be re-broadcast, and suggested my parents might also enjoy it. It was an attempt I suppose to cast off the mantle, to share with my parents something of the cultural and intellectual freedom I had found at Martyrs' Church

But it was a mistake.

We sat listening as Hoffnung's distinctive tones filled the room. By the time he had reached the joke about the woman who had been ill in bed for a month with the doctor, and felt it wasn't doing her any good I was feeling distinctly apprehensive.

It was the item in Hoffnung's 'advice to tourists' – in which he alerted visitors to the fact that every brothel in London had a blue light outside – that did it.

Without as much as a glance to one another, or a word to me, my parents rose in tandem and left the room, heading for bed.

I listened for a little longer, and then, turning the radio off, sat in melancholy silence.

Nothing was said the next morning.

*

But that very first week at St Andrews, I had found new joy. I was beginning, as at Shotts Library to glimpse the secret of choosing joy – my interpretation determined the effect on me of the sigh of the rising tide. And I saw that the God I had been wrestling with aimed not to wound, but to bless.

TWELVE

REINDEER ON THE ROOF

Why not invite Willie Scobbie, the avuncular former County Librarian to play Santa Claus at a Christmas event for children at Carluke Library? I wrote to him proposing this, and he replied gamely accepting the invitation. So off I went to research costume hire, tracked down reindeer, and wondered whether you needed local authority permission to land a sleigh on a hyperbolic parabaloidal roof.

*

I walked back under the distinctive roof on the first Monday in June 1975. Snow was falling. I was in charge of a public library with a staff of three and an annual book budget of £5,000.

By the time I completed the post-graduate course, local government re-organisation had located Carluke Library in the new Lanark (later Clydesdale) District Council. Willie Scobbie showed considerable confidence in me despite my chequered history by putting my name forward for this post. And so without filling in an application form or attending for interview I found myself appointed as Carluke's new librarian. It was the way things were done back then.

I was a committed, popular local librarian, and acquired an extensive knowledge of contemporary literature and local studies. My Christmas party plans had precedents in earlier special events I organized at the library: a painting competition for children, which involved the whole community, and a talk by an expert from the Hunterian Museum on the fossils collected by a 19th century Carluke polymath.

Dr Rolfe brought some of the collection with him to the event which I called *Lanarkshire in the Beginning*, daringly, I thought, as I suspected Dr Rolfe's view of 'the beginning' differed considerably from that of my Brethren friends. The event was attended by a small, though respectable audience, but was marred by the disappearance of one small fossil, purloined, we suspected, by one small boy.

*

I was asked to lead a reflection at a re-union of the St Andrews Scripture Union Team. I had been reading the autobiography of a well-known Christian, Roy Hession author of *The Calvary Road*. My excitement at his vision of Christian living briefly obscured what I knew deep down: that he wrote of something which lay behind a door I had not yet found.

I quoted from the book, sitting on the floor surrounded by the others in Helen Muirhead's house, and then said passionately (or rather read from a script I had previously typed passionately) that it was a question of 'Jesus only! Jesus always! Jesus in the midst!'

Even as I spoke I sensed the leaden emptiness of my words.

*

Ben Schofield, one of the Brethren at Carluke who regularly took services in other Brethren assemblies invited me to accompany him one Sunday to Allanton – this was a regular mentoring practice to train up promising future speakers.

I remember a handful of us, all men, kneeling on the bare wooden floor-boards, heads bent, eyes closed, hands clasped on the surface of the rudimentary benches. We were praying for the open-air ministry and the gospel service later.

We made our way to a street corner and stood decisively at the edge of the pavement with a portable loud hailer. There was unaccompanied singing, a testimony, a short Bible talk, prayer. The street was quiet, no-one passed by, no sign of life at the living-room windows.

Afterwards, we walked back to the hall. We had been faithful. The Word had gone forth.

Later, I sat with Ben on the platform. Before he delivered the gospel sermon which would probably last half an hour I talked for ten minutes. I included the sentimental story – possibly an evangelical myth – of the shepherd boy, lacking formal education to whom a visitor taught the 23rd Psalm. To help him remember the first line, the boy assigned each word to a finger on his left hand. The-Lord-is-my-shepherd.

'Keep hold of your fourth finger when you are saying it,' the Christian tells the boy. 'It will remind you that the Lord isn't just *a* shepherd but *my* shepherd.'

Weeks pass, and the boy is out caring for his flock when, deep in winter there is prolonged snowfall. His body is found eventually, buried in a drift.

'Why is he clinging to the fourth finger of his left hand?' those who found him wondered.

*

Cameos from libraryland fifty years ago:

The customer leaving the issue desk contentedly, cradling her latest choice. 'You're always safe with a lady!' she purred.

Next day, she was back. She slammed the book, now wrapped in brown paper, on the counter.

'That woman,' she snarled, 'is no lady!' (A thump accompanied each of the two final syllables.)

*

Elizabeth Forsyth comes in with her mother, often. I watch surreptitiously as they approach, but I don't dare make eye contact until she is standing at the desk.

Mrs Forsyth chats cheerfully. My gaze is on her daughter as with a self-conscious toss of her head she flicks her blonde hair over her shoulder.

My fingers tremble as I find her library cards and pass them to her. Testesterone raging. My hand for an instant so close to hers...

*

One day, a perky little stuffed bear is left in the library, we presume by a child. I sit him where he can be clearly seen and arrange for his photo to appear on the front page of the *Carluke and Lanark Gazette* accompanied by plaintive details of his inadvertent abandonment among the bookshelves. Later, when he has been claimed (by the Baptist minister on behalf of his children) the bear, with my assistance, writes a letter of gratitude to the paper signing himself 'Browsin' Bruin'.

*

'Is your mum in?'

'Yes,' said the child. 'I'll get her. Who are you?'

I gave my name. There was a clunk at the other end as the receiver was dropped on the floor, and I heard a shrill voice calling.

'Mu-u-u-u-m! It's John Denver on the phone for you.'

*

The woman who went to the *Daily Record*, saying she disapproved of the content of one of our children's picture books, John Burningham's *The Dog*. And there it was, a two-page spread in the paper, featuring her child holding open the offending pages. The mutt was relieving himself at the corner of the lawn.

'The dog peed on the flowers,' read the text.

I wondered (a) how much they paid her for the story (b) whether she thought the cheque a fair recompense for enduring her neighbours' scorn and (c) what, when talking to her kids, was her own preferred vocabulary of urination.

*

The long hot summer of 1976 when the sun beat remorselessly through the glass and the temperature in the library became unbearable. We sat at tables in the open air, serving our customers there, listening on the radio to news of drought and parched reservoir beds, and the first outbreak of Legionnaire's disease.

*

When Liz Craig and I were on the evening shift together, we sometimes read out the last few pages of Mills and Boon romances when the library was quiet just before closing time. I would take the male role, and my colleague the female, while we took it in turn to read the linking narration. This may have been unprofessional, but it was great fun, and in any case Liz was a Christian, a member of Law Parish Church, and with her boyfriend played in a Christian band. They had been to see Jimmy and Carol Owen's *Come Together: a Musical Experience in Love*, an expression of the blossoming charismatic movement of which I had been taught to be dubious.

I asked Liz if she would like to start each day she and I were on the early shift with a prayer-time in the staffroom. We began doing this, and I thought it was going rather well.

But then Liz told me that the library cleaner, who was also working elsewhere in the building at the time, felt uncomfortable at our morning prayers. And so we stopped.

*

During my time at the library I became involved with the fledgling Librarians' Christian Fellowship (LCF) as Scottish Representative, organising events and producing and circulating publicity material to attract new members. I tried, I suppose, to replicate on a small scale what I had seen of the Christian Medical Fellowship, but locally I had little success.

I designed and had printed posters and flyers about the LCF, mailed them to every library in Scotland and as a result drew together a small cohort of Scottish members.

*

Greatly daring, I drove down in the Blue Bug to an LCF Committee Meeting at Brentwood in Essex. It was at a fellow member's house and I stayed over with him. 'Do you want to go up to London?' he asked after the meeting was finished, 'or just stay put?' *Come Together* was being staged, and we could go along. To my later regret I declined his invitation considering 'up to London' an adventure too far.

On my way back from Brentwood I stopped off at York where I made a point of visiting the Mustard Seed, a coffee-and-book shop run by St Michael Le Belfry, a church nestling close to York Minster. The vicar was the Anglican charismatic leader David Watson. I pushed open the glass door and went in. Tranquil music was playing; serene, attractive young women in long, Laura Ashley style dresses served coffee. I had the not altogether unpleasant sensation that I was standing on dangerous ground.

David Watson had written extensively about renewal, a new and deeper encounter with God through the Holy Spirit, and about the associated supernatural gifts which some claimed to have received – the ability to praise God in 'tongues' (unknown languages); the gift of healing (enabling them to reach out to others as channels through which a transforming divine power brought spiritual, emotional or physical restoration); the gift of knowledge (by which those so gifted received from time to time supra-rational insights into the needs of others).

All this was viewed with deep suspicion by many of the Christians I knew. They did not doubt that when the church was young and the books of the New Testament had not yet been committed to parchment gifts something like these had indeed been given to believers. But now? Surely everything required for salvation was to be found in the pages of Scripture? Surely we had no need of a further divine intervention?

My presence in the Mustard Seed that morning indicated my longing for a deeper awareness of God and my sense of inadequacy. Perhaps the mustard seed of faith had been sown within me, but it had not blossomed and flourished as I expected. In my dissatisfaction it was easy to forget or at least to downplay the joy which at times enveloped me as I immersed myself in the Bible or in a volume of Lloyd-Jones sermons. Most of the time I was aware more of God's absence than God's presence. I had little sense of that relationship with the divine which ought, so I concluded from what I had heard and read, to be central to the Christian faith, little sense of divine empowerment or direction in everyday life.

I often felt as if I were outside the household of faith, standing in rain-swept darkness looking through the window. Inside I could see the large family, sometimes sitting round the fire, sometimes eating and drinking, sometimes dancing with an energetic joy, always oblivious to my presence. I longed to join them, but I couldn't find the door, or else the door had no handle, or else the latch would not lift.

I drank my coffee, bought some stones on which encouraging verses from the Bible had been painted, and left the coffee shop without expressing my longing.

*

The shift patterns at Carluke Library involved working every second Saturday and every second Wednesday morning. I made good use of my Wednesdays off. Sometimes I went to WEC's building in Prince Albert Road in Glasgow, where I made slow progress cataloguing the library. Sometimes I drove to Tweedsmuir where a family friend was the head teacher – as I drove, I'd listen through South Lanarkshire and on into Peebleshire to cassette tapes of worthy Reformed sermons. Sometimes, and most precious of all, I visited my sole surviving grandparent, Archie Jackson in Airdrie. I'd arrive about 10.30am; we'd talk over coffee; and then about mid-day he'd put on his coat, seize his hat from the hall-stand (with his usual Ghandi joke 'My-hat-an'-ma coat') and lead me down the echoing close into Clark Street. We'd stride briskly through the town centre to the Tudor Hotel where he stood me lunch. I recall little we spoke about, but I knew it was good to be with him.

*

I found it hard to be positive about my achievements at work; at times I felt driven as much by a hunger for personal significance as by a commitment to helping others. Immature as I was and uncertain how to unfurl the wings of adulthood, I still found it difficult to relate to people out-with the Christian nest.

At the end of my Strathclyde course I had been awarded the Dunn and Wilson Public Library Management prize, but I had been given no practical guidance on managing staff, and no training of any kind was offered when I took up my new post. I was conscious that the very experienced library assistants knew more about the practicalities of the job than I did. I was on friendly terms with them but suspected in my paranoia this was due to their forbearance rather than to any qualities in me.

I found difficult to give my staff instructions about the changes in practice I thought would be helpful, or to point out when I thought their commitment fell short. And it wouldn't have occurred to me to approach decisions in a collegiate way. Whenever I did or said anything I thought might be even remotely controversial and then saw my colleagues talking quietly together at the other side of the library, I was quite convinced that I was the subject of their conversation and that it was prompted by what I had done, or said, or by the mere fact of me being in the Brethren: any confidence I had sank rapidly in the quicksand of insecurity.

Nor did I have the courage and common sense to discuss the best approach with my managers and seek their advice. There was no encouragement to approach senior staff in this way. When I did make mistakes – for example trying to circumvent a management decision by enlisting the support of the local councillor – the District Librarian was judgmental rather than understanding of an honest mistake made from the best customer-focussed motives.

His relational style was marked by an insensitivity, a lack of empathy and supportiveness: he failed to connect with me, failed to provide the encouragement and leadership which would have helped me overcome my weaknesses and value my strengths. Perhaps he resented having me thrust upon him by Willie Scobbie. Afraid to be real with him, I buried even more deeply the sense of desolation I often felt despite the patina of levity.

*

One day when I was feeling particularly vulnerable, Fred Bell, a warm and friendly senior colleague roared into the car park on his motor-bike.

As he stood in the staff room peeling off his gloves and yellow jacket and unstrapping his helmet, once again I felt as if I was in an Enid Blyton novel, and the parents had turned up when the adventure had gone pear-shaped, and there was someone to lean on. After Fred emerged from his bikers' gear, I could have flung my arms around him.

*

'Christians are (or should be) dangerous people, since they claim total allegiance to a self-revealing, personal God, and thereby challenge accepted ideas and value.' Thus I began a literate and confidently dogmatic article which I was asked some years later to write about Christians in librarianship for the *New Library World*.

The received wisdom was that librarians should, in their professional role, have 'no politics, no morals, no religion'. 'For me at least,' I wrote, 'this is impossible, since total allegiance to God involves bringing under His authority every aspect of life, not least work, or, to put it in another way, being my Christian self in every situation.'

Rather arrogantly I claimed that 'my attitude to professional issues is formed not by dancing to the tune of personal prejudice or conventional wisdom, but by biblically evaluating the factors involved,' though I did have the grace to concede that there would not always be agreement on a definitive 'Christian attitude' to a given professional issue.

I then outlined what I saw as the relevant 'fundamental principles'. 'The Christian owes his [sic] choice of career to the call of God' and therefore approaches work with 'a sense of purpose and responsibility'. I wrote of having 'willingly and joyfully chosen what I saw as being God's will for me'. This statement astonishes me, and is at odds with my recollection.

'The Christian must live in a fallen world which has by and large turned its back on God.' I must therefore 'learn to co-exist in that society without…compromising my principles.'

I mentioned thirdly that 'all truth is God's truth. Everything which is true, whether in a scientific or philosophical sense, properly originates from, and belongs to God.' Wherever a book has something in it of beauty and truth, that is a reflection of the divine.

I mentioned 'the supreme value of the individual – created a free agent in the image of God' and explored the implications of this for relationships with colleagues, library customers, people of other faiths and for the challenge of working for a better society.

But on one issue I was quite emphatic 'While having every sympathy with those whose orientation is homosexual, I cannot countenance homosexual practice.'

*

Andrew came along to some Librarians' Christian Fellowship meetings and then withdrew. He wrote to me to say he was gay, and that he had found more support in the Gay Christian Movement.

Two things struck me forcibly. There was immense relief that, though I faced challenges managing my heterosexual yearnings I was not gay. And there was a compassion for Andrew, and a sense that we, that I, had failed him.

*

A fifth principle, I continued, was 'the pre-eminence of spiritual values'. I believed that 'the pursuit of social and political amelioration without regard to the spiritual roots of world problems is bound to fail heartbreakingly, for there can be no ultimate peace, joy, satisfaction and goodness until the individual has found rest in God.' Sixthly:

Whatever the expressed needs of a reader, this perception is bound to colour my approach. And while I would not manipulate the work situation so as to create opportunities for Christian witness,

I believe that such opportunities will inevitably arise when one is one's Christian self in every situation.

And 'the final over-riding principle [was] that Jesus Christ is Lord, the only way to God.' This meant that

I have no truck with 'enlightened' liberal opinion which sees all varieties of religious experience as being equally valid and valuable, and I am neither being true to myself, or my Lord, if for the 1680 hours per annum I am at work, I act as if I shared the majority view.

And I concluded with a rhetorical flourish:

The early Christians turned the world upside down. Jesus had been indistinguishable from his message, and those first followers of his inextricably linked belief and practice. Today the light is sometimes shrouded, the salt savourless, the living epistles illegible and inconsistent. As Christian librarians, we are dangerous. But perhaps not as dangerous as we should be.

*

Two issues particularly troubled me during my time at Carluke Library: trade unionism and book selection.

As was common at the time Lanark District Council operated a 'closed shop' – only trade union members were employed. And so I became a less-than enthusiastic member of NALGO (the National and Local Government Officers union). In the autumn of 1976, the Council decided to make financial savings by stopping paying library staff a 12.5% shift allowance, and to remove the shift element of working practice, while at the same time not altering library opening hours.

This disturbed me, I was in favour of Union membership, but had issues with the 'closed shop,' which I felt, as I said in a piece written at the time, was 'a worrying restriction on personal freedom… It is bad if, before we can practise the job to which we have been called by God, we must join an organisation run by men [the sexist bias I was unconscious of!] whose whole outlook may be apathetic to Christian things, or downright atheistic'. Nevertheless I reasoned that God in calling us to a certain job may want us 'to accept the Union as we accept other less-than-perfect institutions in our fallen society'.

But when it came to strike action, I felt there could be no compromise, and I had biblical texts to back up my position. All authority was delegated by God, it was my duty to be obedient to management rather than to the Union – even where injustice was involved. 'My principal loyalty,' I wrote, 'was neither to my colleagues nor my bosses but to God, who can never accept the possibility of his servants withdrawing their labour.'

There's a deep contrast between my recollection of the confusion I felt at the time, and the confident dogmatism of this statement, which was written for consumption by an audience of Christians. It was perhaps a bid for solid ground, a bid for acceptance and recognition by the community I was desperate to be part of.

Ten years later, I was on strike for a couple of months over School Librarians' pay. By then, I had persuaded myself (or perhaps it was convenient to believe) that in a just cause, withdrawal of labour might not simply be permissible, but a duty. Was I, in 1976, or 1987, or on both occasions, moulding my understanding of God's heart to meet the pressing necessities of my own?

*

The second issue concerning me was selection of stock. In my *New Library World* article I wrote that I was

> greatly tempted to censor my stock – was not God a greater master than the District Librarian? But I realised that, for the Christian

librarian, living in a fallen world means providing the community with good examples of material on any subject requested. I confess to linger unease over this attitude, which seemed perilously close to compromise. You may be sure, however, that requests for material written from a Christian perspective were enthusiastically met.

The background to this was my belief that books on say witchcraft, occult forces and atheism could damage people spiritually and my personal awareness of being both repelled and naively attracted by explicit descriptions of sex. ('I guess that's not about a construction site?' said my reader Hazel as, a glint of anticipation in her eye, she headed home to enjoy Mickey Spillane's *The Erection Set*.) It didn't occur to me that for example portrayals of opulent materialism could similarly be spiritually damaging.

It troubled me that since I was responsible as librarian for the stock on my shelves it was logical to assume that I was morally accountable for any negative affect of that material on folk who borrowed it. Hence my initial tacit support for censoring materials, although I can't in fact actually remember refusing to stock any book – my convictions, when faced with the challenge to action, were clearly not sufficiently strong.

Over the years however I realised that the Christian call to be a librarian is implicitly a call to be a good librarian. A good librarian provides access to books and information published within the law on all subjects, with the proviso that the books stocked should be the best-written and best-designed of those available on the subjects in question. The Christian librarian's responsibility is thus to provide the material which he or she is contracted to supply – what the reader makes of it is their own responsibility.

*

My *New Library* World article was heavily influenced by the thinking of evangelical leaders such as John Stott and Martyn Lloyd-Jones. It was, I suspect, a statement of the kind of Christian librarian I aspired to be, or thought I should be rather than the one I actually was – an attempt to write into being that evangelical self. I judged myself lacking in courage, too quick to compromise in the interests of my own comfort.

But I suspect in practice I was lovely and gentle and caring with my customers, and while I might write dogmatically in black and white terms I lived with compassion, inhabiting the many areas of grey. My readers would not have seen the dogmatic controversialist, but they might have glimpsed in me something much more real, and more important – grace. Which, I would have realized had I only thought clearly, was a key characteristic of Christian faith. So perhaps I was negotiating my life in the two kingdoms of earth and of heaven much better than I realized.

*

No sooner had I begun working at Carluke Library, than I began to think about leaving. I had suspected during my post-graduate course that work in an academic environment would be appealing, but the impetus to move came chiefly from my parents. For my mother at least, employment in academia was more professionally respectable than working in a public library – though she was quick to point out to the young shop assistant who mentioned having seen my 'stacking shelves' in the library that there was no comparison between a job in the Co-op and my exalted responsibilities.

There was a vacancy in Strathclyde University Library; Professor Tyler agreed to give me a reference. From my parents' point of view I was a shoo-in. Wasn't I one of the Prof's star pupils? They insisted on taking me in to Glasgow on the day of the interview. I had limited understanding of the interview process, and had done very little research into the job – there was no emphasis in the post-graduate course on interview techniques. I answered the questions as best as I could, expatiating at too-great length about my rather shallow passion for Scottish Literature.

The candidates were told to return in the afternoon. My parents and I had lunch and then they returned to the car to await my joyful return. The hopefuls were kept waiting for a couple of hours while the interviews were completed. I was not successful.

I returned to the car, where I found my parents seemingly cross at the delay, and especially cross that I had been foolish enough not to get the post. 'We thought you were being shown round your new workplace.' I ask myself if I was projecting on to them my own disheartenment, but I recall no words of solace or comfort.

*

One January morning I was again in the car with my parents, this time heading down the interminable Lang Whang road (the A70) for an interview at the Scottish Office Library in Edinburgh. I had applied simply to please my parents in the hope that I wouldn't be called for interview; and was full of dread at the thought of having, were I successful, to find a place to stay in the city. It was the day of the strike over shift allowance, and so I was legitimately absent. My commitment to my principles was not tested.

Again I failed to hone my interview skills or even research the job in question. I sat in St Andrew's House being grilled by an intimidating panel of civil servants, fielding impossible questions, longing for it to be over.

Another silent, dejected car journey, homeward bound.

*

There was a job vacancy at the Duncan of Jordanston College of Art in Dundee. I applied, again simply to please. It was a foolish move for my knowledge of and interest in art was negligible. In my father's line of work it was common practice when you were applying for a post to visit the workplace both to show face, and so that you could talk knowledgably at the interview about the specific work context. He suggested I should do the same and it didn't occur to me to question this.

I arranged this with the slightly bemused library team at the College, and headed north on the arranged date, driving myself this time. I remember the sunshine, the liberation I felt as I pointed the car up the A9 towards Perth, the reports on the radio of Jimmy Carter campaigning for the US presidency, my thankfulness on opening my lunch-box and seeing the care my mother had taken in making sandwiches.

'This is where your desk would be,' the young librarian said in the course of my guided tour round the library.

Home via Stirling – I'd contacted mission team leaders Hugh and Margaret, and they'd invited me to visit. That night the Swedish gospel choir *Choralerna* were performing nearby, and many of my friends from the team were attending. I joined them, the music from the great speakers blasting my ears with joy.

I wasn't even called for interview.

*

I had been taught to expect God to guide with specific, unmissable clarity though I had no experience of this guidance, nor was the method by which it was to be received ever been made clear,

At one point, my parents very generously gave me £2,000 for my future.

Shortly afterwards, once the money was safely in my bank account, I read an appeal from a Brethren missionary for the funds to build a hall in a town in South America. The sum required was £2,000.

A 'yes!' welled up in me. Yes! I should give my £2000 to this worthy cause. What I took to be an unmistakable call of God – and hadn't it been confirmed by the exact equivalence of the sum required and the sum I'd been given – came to me with clarity and conviction.

I told my parents what I planned to do.

'You can't do that!' they said, understandably. 'We gave you the money for *you*, for *your* future.' (And £2000 was a lot of money back then. My first car, a Mini, cost £750 new in 1975.)

'But it's *my money*,' I argued back. 'And I feel this is the right thing to do.'

I see their point of view, but they did nothing to show they understood my perspective. Nor did they say anything to explain the mismatch between what they were telling me, and the stories and teaching we inhabited and the books we read. Stories of a God who invites our obedience, and blesses us as we obey, a God who honours sacrifice.

But I did not question my parents further: this must be a special case, I reasoned, in which the principle of generous response to the call of God was held in abeyance.

The sense of calling to give was strong, and I felt, clear-cut. What was its source? Was it simply an obsessive reflex, or did I imagine that by giving, I would be in God's debt and thus persuade God to open the forward-leading door? Or was such a gift a material expression of the wild spiritual surrender I yearned to offer?

I did nothing, and lived with a burden of guilt that I had been called, and found unfaithful.

*

One day, early in 1977 an advertisement caught my attention – indeed, exploded into my consciousness – as I read *The Bookseller* in the library office. It had been placed by Scripture Union in England who were seeking a Bookshop Manager for their Carlisle shop. I knew at once with a deep certainty that this was a 'call,' that I should apply for this job, even although success would mean moving away from home.

I spent a weekend agonising over telling my parents about this, fearful, I suppose that they would feel I was abandoning my profession. However, they were largely supportive.

I applied for the job, but in the end was not even called for interview. However one Wednesday I saw Scottish SU General Secretary John Butler in the Glasgow SU bookshop, and told him about my Carlisle aspirations. It transpired that he was looking for a manager for the shop in Falkirk's Cow Wynd. After spending an afternoon with him there, I was appointed to the vacancy, taking a cut in salary to £1,700 per annum.

*

One morning, in the kitchen of the house in Carluke's West Avenue where we were living by then – a home for life, my father thought ('Just what the doctor ordered,' wrote the solicitor doing the conveyancing).

My mother was writing a letter.

'I think you should let John read it before you post it,' said dad.

She handed it over to me. It was addressed to a Christian periodical, and expressed her pride in me for the step I was taking in moving to Christian employment.

The language was sentimental and euphoric – I had never seen anything quite like it in print.

'I'd rather you didn't send that,' I found the courage to say, having been given permission by my father. I think I said it more to enjoy the freedom of being able to say it than because of any deep unease at the wording of the letter.

It ended up in the waste bin under the sink.

I was ungrateful, not accepting my mother's real pride in me. But I wish she had been able to express that pride directly, rather than to a third party. And I wonder whether part of her motivation for writing the letter was the thought that having a son in 'full-time Christian work' would reflect well on her?

And what about that 'call'? Again it seemed genuine, undeflectable in its intensity. The words in the advertisement grabbed my attention, and somehow I recognised their significance even before I'd fully understood what they were saying. I can see this 'call' might have been the fruit of a desire to get my parents – with their frequent prodding to get another job – off my back. Or of a desire to remove myself from the troublesome ambit of trade unionism. Or was I thinking that, by associating myself with Scripture Union I would finally be bidding farewell to the mantle of my former self, and that it would be forever summer in St Andrews? I was certainly proud of that pay-cut. It was a statement of faith, a minor martyrdom, signifying commitment to the cause.

I saw it, genuinely, as a call of God, one which my parents could not deny or argue against. I was extremely apprehensive about what lay ahead, but for only the second time in my life I had personally made a major decision. I had chosen a job! Now, my future was secure. I would work with Scripture Union for the rest of my life.

*

Late one Tuesday evening in the early spring of 1977, I was lying in bed reading one of Martyn Lloyd-Jones' sermons on Ephesians when the phone rang. It was the police – the library was ablaze!

I got there as quickly as I could – the familiar car-park was bustling with police and fire-fighters, who already had the outbreak under control. The interior of the staff-room at the front of the building was black and smouldering, and in the heat the tiles above the front desk in the public area were showering down dripping globules of molten plastic.

There was no physical damage to the rest of the building, but the space under the arching roof was heavy with acrid smoke. With the fire officer's permission, I went into the building, and as every good librarian would have done in those pre-digital days, I carried the precious wooden trays of orange cards to a relatively safe place.

Less than a week later we were back in business. The District Librarian arranged for the commercial cleaners to come back to deep-clean the undamaged part of the building; my colleagues and I washed the covers of all the books with soapy water; and we set up tables in the centre of the library to work from.

In the library office, one wall had been lined with deep shelves. Most of them were filled with books, one was packed with folded back-issues of the *Carluke and Lanark Gazette*, and one housed a Baby Belling cooker. It was plugged in to a socket on the wall at the back of the shelf, so that to switch it off at the mains you had to reach behind the appliance. It appeared the fire had been caused by the cooker igniting the newspapers.

When I was discussing with the District Librarian the need to employ contract cleaners to get the library back to a state where we could safely open to the public, he pointed out that the fact that the cooker had been left switched on was my responsibility, and that if I made it difficult for him by insisting on a higher quality of cleaning than he was prepared to fund, then I might find myself facing the consequences of my mistake.

This felt like the ultimate betrayal, but I lacked both the courage and indignation to argue back.

*

A few weeks after the fire, before the damage had been repaired, I stepped out from under the distinctive roof for the last time.

I enjoyed my time at Carluke Library. I had much latent ability which could have been nurtured. I was ahead of the game in advocating community engagement in libraries. But having an unsupportive manager, and parents who repeatedly urged me to move on left me struggling.

Word of my plans for Santa's visit must have reached the District Librarian, presumably via whoever typed Willie's reply, and one day he said to me 'What I'm hearing about Willie Scobbie playing Santa at your library can't be true, can it?' His tone indicated that if this were the case, then my plans would meet with his severe disapproval, and lacking the guts to stand up to him, I lied. 'No,' I said.

The sleigh never landed on the hyperbolic parabaloidal roof.

THIRTEEN

'GOODBYE OCTOBER'

We often played music in the Scripture Union bookshop in Falkirk's Cow Wynd. 'The Bible Shop,' locals called it. Falkirk Christians, certainly the ones who bought their music in the shop, seemed to be very conservative in their tastes – we sold many albums from the 'Banners and Bonnets' label, (forever accidentally mispronounced by me as 'Bonners and Bannets') which originated in Ulster Presbyterianism.

But we also sold some contemporary Christian music offerings, including Adrian Snell's album *Goodbye October*. The title track was a sweet, beautiful song about the changing seasons, and our tendency to rush through the years failing to make 'time for Jesus and the things he wants to teach us. Can he reach us, do we really want to hear?' It was the haunting melody which gripped me, rather than Phil Thomson's lyric or the theology.

Hello forever
Let me rest in Jesus' arms
With his love around me I can reach the skies
Well I wonder as the seasons turn
And autumn slowly breaking
Are we waking with his summer in our eyes
With his summer in our eyes

But these final words, about finding security and summer in Jesus encapsulated my longing. Working in Falkirk was a chance to get away, to be who I was, to shape the rough draft of my identity, but I blew it. Even at the age of 25, finding a flat near the shop was an uncertainty too far.

Initially, I stayed over Monday-Thursday with Mrs Chisholm, a stalwart of the local Brethren fellowship. (I recall how pleased she was to receive a letter from Magnus Magnusson when she wrote to complain about his controversial TV series *BC: the Archaeology of Bible Lands*.) This had been arranged some weeks before when my mother and I, both nervous, she more so than I ('I've never done anything like this before,' she said) visited my future landlady. It was always understood that the arrangement was temporary until I had time to find permanent local accommodation. Unaccountably, I did not take this step, and eventually my landlady began to quietly hint that it really was time for me to move on.

My weeks with Mrs Chisholm came to an abrupt end when she fell ill with labyrinthitis. But even this, on top of my having been 'welcomed into fellowship' by the local Brethren one Sunday when I was at the Falkirk morning meeting was insufficient to prompt me to action. It was as if in fear and lack of self-confidence I had closed my mind to the possibility of settling in the town.

For the rest of my time in Cow Wynd (I was only there for a year) I drove home to Carluke over the moors. But I worried about the prospect of snow, and blocked roads.

*

I had an introduction to the arcana of stock control and cash handling at the Glasgow Scripture Union bookshop where I reported on the Monday morning after leaving the Carluke Library, feeling both relief and expectation. I'd be working in a Christian environment with those I regarded as Christian brothers and sisters. And indeed I enjoyed my time at the Falkirk shop, and most of my time at the Glasgow outlet where I became manager in late spring of 1978.

The happiest of my bookshop days were probably those in Falkirk. I remember Saturdays in the office there, with Saturday girl Mhairi Todd (who was once addressed on a computer-generated label as 'M hairi 3 odd') and Fiona, a teenager from one of the villages close to Falkirk whom I'd met at the St Andrews SU mission and who would sometimes drop in. We'd buy millionaire's shortbread from the bakers along the road, there would be *Mull of Kintyre* on the radio in the office, we'd sell books and joke with the customers, and life was sweet.

I had a leaflet printed to promote our work, with the slogan 'More than just another shop'. It emphasised both the spiritual value of the merchandise we were selling, and also our hope that people coming through the door would detect in the atmosphere and in the friendliness of the staff something special, something of God's grace and love. I was certainly motivated to reflect this in my own interactions with people, although (mistakenly as I can see now) I felt something of a failure because I never seemed to engage any customers in conversation on spiritual issues apart from discussing the subject-matter of books.

There was a weekly open-air market held in car-park near Falkirk College, and I was drawn to have a regular presence there, selling Christian books. I had a strong sense that this was something I was called to by God, something I should do. But equally it could simply have been an idea – my concept of 'the sort of thing Christians should do' – springing from guilt, to which my obsessiveness attached itself. I am still inclined to believe that the 'calling' came from beyond me.

One Saturday I went down to the market, and looked at the metal frames the stalls were supported on, and the protective tarpaulins over them, and I felt daunted. The people doing business looked like guys with whom I would not feel at home. My vision of a regular presence there was completely realisable, had I got a team together to talk through the issues involved and actualise the dream. But I lacked the confidence and drive to make this happen.

When I was invited to take charge of the Glasgow shop I was troubled. The offer attracted me, because Glasgow was a bigger shop and easy to reach from home on a daily basis. I was being offered a promotion, yet something drew me to remain in Falkirk, to commit to the town. I accepted the Glasgow job.

As I walked up St Vincent Street in Glasgow from the station on my first morning in the new post, I still felt I was making a mistake, and yet did nothing to correct it. A Saturday or two later I drove up to Falkirk with a bundle of Christian tracts, and stood beside the entrance to the market, resolutely handing them out. It was an attempt to atone, to wipe my conscience clear of the guilt I felt at having taken the easy option.

*

Along with my team, my responsibilities as bookshop manager included ordering, displaying and promoting stock: Christian books and music, greetings cards, stationery and the SU Sunday School materials and Bible reading notes of which we sold enormous quantities in the Glasgow shop. Annual turnover at Falkirk was £20k, and at Glasgow £75k. From the latter shop, I supplied Scottish Scripture Union camps and missions with bookstalls, designed mail order catalogues (in the days before desktop publishing) and reviewed books for *Tell SU Scotland's* quarterly news-sheet.

(In concluding a review of a book which presented rock music as an ally of the church. I expressed my doubts as to whether 'Jesus will ever be found dancing to the savage beat of rock'. It was, I knew, a powerful phrase with a shade of ambiguity, but even as I wrote it I wondered if it were actually true.)

*

The soundtrack of my days at St Vincent Street was provided by recordings by the Fisherfolk, part of Graham Pulkingham's charismatic Community of Celebration then based on the Isle of Cumbrae; by Chuck Girard singing *Sometimes Allelujah* and Bob Dylan *Slow Train Coming*; by Andrae Crouch leading *Through it all*, and *Take me back* in which he begs the 'dear Lord', to restore to him to the joy he experienced on first encountering the divine; by Scandinavian singer Evie Tornquist assuring us that the 'hard times' in fact strengthen you.

Shortly before I woke on the day I was due to start work in the Glasgow shop I had a dream, in which I remembered that Helen Arbuckle, the girl I had stood beside on the veranda at Crieff Hydro when I was fifteen, the girl for whom, obsessed, I had written the poem beginning 'Myself and her and silence eloquent' was now working somewhere in Central Glasgow. She might conceivably, my dream told me, come into the bookshop where I'd have a chance to renew acquaintance with her.

On waking I realised this dream was probably woven by my mind's wishful and lustful thinking. But just a few hours later Helen walked through the swing doors into the SU building at lunch time. Surely, I told myself, this wasn't co-incidence. Surely this was the fulfilment of my dream. Surely the dream must therefore have been a sign. Surely this was the girl God had for me.

Helen came to the office reasonably frequently over the next few weeks and I used to fantasise about marrying her. Already, I had composed the last, rolling, grandiloquent sentence in my bridegroom's speech in which I announced my joy that the silence of which I had written in my poem, 'this long silence (pause here for effect) has been (longer pause) irrevocably broken'.

I think I had courage to ask Helen out to her face; I certainly recall later writing a letter to her posing the same question, but on both occasions her answer was 'No'. I went to an evening class at the Glasgow Bible Training Institute, in part following in the footsteps of my mother who still had her neat notes, written in blue ink, on St

Paul's Epistle to the Romans, but largely because I knew Helen was taking the course. I was, I suppose, stalking her. I didn't sit close, but it was enough to say 'Hi' as she passed.

I was still expecting direct guidance from God, and anticipated (taught by the 'testimonies' I'd heard) that it would come by vivid and undeniable means. I rationalised that if God had made clear to me that Helen and I should get together, then God would give her equal clarity. It was probably obvious to her that I had very little experience of friendship with women but I was wounded that she was not prepared to get to know me better. Any self-confidence I had was crushed by her rejection and by the imagined crescendo of laughter as she described to her family my hesitant advances.

My father still worked with Helen's dad, and occasionally he and his wife would be invited to dinner at our house. I was included. Sitting across from Mrs Arbuckle at my parents' table I saw in her features the face of Helen, looking back at me.

Still Helen came into the bookshop. I remember serving her once, full of pain and longing, as in the background Evie Tornquist's strong voice sang of finding strength in those empowering 'hard times.'

Sometimes I wondered.

*

I attended the Christian Booksellers' Convention twice during my years at Scripture Union, when it was held at the Wembley Conference Centre. This was a trade fair for Christian publishers and booksellers, accompanied by a programme of speakers. On both occasions through my father's generosity I stayed at the Eurocrest Hotel, adjacent to the Centre.

On the first occasion, new to London, I thought all I had to do was to ask a taxi at Euston to take me to Wembley, but the driver looked at me as if I were an imbecile.

'You'll have to get a train, mate!'

The first year I spoke briefly to Joni Eareckson an American author whose book *Joni* described her discovery of faith in God after she had been paralysed from the neck down in a diving accident. The film based on the book was premiered at the Convention. I also had lunch – in the sense of sitting across the table from – the Irish preacher/politician Dr Ian Paisley. He spent the meal talking to his team, who were also present, with his trademark certainty and emphatic delivery, and I found I had nothing to say to him. What made the most impression was the meal I ate at a table where a young woman missionary was sitting, surrounded by her publishers and key booksellers. Her book about her experiences of God in her work had just been published. I was surprised to feel a certain distaste. Were these besuited male publishers using her? Was it right to take precious things God had done in people's lives, and commercialise them? Would her life from now on be an endless quest for material for the next book?

When I returned home, my mum had created in my absence a big cushion – cheery fabric packed with stuffing. It was something I could lean against when stretched out on the floor beside the radiator, reading.

*

In the Summer 1979 issue of *Tell* I wrote about my policy when selecting stock for the shop. Scripture Union was and remains an evangelical organisation, and it was to be expected that the books sold in its shops would represent a broadly evangelical theological position, but I wasn't given any guidelines to inform my purchasing. Each of the other bookshop managers in the Scottish Scripture Union network, while maintaining a standard, staple stock had their own distinctive emphases. Chris Andrews in Edinburgh, for instance, had a particular interest in books reflecting the more mystical, contemplative tradition, and this was reflected on her shelves. Chris had a mouse on her desk called Timothy, made of canvas, with blue ears and long whiskers.

I, however, was still theologically naïve. I told *Tell* readers:

I have real qualms about stocking any books whose author does not substantially subscribe to the SU basis of belief. While I profoundly dislike slapping labels on people – eg 'He's "one of us" therefore his book must be OK' – and while I also recognise that non-evangelical writers can give us the occasional valuable insight, I could not with a clear conscience stock books which might shake the faith of any of my customers on core doctrines. Great is our responsibility!

On peripheral doctrines – baptism, the charismatic movement and the rest – on which Christians agree to differ, I am content so along as my shelves reflect both sides of the issue.

That phrase 'occasional valuable insight' seems condescending. What I said might be acceptable as I was serving a Christian youth organisation with a particular theological slant, but I'm uneasy about the role I perceived myself to have as a gatekeeper, protecting my customers from what I deemed might harm them. Thus we stocked *The Truth of God Incarnate*, but not *The Myth of God Incarnate* to which it was a rebuttal.

I was disturbed to discover that my predecessor at the Glasgow shop had ordered from the Collins representative twenty copies of a novel which, though it may have been written by a Christian didn't seem to me to be particularly Christian in emphasis when I dipped into it. It even included a fairly explicit description of a naked woman. This I couldn't handle and I persuaded the poor uncomprehending rep to take the volumes back for credit.

However I was comfortable stocking books discussing sex and sexuality from an evangelical perspective, such as *Intended for Pleasure* (a Christian equivalent, I suppose of *The Joy of Sex*). Somehow I frequently found myself drawn to its stirring pages and in particular the line drawings it contained.

I was concerned about commercialism and the balance between sacred and secular objectives when Christianity and business are linked. Initially I was excited by the regular visits of the publishers' representatives with the latest catalogues announcing new publications which I could promote and sell. But I soon began to wonder whether in fact so many new titles were necessary. I found myself tempted to promote new titles as 'must haves' for my customers. But were they really all essential reading? Would they really have a significant impact on people which existing works could not deliver?

Sometimes the answer to this was 'yes', but more often it was 'perhaps' and sometimes 'certainly not!' I wrote in the article in *Tell*:

> *Doctrinally impeccable a book may be, but the manager must still decide if it is a worthwhile addition to his [sic] stock. Teaching? Does it shed new light on its subject, or is it merely the latest in a long line of titles covering the same ground? Biography? Is the subject's life and experience treated in a way which will truly deepen the spirituality of the reader?*

I was beginning to understand because I recognised the tendency in myself that people conscious of a mismatch between their own inner sense of God and that promised by evangelical Christianity were prone to consume new books and recordings, and to attend conferences and events in search of an elusive inner wholeness. A book, a recording, a conference could inspire you to believe that you could share the author, artist or speaker's experience, and that hope sustained you until you realised once more that God was not as close to you as you had hoped, and the whole cycle would begin again. Living vicariously through other people's experiences is perhaps an indication that we have not yet learned to be comfortable in our own skin – we are seeking to model our spiritual lives on what we see in others rather than exploring our own uniqueness.

At times, I felt I had stepped on to a treadmill of commerce, promoting new titles simply to maintain cash-flow. I was horrified by some of the 'Christian' products we were offered – ordinary items 'Christianised' with verses from the Bible – such as the Pritt glue tubes each bearing a small round sticker printed with a biblical text in a minute font. This seemed a blatant exploitation of the Christian market. And I found in a supplier's catalogue a photo of a fish-shaped piece of leather, designated 'Winnie the Whale'. It was clearly designed for disciplining your kids – for it bore the words 'Spare the rod and spoil the child'.

As I admitted at the end of the article, 'theory is easy, practice much more difficult'. I urged my readers to 'read less and read more deeply', and concluded (it was again, perhaps, a desire rather than a statement of absolute truth):

> My basic management principle is simply this – God honours those who honour him: the less I get in his way as he runs his shop, the greater will be the profits, spiritual and commercial.

Interesting how self-effacing that statement is as I emphasise 'not getting in God's way' rather than positively acting as God's agent and partner in a valuable work.

*

'See you later alligator,' I'd say to Wendy on my way out to lunch.

'In a while, crocodile,' she would respond, dutifully, but with a smile.

Keen to have the last word, I always added my own concluding line: 'Not on your Nellie, phantellie.'

I enjoyed working for Scripture Union. I appreciated the Christian ethos of the organisation, and the friendliness and supportiveness of the staff, in particular my bookshop team. I did a good job with an enthusiasm which was appreciated by colleagues and customers alike.

When I left in May 1980 I did so reluctantly, against my will and against my better judgement.

I had not journeyed from autumn to a warmer season; I had not cast aside the inhibiting mantle. Rather I was burdened by emotional pain, and far from waking into Christ's summer I found myself trudging through an endless wintry landscape.

FOURTEEN

A SHAMEFUL SECRET

The job appointment was conditional on my passing a medical.

My father drove me across to Hamilton where the Council's medic was based. 'Now remember,' he said on the way, 'your anxiety is something between you and Dr Duthie. You don't need to be mentioning it today.' Dr Duthie was my GP.

As the doc ran his tests and asked me questions, I sat with a sense of anxious detachment hoping that I was successfully masking the truth while at the same time suppressing both my ethical concerns over remaining silent and the urge to call out 'Help me!'

Afterwards I walked back to the car, my seemingly shameful secret intact.

*

In 1977, newly started working with Scripture Union, I was asked to attend the evangelical Christian conference which had for years been held each autumn at the Butlin's holiday camp at Filey in Yorkshire. There I was to help a colleague from SU in England to promote Scripture Union publications. I found the long hours, the unfamiliar routine, and especially the unconventional personality (as I saw it) of the man I was not just working alongside but also sharing a chalet with cumulatively very stressful. He was open about the sexual arousal he felt when watching Evie Tornquist perform, and this perturbed my prudery. Such a reaction and such openness were surely inappropriate in a Scripture Union staffer!

I remember walking up the dark stairwell leading directly into the brightly lit auditorium one evening after a conference session had begun, feeling the empty poignant sadness of exclusion as the crowd sang, apparently in a deep communal yearning to see Jesus, to encounter him, to express their love to him.

On the final evening of the event, I spent a hectic hour shifting unsold Christmas stock to my car to take north to my bookshop in Falkirk. The next morning after a restless night I left Filey and headed for Scotland. After a few miles, completely unexpectedly, I was overcome by an intense conviction that my journey would end in a fatal accident. Mile after mile I drove in terror, tensely gripping the steering wheel, fearfully eyeing each oncoming vehicle. Would this be the one?

I stopped at a motorway service station on the M6, certain that my death was imminent. With difficulty I restrained myself from phoning my parents telling them not to expect me back. It was only when I reached Lanark, a few miles from home, that I could admit the faintest possibility that I might after all complete the journey safely. Eventually I turned into our drive, switched off the engine and slumped back in my seat.

This experience on the road back from Filey was more severe than anything I had endured previously. Although the anxiety did not remain constant at this intense level, that day signalled the start of a 13-year period of emotional pain which forced me to acknowledge that I had a mental health problem.

*

In the mid-1970s, my parents and I had begun travelling across to Airdrie twice on a Sunday and once mid-week to attend Ebenezer Hall, a Brethren church in Coatdyke.

We had family connections with Ebenezer – my paternal grandparents had been members there, and my parents had worshipped in its bench pews during their first years of married life.

In part the move may have been intended to introduce me to a wider range of Christian people – an attempt on my parents part at social engineering – but the immediate trigger was a disagreement between my mother and some of the folk at the Carluke Assembly.

*

The morning meeting at Ebenezer Hall was the usual mix of prayers, reflections on biblical passages, and hymns from the *Believer's Hymn Book*. Sometimes as was expected of me, but not without real faith I would stand up and pray, or share some Bible-based thoughts.

Afterwards, in the car, I'd ask mum and dad 'Was what I said OK?', hungry for affirmation. I'd feel wounded if their response was not as fulsome as I'd hoped for. In participating in this way I was seeking more to please my parents than to please God, yet often in passing on thoughts I had received with some sense of 'givenness' I was aware of an accompanying spirit of love and grace. Later I came to realise that the only times I had any sense of joy in church was when I was contributing to the service.

*

It was so different one snowy winter's day when my father judged it would not be prudent to risk driving to Ebenezer and said 'Why don't we have our own little meeting here?'

We sat, the three of us, beside the radiator in the bow window. Outside, a cold sun reflected on snow-covered garden bushes.

We did not sing. I expect my father read from the Bible and prayed. Probably he hoped I would contribute.

But I was frozen with embarrassment, wishing to be anywhere else but there.

I could not be honest and intimate in that context when so much of my inner life was concealed.

*

One afternoon in spring 1978 my father stood holding the telephone receiver.

'Are you happy we do this?' my father asked mum and me as he was about to dial the solicitor's number?

I nodded – it was his choice.

He had decided to move on from the house he had expected to be his final home to Airdrie and was putting in an offer for a property very near my mother's childhood home.

I suppose the move was to avoid the Sunday double-journeys from Carluke. Perhaps there was also a desire to make it easier for me to make the Christian friends they yearned for me to have.

But my years at that house in Motherwell Street Airdrie were the unhappiest of my life.

*

Many of my journeys from Falkirk back to Carluke after I was no longer living with Mrs Chisholm took place after dark. The drive took about fifty minutes of which I found the first few miles over the moor to Slamannan the most difficult. On frosty nights the sky would be clear, the stars twinkling brightly. I was aware my own smallness and vulnerability as I drove across the earth's crust utterly insignificant in comparison with the vastness beyond, afraid that I'd fall off into space, or that some great darkness from above would pursue me.

Supposing the car broke down? I'd work out how many minutes it would take, once I found a phone and called my father, for him to reach me, pluck me from jeopardy and take me home.

But inevitably, if the forecast predicted snow Mary Fischbacher would phone me or drop in to the shop to enquire if I'd like to stay over with them. Her husband Eric was a GP who had trained with my father: I was touched by their generosity and indeed found a degree of healing in the warm acceptance in which the Fischbachers enveloped me. I experienced for the first time how joyful Christian family life can be. There were prayers, jokes at mealtimes, speakers scattered around the house connected by long cables to record players so that folk could listen to their music wherever they happened to be. Sometimes Eric and Mary's two younger daughters Moira and Fiona sang together, accompanied by guitar, in front of the flickering coal fire, a recent, reflective song about the morning star loveliness of Jesus.

The stories of everyday practical concern showed by family members to others on a regular basis pierced me with guilt as I reflected on what I saw as my own selfishness.

There were nights when travel was impossible because the roads were thick with snow, and we'd be snug in front of the fire and Eric would say 'The snow doesn't matter when I've got all my family safe under my roof.'

I'd lie in bed utterly secure and listen as outside in the cold snowploughs cleared Ercall road as far down as the house in case Eric had to visit patients in the middle of the night, and the yellow light on top of the cab pulsed on the bedroom wall. I do not think I had ever before felt so loved as I did under the Fischbachers' roof.

*

One Sunday at Ebenezer, just after the morning meeting, an older woman stood in the vestibule, about to leave.

'Wasn't that *wonderful*?' she said, eyes bright.

Conscious of telling an untruth, I muttered a miserable 'Oh yes,' and smiled.

But what had she *felt*, I wondered, what had she *felt* as she'd listened to words of prayer and exhortation, and sung hymns, and taken bread, and wine?

Did everyone *feel* as she felt? And if so, why did I feel numb, and untouched? No angel had stirred the waters of my soul.

*

The Baptist Church at Denny had asked for a representative from Scripture Union to give a presentation on the organisation's work at a Wednesday-evening meeting, and I'd offered to go. As I drove Dennywards through the darkness at the end of a busy day, I felt a rising tsumani of panic.

There wasn't a large audience: all I had to do was to give a short introduction, and then talk the audience through a series of colour transparencies. But the anxiety mounted as I set up my equipment. I went to the loo, and took a Valium.

When I stood up to speak, my heart was racing so fast I felt it would explode. I could hardly breathe; my every impulse was to run and run and run through the darkness, anywhere. Yet despite this it seemed easier, braver, more face-saving to keep going rather than admitting something was wrong and asking for help. I uttered one painful word after another while struggling to contain the panic. My brain, it seemed, had detached itself from my body: at one level, I was acutely aware of the physical turmoil, the trembling hands, the pounding in my chest, whilst in a calmer centre, high above the storm my mind continued generating thoughts and words and sentences which my lips were able to express. Eventually the fear subsided somewhat, and I made it through to the end of the meeting, totally exhausted.

But what had happened, and would it happen again?

*

Occasionally I was asked to speak at Ebenezer Hall in the half-hour slot assigned for 'ministry' at the conclusion of the morning meeting, and I discovered that as Ben Schofield had noticed I had a gift for exploring what the Bible taught and applying it with sensitivity and relevance to everyday situations. I found it especially powerful emotionally to explore the creative tension between Bible stories and the biblical themes which they illustrated and symbolised – or, as the theologians put it, to juxtapose type and anti-type. For me three words in the Old Testament story where Joseph reveals his true identity to his brothers – 'I am Joseph' – had far more resonance than almost anything else in the Bible. Here Joseph was a 'type' of Jesus, revealing himself to those who did not know who he truly was. Even at that date, I found story had more life-giving potential than dogma.

Preaching I found stressful and yet fulfilling, rewarding, but my preaching was invariably sustained by Valium. There was always a fear of another panic attack.

Once when a sermon was being recorded, the microphone caught my final whispered words after I had successfully reached the end: 'Thank you, Father, Thank you.'

*

There was healing joy one Christmas when I was preparing a talk for the Youth Fellowship (which I helped to organize) which compared the verse from the gospels about the baby growing in Mary's womb with St Paul's description of Christ 'being formed' in believers as his character grows progressively more dominant within them. I don't quite know what this meant to my audience of teenagers, but it was significant to me.

The Youth Fellowship leader decided that it would be good to give the group an overview of the books of the Bible. He and I would speak on alternate weeks. To me this was impossibly demanding as I felt I had to have a detailed overview of a book before I could conscientiously speak on it. Genesis, I managed. Leviticus was more of a challenge.

There was a train driver's strike. One day I stood on a packed double-decker bus heading through the dark, blustery morning towards Glasgow my head bent to the left because the ceiling was too low, my nose buried in Banner of Truth's reprint of a very verbose 1852 commentary on Leviticus.

*

One thing I knew I should be involved in as a Christian was 'evangelism' – reaching out to others with the good news.

In membership at Ebenezer Hall was a school janitor named Duncan ('Dunky') Donaldson. Earlier in his life he had been one of Airdrie's most notorious drunks until the day he heard and responded to the Christian good news and from that moment was genuinely transformed. His presence, a constant reminder of God's ability to change lives, was a perpetual inspiration and challenge to the rest of the church in their efforts to share their faith.

This expectation that we should share our faith and in sharing see evidence of its power had been the impulse behind my dream of a market bookstall in Falkirk. And I felt the same impulse while working at the Glasgow shop despite the fact that the whole purpose of my job revolved round outreach. I felt a more personal engagement was necessary.

*

'Would you like to set aside a shelf for Christian books? I would give you them sale-or-return, with a 20% discount?' I had found the courage to speak to the owner of a shop in Airdrie which sold books among much else.

He thanked me, but said that this wouldn't be possible.

*

On Friday nights, we'd meet at Ebenezer Hall for prayer before walking along to the town centre, usually in pairs, handing out leaflets about the Christian faith and trying to engage folk coming out of pubs or standing on street corners in conversation about the spiritual dimension and the reality of God. I found this incredibly difficult.

My understanding at that time was that though God often entrusts things to us which we are good at and obviously made for sometimes we are also called to do hard things. When you do the hard stuff in open-ness to and dependence on God then God's presence is with you, but if you refuse to face the challenge you are somehow diminished.

I remember one evening getting into halting conversation with someone who had just left a pub. For some reason I'd become separated from my partner and so there were just the two of us. I guess Brian must have been showing some interest in the faith because I invited him back to the church hall which was a quarter of a mile away for coffee and a chat. He and I walked side by side along the dark pavement. I struggled to think of things to say. When we reached the church, I entrusted Brian with a sense of relief to someone else's care and before long he had committed his life to God, and began what was to be an enduring Christian journey. I was amazed and encouraged to be part of his story.

And yet I know that in all this I acted to assuage my supergo-driven guilt rather than through any love or concern for individuals.

*

In the weeks before my second visit to the Christian Bookseller's Convention in 1979 I'd been anxious and low and probably should have abandoned the trip. But I went ahead driven perhaps by the determination which got me to the end of that meeting at Denny. Perhaps carrying on with what has been planned, despite its painfulness is the easy option, less stressful than acknowledging reality.

The night before leaving, I watched the last episode of one of the early TV series of *All Creatures Great and Small* based on James Herriot's books about a vet practicing in Yorkshire in the late 1930s. I'd seen most of the previous shows and enjoyed these gentle rural stories with their minor personal and veterinary crises which for the most part came to positive, satisfying conclusions.

But the story I watched before my trip to London ended with Herriot heading off to serve in World War Two, sitting in a black taxi, sadly waving goodbye to his wife as he was driven away into uncertainty. Watching this on a bleak, black-and-white screen I was engulfed by a clammy cloud of desperate melancholy. Herriot was turning his back on the joy, security and routine which he (and I as a viewer) had come to love. My anxiety at the thought of leaving for London fed on the sadness of his departure.

Immediately after the taxi faded from the screen, I switched channels just in time to hear a trailer in which a sepulchral voice intoned 'Possessed by the devil' over eerie, flickering graphics. I turned off immediately, but not before I was pierced by these words. Were my negative, painful thoughts animated by a demon within me?

Next morning, I grimly caught the train at Glasgow Central Station and headed south to Euston. I forced myself through the daily routine of attending conference proceedings and viewing publishers' stands but nothing I did seemed real. It was as if everything I saw, everyone I spoke to was on the far side of an impenetrable sheet of plate glass; or as if I was shrouded in an anaesthetising mist which prevented me connecting with reality. I knew several of the other delegates and could have asked any of them for help and encouragement but the thought of revealing my vulnerability – my shameful secret – raised tension levels still more.

The only positive experience I remember in the course of the week was sitting back in my hotel room and watching a programme from the brilliant Whitehall comedy series *Yes Minister* – it was the first time I'd come across this, and the wit and ingenuity of it gave me a brief, healing respite.

I'd booked a seat on a late afternoon train on the day I was due to come home to give me time to explore London before catching it. But a claustrophobic Tube journey, and the agonisingly slow progress up in the lift from a deep station platform close to the Imperial War Museum left me so on edge and detached from the present that I was totally unable to concentrate as I wandered round the Museum.

I wanted to get home and decided to catch an earlier train. Since my ticket wasn't transferable, I bought a new one at Euston. Too restless to stand patiently in the 2nd class ticket queue, I went to the queue-free 1st class window, and bought a single to Glasgow. It cost me £35.

My parents met me at Central Station. I saw them standing on the concourse as I walked along the platform towards the ticket barrier. My mother seemed stony-faced, grim. It may simply have been the face of her concern for me, but in my state of mind I read her expression as denoting judgmental revulsion. Certainly there were no reassuring hugs.

*

In the event I never delivered that talk to the Youth Fellowship about Leviticus. I was laid low early in 1980 by a debilitating virus which confined me to bed for several weeks.

My illness, sufficiently severe to give rise to a house call from Dr Duthie, rare even in those days, must have been a further concern to my parents. It weakened me for a while and left me more susceptible to emotional angst.

*

In the spring of 1980, my parents planned a week's holiday. Since I was still struggling emotionally, they felt it wouldn't be wise to leave me on my own at home – perhaps they feared I might be suicidal. Remaining in the house would have been my preference, but the matter was never discussed with me. They arranged for me to spend the week at the former WEC College in Glasgow where I had helped to catalogue the library. It still belonged to the mission and was used as a residence for Christian students studying at the university and local colleges.

I'd met Roy and Daphne Spraggett who managed this facility but I did not know them well. It was with a sense of foreboding, a feeling of abandonment that I set off to work that Friday morning from Airdrie lugging my case. Later in the day I dragged it up Clarence Drive in Glasgow's west end on my way from Hyndland Station to Prince Albert Road.

Roy and Daphne welcomed me, and showed me to my room. I suppose they knew the shameful secret, but it remained unmentioned. The next day, the Saturday, I was working, but back at the College in the evening tension began to mount. Gripped by the old familiar feeling that I was just managing to keep the lid on some disastrous emotional explosion, I sat at the table in the library forcing myself to fill out a catalogue card for the next book in the pile. I was invited to attend a Saturday evening church service but politely declined.

*

The next morning in bright sunshine I walked across Kelvingrove Park to the Sandyford Henderson Memorial Church of Scotland with the Spraggetts' daughters and some of the students whose accommodation I was sharing, and sat down in the cool interior of the old building. The only thing I remember about the service was a verse from the Book of Job which the Rev George Philip quoted in a prayer – 'Though he slay me, yet will I trust in him'. (Job 13:15 AV) I had never before, to my knowledge, heard these words, this naked expression of faith in God no matter what, this apparently insane conviction that despite incomprehensible darkness and pain all would be well.

The translators differ over whether the words George Philip quoted from the King James version of the Bible are in fact an accurate equivalent of the original Hebrew, but no matter. For me that morning they were words I needed to hear, not just for that day but for the days to come. I found I could identify both with Job's sense of alienation and bleak abandonment and with the faith in which he was able to say, in effect 'I don't know what you are doing, God. I don't know why you are inflicting this terrible pain on me like a malicious sadist, or at very least sitting back, it seems a spectator in the arena of my suffering, but I believe. I believe you are love. I believe that somehow in this your love is present. Whatever happens, I believe.'

As I gladly took those words 'though you slay me yet will I trust in you' and made them my own, I found an oasis of peace in the eye of the storm, and I remained there throughout the day. That afternoon, back at the College I worked in the library, much calmer. Out on the glazed verandah, venerable retired missionaries sat in the sunlight talking of the Lord's goodness in their lives. Their level of spirituality seemed from their words to be so much deeper than mine, so much 'other' than mine. Yet I was confident that I could trust God in the darkness, and that was enough.

*

The next day, my parents called. How was I? I'd had a bit of a tough time to start with, but I was much, much better now, I replied. My mother seeming to hear just the first part of what I said, decided they should abandon their holiday and come home. 'No, I'm fine now,' I said, 'You just stay where you are.' But they insisted on returning: I was frustrated – first I'd felt abandoned, now I was full of guilt because their holiday was coming to a premature end and it seemed to me that I was to blame.

Again, I'm sure their actions were prompted by love. I wish they had found a more tangible way of helping me to feel reassured, accepted and accompanied – but perhaps at times I was beyond reassurance.

*

One Saturday when I was working at the Falkirk book-shop, I was burdened by an impulse, neurotic in its intensity to ask to be baptised again at the baptismal service I knew was scheduled to take place at Ebenezer Hall the following day. It would, I recognised, take courage to broach the subject with my parents and with the church leaders but it was something I felt I had to do. My initial baptism which I went through in full knowledge that I was not a believer, must have counted for nothing in God's eyes, must indeed have been an abomination to God. This impulse was surely a gracious divine invitation to get it right. A re-baptism would surely in God's eyes be a first, genuine, glad, liberating immersion into a fuller life.

Perhaps I thought that in this action I would find healing and be as other Christians were.

As I was locking up the door of the shop in Cow Wynd in the late afternoon sunshine I held the handle longer than I needed to. 'The next time I touch this,' I said to myself, 'I will have been baptised properly.'

*

Monday came and I wrapped my fingers round that handle again but I had not 'passed through the waters' in the interim. I'd told my parents of my wish to be re-baptised, but they had persuaded me that this was unnecessary. Or perhaps I resigned myself to not receiving their blessing without which, not yet sufficiently my own person, I lacked courage to proceed.

*

In early 1980 my parents, especially my mother, urged me to find another job. In this suggestion I saw no logic. There was absolutely no connection between my anxiety and the job which when I was well I enjoyed immensely, though I'll never forget how rude I was to an over-persistent carrier-bag salesperson one day when I was not myself.

The train journey from Airdrie to Glasgow Queen Street was a twice-daily walk into the jaws of claustrophobia, as was its fear-wracked alternative, the drive along the M8 into the city. I wanted to remain with Scripture Union but lacked the emotional robustness and clarity of thought to argue with mum and dad.

'Do you want me to speak to your mother and tell her you want to stay?' my boss asked me. 'No, just leave it,' I replied miserably, in no mood for a fight, and knowing how angry she would be if he intervened.

My parents – with a singular lack of perceptiveness – had hinted that I might find work in a school library congenial, and when I saw an advertisement for the post of school librarian at Linwood High School in Renfrewshire I dutifully sent for an application form and completed, it sick at heart. The thought of living and working away from home horrified me at that point and a daily commute to Linwood would have been difficult and so I tore the application form into small pieces and dropped it in the bin.

But then inevitably, I began to worry in my neurosis if I'd done the right thing. Perhaps God was calling me to Linwood, and I was resisting? I phoned asking for another copy of the application form, lying that I'd made a mistake when filling in the first one and I sat one lunch-time at the big table in the room where the SU Council held its meetings completing it. Later I walked down to the foot of St Vincent Street and dropped it into the post box with resolution and dread.

I had contacted William Scobbie who was now retired asking him if he would give me a reference. Yes, he told me, he would be happy to oblige, but did I know that there was currently a school library post vacant at Airdrie Academy? If I was interested, he said, I should contact Margaret Sked his successor.

This I did, and at her invitation, I took the train out to Hamilton one afternoon to meet her. It was in no sense a formal interview. Margaret described the duties of the post to me and I listened, growing increasingly dubious about my ability to cope with the work. The shameful secret was left unmentioned. I said politely to Margaret that I'd think further about the job and give her a ring to let her know my decision. But no, I told myself as the train rattled its way back to Glasgow. This job wasn't for me.

A day or so later I phoned Margaret, quite resolved to say 'No!', but somehow after we had talked for a bit, and she had tried to persuade me to accept, I heard myself saying that I would take the job, and I still don't understand why I said 'Yes'.

*

We were entitled to a generous staff discount at Scripture Union, and the day I left, I bought around £40-worth of theological books, and struggled out to my father's car when he came to collect me, laden with two large book-filled carrier bags. I still believed that the Bible's teaching could be summed up and clearly articulated once and for all. My purchases that day, I surmised, would be all I would ever need as I tried to shoehorn my life into the theological framework I accepted as a given.

*

I still had no idea of how God's guidance worked. My neurotic indecision over the Linwood job application showed both an obsessive desire to seek God's will, and a complete lack of clarity over how that was to be discerned. What in fact happened – that unexpected entry of Airdrie Academy into the equation, and that telephone conversation which had the opposite outcome to what I'd anticipated – could just possibly be interpreted as divine promptings – but only with hindsight.

But the fact that I did say 'Yes' was why I found myself en route to Hamilton that afternoon, my father driving.

'Now remember! Your anxiety is something between you and Dr Duthie.'

And so I started my new unwelcome job bearing this shameful secret.

FIFTEEN

BAM-BAM-BA-RAMBAM

'Bam – bam – ba – rambam.'

The kids at Airdrie Academy quickly gave me a nickname. Detecting a faint similarity in appearance between me and the bespectacled, intellectual quiz-master Bamber Gascoigne, they dubbed their new librarian 'Bamber'. Now this could have been regarded as something of a compliment, but 'Haw Bamber wee man!' chanted by mocking youths was enraging. So was the incantation, conceived with malicious brilliance and modulated: sometimes whispered nerve-jarringly *sotto voce* as I traversed the school corridors, sometimes bellowed with an accompaniment of fists drumming on library tables – 'Bam – bam – ba – rambam. Bam – bam – ba – rambam'.

I absorbed this daily because I thought I had no choice.

As I walked across to the House Block for lunch, elbowing my way through what seemed a miasma of mockery and aggression I'd see the Special Needs teacher, who had long-standing discipline problems, lurking outside his classroom door: face worry-haunted; tense fingers white, nail-bitten. Was this my destiny?

*

I began working at the school in early June 1980, and spent the first few weeks getting the library in order and acquainting myself with the staff. At the basement level of the school's main classroom block, built in the 1930s there was a long, open recess about eight feet deep and thirty yards in length, supported at the front by brick piers. This recess, overlooking grass and sparsely-populated flower beds, had originally provided a place for pupils to park their cycles but later the space between the piers was filled in with glass panels, each with an opening window at the top. Half way along, a glass door gave admittance to my new domain, 'the library in the bike shed'. A rather sad-looking collection of books crammed the shelves on the back wall, and one island unit at the far end.

Other than my fortnight's holiday, I spent my first summer conscientiously at the library – my line manager was the headteacher rather than the Principal Schools Librarian, and no-one seemed particularly concerned whether I was present during the holidays. I sat contentedly in the sunshine reading teenage novels, and writing Christian articles.

On at least one occasion there was cross-fertilisation from the first of these activities to the second. In an article published in the Brethren periodical *The Harvester* I wrote:

In her teenage novel Pennington's Heir, *K. M. Peyton has her young pianist hero meditate on his musicianship. He wants to be 'Beethoven's medium, his ghost, realising his incredibly perfect… tune'. Fulfilment is 'For Beethoven to nod his head and say "yes, that's what I meant"…Not to have people clap because you were good, but because you showed them the composer's intention. Not to be big-headed, self-opinionated, a jumped up finger-gymnast. "Oh God," Pat said to the piano, "If only it was easier."' How closely that parallels our Christian service, representing God's intentions. We often say 'if only it were easier.' Can God say of our life and work 'Yes, that's what I meant'?*

*

When term began, pupils from the first three years had a regular period in the library when accompanied by their English teacher they came to change their books. At the start of the session, I introduced them to the arcana of library organisation.

My budget for selecting new stock was very low – around £1000 per annum. The paltriness of this sum reflected the head teacher's slender estimation of the value of the library to his pupils' education. I regularly visited the Education Resource Service HQ – the familiar building in Hamilton's Auchingramont Road – where I attended meetings and training sessions with other school librarians, and borrowed resources to meet the specific needs of pupils or teachers at my school.

I didn't fully understand initially what was expected of me – there was no pre-entry training. Margaret Sked and her senior team shared a progressive vision of the importance of libraries in education. Librarians should have a central role in their school's learning environment, organizing resources so that they could be accessed inter-departmentally and targeted to support pupils in their studies, and working alongside children both to inspire them to read fiction and encourage them to develop their study skills.

Airdrie Academy was not fertile ground for testing new visions of the school library's role. Other than Iain Morris in the English Department, most of my Principal Teacher colleagues were not in the habit either of using the library themselves or of encouraging their pupils to do so and though I did consult them all as part of the selection process, inviting recommendations of titles for purchase, I did not succeed in stimulating much library use 'across the curriculum'.

But my main problem was the sense that I had somehow 'ended up' in the job I was doing rather than making it a positive choice. At that point I lacked the professional confidence, emotional resilience and personal commitment to this new vision of the school library to be able to promote it tenaciously in my dealings with the head and other senior staff. Something shrivelled within me as I heard my colleagues at the Hamilton meetings discussing curriculum change and parallel library developments. In my state of mind these sessions seemed both uninspiring and threatening. This kind of librarianship, I concluded, simply wasn't 'me'.

For their part, not having any real understanding of the role a school library could potentially play, the school management's expectation was that I would act as an on-site public librarian rather than as a fellow-educationist. The best that can be said for my time at Airdrie is that I fulfilled this limited role to the best of my ability.

I spent a good bit of the time between class visits reading. And I would wait with trepidation for the banging of the corridor door and the clatter of feet on the path outside heralding the arrival of the next class. When, ten minutes into the period I was still on my own I could safely conclude with a sense of relief that the teacher had decided not to bring the pupils down that day.

*

I remember the kindly, irascible English teacher John Macdonald, who coped brilliantly with a physical disability. He often brought a class to the library late on a Friday afternoon. He'd tell me how careful he was on Fridays not to lose it with the kids, as if he did he'd spend the weekend worrying about possible repercussions. I loved his gruff gentleness.

One Monday John wasn't in his classroom. They found him dead in his flat, the victim of a virulent influenza.

*

Would I be able to make it to the end of my short introduction to the Dewey Decimal System without collapsing on the floor, or fleeing the scene in panic? Would I be able to keep functioning, stamping one book after another while teenagers hubbubed around me until the ragged queue diminished? Dealing with groups of pupils visiting the library often provoked acute anxiety.

What troubled me most was my almost complete inability to control the students. I had no sanctions to threaten or deploy. There was always a teacher present when classes were visiting, but at lunchtime and intervals I was on my own. I had received no guidance in working with groups of children, and my natural instinct was to be as supportive as possible. But the kids did not have to be particularly perceptive to detect my weakness and lack of confidence. Mayhem ensued.

When I unlocked the library, some students came in quietly to work or to select books, but most stormed past me intent on creating havoc and I knew they'd soon be climbing out the windows or opening the fire doors to allow their mates in. I did have a small team of pupils whom I had enlisted as library helpers and some of them did their best to assist me by marking books in and out, and re-shelving returned items. Some of my other volunteers were not particularly well-chosen and if anything contributed to my problems, yet I lacked the confidence in my authority to manage them properly. I tried to control entry to the library by assigning a named card to each pupil and insisting on this being produced before a child was allowed in. But this strategy failed as I didn't know all the pupils by name, and once inside children would pass their cards through the windows to others outside.

Though deeply ashamed of my problems I discussed them fairly openly with colleagues – to whom what was happening must in any case have been obvious. For a while Iain Morris sent one of his staff down for half an hour at lunchtimes to stand watch over the library door on my behalf, but needless to say this was not popular with his team and eventually I kept the library closed when pupils were not in class.

I struggled with a sense of deep failure. I remember once, shortly before a holiday, locking the library door one afternoon and tidying up the shelves which were invariably in a state of chaos following the lunch-time invasion: in truth I spent most of the time dipping into promising-looking books. I concentrated on the island unit, working on the far side. From outside, all that could be seen of me through the window was my ankles and feet below the level of the bottom shelf. Each time I heard the corridor door banging, signalling that someone was walking through the garden, I sat down on the chair I had placed conveniently behind me, and put me feet on a shelf so that no-one outside would see I was there.

*

Very shortly after starting work at the Academy, I remembered Professor Tyler's invitation to undertake research in his department, and I contacted him. The project I had in mind related to the history of theological and Christian publishing.

In the school library I had found a reference in Ian Watt's book *The Rise of the Novel* to a fascinating piece of research. A PhD student in the 1930s had, long before the advent of computers, analysed all the religious titles contained in the 18th century British Museum catalogue according to their place of publication and the religious denomination to which the authors were affiliated.

Partly propelled by a desire to do something of significance I wondered whether it would be possible for me to analyse the 19th century section of the catalogue in a similar way. I soon realised that because of the explosion of publishing after 1800 this would be impracticable. Could I, I mused, write a study of 19th century theological publishing? I began some preliminary research, tracking down printed material and archives. On-line searches were in their infancy, and were conducted on the student's behalf by professionals. I paid £40 for a search, which revealed hardly anything of use.

But when I discovered the riches of material available I refined my field of interest, homing in on Scottish 19th century religious publishing. I discussed this area with Graham Jones, the supervisor I was assigned when I committed to writing a Masters thesis, and finally decided to study two Scottish publishing companies, Blackie and Son, and Thomas Nelson and Sons. In the early years of both businesses there was a heavy emphasis on religious titles.

Inspired by my own experience of the Christian book trade, I wanted to look for evidence of the religious, or spiritual motivation at work in Blackie and Nelson's publishing. How easy was it for them to balance a commitment to mission, and the making of profit? And what happened when the second and subsequent generations took over the companies? Was a sense of mission still a driving force; was there increasing focus on the bottom line?

This project was undertaken in my own time – I visited archives in key Scottish centres; I spent hours in the Mitchell Library in Glasgow reading through 19th century issues of *The Bookseller*. The thesis was completed by the summer of 1983.

My father very kindly helped fund this degree, which I had to pay for myself. He may have hoped that it would help me find professional advancement. For me it was enough that it gave me something to focus on and both the process and the achievement gave purpose and satisfaction.

I think my parents were proud as they sat in the City Hall that October day in 1983 and watched me graduate MA for the second time. It was a far more cheerful event than my first graduation. I felt more in control; felt I had achieved something.

*

There were some positive aspects to my time at Airdrie Academy. I tried to get involved in out-of-school activities, accompanying a quiz team to participate in inter-school events, and helping at the school gala at the local swimming pool. For this, I needed trainers and was so naïve and inexperienced that in the sports shop I pointed at tennis shoes instead, only to be ashamed as my inappropriate footwear attracted scornful glances by the poolside.

What preserved me from utter despondency during my years at the Academy was the companionship and support of the English department staff who valued what I did for them and for their pupils despite my difficulties. I made my home at breaks in the English department where I had full coffee-drinking rights, and joined the team for end-of-term meals.

My major source of encouragement while at Airdrie Academy however was the school's Christian Union group, run by a team of around ten staff including Iain Morris and attended regularly by around forty pupils. The leaders of the CU welcomed me on my arrival, and I helped organise the regular meetings and special events including visits to local churches at which pupils took part, singing or speaking, and at which I sometimes preached. Along with a colleague in the English department I organised a regular morning prayer meeting for staff and pupils. This involvement was uplifting. Without the friendship of the staff and pupils connected with the Christian Union my time at the school would have been very bleak.

*

Walking upstairs in the House Block to one of the House Canteens where we were holding a Christian Union parents' evening. Around me were pupils and their families. But there was an evening peace in the stairwell; a calm sunset sky; the daytime turmoil – shouting, thudding feet, catcalls – was stilled. The House Block, I reflected, was no longer an alien environment.

*

One summer day in 1981 I entered 38 George Street in Edinburgh home for well over a century to the theological and legal publishing firm T. & T. Clark. Ramsay Clark had sent me a brief printed history of the firm, and I wanted to discuss with him what data on their history still existed. It was then that I heard of an extensive archive deposited in the National Library of Scotland which I discovered was particularly rich in material from the 1880s and 1890s.

I spent weeks in the summers of 1981 and 1982 sitting in the Manuscript Room at the National Library having absented myself from school where I knew no-one would miss me. Day by day I poured over letter books and accounts, making extensive notes in pencil, deciphering handwriting, scanning words which probably had not been read since shortly after the day they were written.

I came to know that office in George Street as it had been a century before; I could imagine myself working there among Ramsay's ancestors, correcting proofs, ordering print, welcoming authors, liaising with curmudgeonly translators of German works, debating whether to publish contentious biblical criticism, negotiating language differences with transatlantic partners. Outside, horse-drawn carriages clattered on the cobbles. It seemed a more benign environment.

The National Library was still rather intimidating in the early 1980s; there was a severe silence in the entrance hall as you handed over coat and bag and submitted your writing folder to a security guard for inspection. The Manuscript Room was an inner sanctum reached through the general reading room, a holy of holies dedicated to scholarship. A priest, one of the librarians, mediated the riches bringing them to your table, invigilating to ensure that there was no sacrilege.

At lunchtime, I'd go across to a café in Victoria Street for a sandwich, cake, and coffee. I felt reasonably positive. I loved wandering around the heart of the city after I'd had done enough work for the day, exploring bookshops before walking back to Paisley Avenue where I was staying with family friends.

*

At night I lay in bed listening to the sounds of the city. They seemed eerie and threatening, disturbing my unquiet soul. When I caught the bus into central Edinburgh in the morning, I saw morning by morning the sign above one of the doors. EXIT. I tried to ignore the word, but it filled me with dread, luring me to think of the eponymous organisation which promoted assisted suicide.

Get to the library; don't walk too near the kerb; don't look over the railing when you're crossing George IV Bridge; retrieve your manuscript; read, concentrate, focus.

Strathclyde University accepted me as a PhD student.

*

Sitting in an Airdrie church the Sunday after Margaret Thatcher's task force set sail for the Falklands. Sunlight shone on the dusty old beams. Was this what it was like when people sat in these very same pews at the start of the two world wars?

In Iain Morris's classroom at lunchtime. The television was switched on. Mesmerised, we were watching footage from the South Atlantic. I was driving along Kildonan Street in Coatbridge when I learned of the sinking of the *Sheffield*. I watched Brian Hanrahan counting them all out, and back.

Why this conflict, I thought? Surely it's self-evident that these islands are off the coast of South America and properly belong to the adjacent nation?

*

In December 1982, I was interviewed for a promoted post, based at Education Resource Service in Auchingramont Road, Hamilton. The Head Teacher at the Academy must have given me a favourable reference; I'd researched the job description by visiting a local primary school and chatting to the head; and (prompted by my father) I had shown myself to be future-oriented by signing up for a week-long computer programming course in the Basic language at Strathclyde University.

I arrived home from the course on the Friday night. My mother was waiting. 'Greetings, Primary School Library Advisor,' she proudly proclaimed.

Margaret Sked had phoned to offer me the job.

I took up post in early January the following year.

I knew that the increase in salary meant that it was at last viable for me to consider purchasing a place of my own.

No more 'Bam-bam-ba-rambam'. No more apprehensively lurking behind the island unit. The cruel rhythm had not broken me.

SIXTEEN

'GOD LOVES YOU'

Shortly after leaving the M6, I pulled into a layby on the edge of woodland to take a pee. I was stilled by the deep calm, the freshness of pelting rain on bright green foliage. But I was emotionally numb. Having a holiday was a hoop I felt I must jump through. Going to Keswick was as good as anywhere.

I'd booked myself into a Guest House in Keswick's Wordsworth Street, planning to attend the two weeks of the 1980 Keswick Convention – an annual Christian conference and celebration held since the 19th century. My accommodation was in a part of town where the very street names have entered into evangelical mythology: – Skiddaw Street, Blencathra Street, Helvellyn Street, Southey Street.

I found the place and unpacked my stuff including the books I'd taken to read – Jenni Calder's new biography of Robert Louis Stevenson, and Ron Sider on *Christ and Violence*. They sat me at a table with the only other solitary guest, an elderly gentleman with whom I tried mealtime by mealtime to make polite conversation while concealing my boredom. Later in the evening, we'd watch the Moscow Olympics on the television in the lounge.

Attending many of the meetings in the Convention tent gave shape to my mornings and evenings. But far from being encouraged by the Bible expositions and sermons, I still felt 'on the outside,' unable to connect with God as others in the great audience seemed able to do effortlessly. I had a strong impulse to go forward in response to the invitation at the end of these meetings – to commit, to be prayed for – but I think I understood that the impulse was obsession-driven. Holding within me the pain of this urge I did not yield to it and kept my seat knowing that it would subside eventually.

One day family friends Archie and Grace Roberts from Inverness invited me to visit them in their caravan after the morning session. I remember trying to talk of ordinary things while suppressing the cry for help which screamed within me – submerged, but not far beneath the surface.

The rest of each day at Keswick I was on my own except for the middle weekend when my parents came down to visit. I filled my time as best I could, always conscious of restless anxiety.

I visited every shop in Keswick at least once, took long, long walks round Derwentwater, toured the Cumberland Pencil Museum. One afternoon I drove to Cockermouth and visited William and Dorothy Wordsworth's childhood home. Another day I went to Brockhole, the Visitor Centre on Windermere, and sat in sunshine whiling away the hours reading the *Daily Telegraph* from cover to cover. I walked beside the River Greta in Fitz Park in Keswick in the cool of evening the day Peter Seller's death was announced (he died on 24th July 1980), reflecting on the ultimate sadness of his life. I planned writing some articles as I instinctively sought the healing touch which accompanies the act of creation.

I survived the fortnight. It was not all struggle: some whisper of calm crept into my soul mediated not by the Convention so much as by the sacrament of Lakeland beauty.

*

On another occasion I was attending a Brethren Christian conference for youngish people at the Abernethy Centre, Nethy Bridge. I felt low and fearful, with no stamina for interacting. On the Saturday afternoon when everyone was away walking the hills I lay in my bunk reading the Penguin edition of Daniel Defoe's *Robinson Crusoe*, borrowed from Airdrie Academy library. I was consoled by its reassuring portrayal of a personal world which even in times of extreme crisis was God-centred.

Later talking to a young woman in the foyer I discovered that she too felt not entirely at home. I shared a little of my experience, and sensed that our conversation had uplifted her.

This insight surprised, humbled me.

*

My GP referred me to a clinical psychologist at the local hospital to help me confront and cope with debilitating panic. I saw Eileen just once. The way to her office led through the psychiatric wards. I walked past people who were visibly suffering from mental health problems, and found this both terrifying and fascinating. I tried to distance myself from what I was seeing while at the same time knowing that I was one of them.

I remember clearly the day I realised I was mentally ill. I was sitting at a meal table, panicking that I wouldn't be able to make it to the end of the main course without meltdown (one forkful after another, John, slowly, slowly, keep calm, keep calm, now for the next forkful, listen, listen and talk, John, slowly, calmly, calmly). Naming the demon diminished it, marginally.

It was an insight I don't think my mother ever accepted, either in relation to my life, or her own. Day after day I would arrive back at the house from Airdrie Academy, suspecting that yet again my mother in her sadness would make negative comment after negative comment.

I kept my pain to myself as much as I could. Once when I was trying to explain what I was experiencing to my parents, my mother said 'Stop! If I hear any more I'll end up in Hartwood.'

Hartwood was the local mental hospital where cruel rumour had it that Maggie Cassells my disconcerting Carluke Primary School teacher had been confined.

*

For a Christian in those days, to seek professional help with a mental health issue was to face being stigmatised by many other Christians: you were regarded as having somehow 'let the side down'. They reasoned that the transformation which takes place in you when you embrace God affects your life in its every aspect – not just spiritually, but emotionally, mentally and psychologically. And so it was often concluded among evangelicals that when a Christian had mental health problems it was indicative of moral or spiritual failure, and that the appropriate solution was not psychiatric support but spiritual counselling, and greater obedience to the Word of God.

I think this stigmatising sprang from fear of mental health issues, fear of anything 'other' which did not fit easily into theological schemes. This was profoundly damaging especially since some harsh doctrines taught in churches actually contributed to the sufferer's mental pain.

*

I sat down in Eileen's room. She smiled, and we talked. My knowledge that she was a believer made it easier for me to accept her help. To see a Christian professional was deemed by those of my fellow-Christians who were judgmental of people with mental health concerns to be somehow less dangerous, less culpable. A Christian would be aware of the transforming divine power (so the argument ran) as well as the dubious God-excluding theories of Freud and his successors.

Eileen listened to me sympathetically. She proposed a course of what she called 'aversion therapy', which would involve me exposing myself gradually with her presence and encouragement to the things

I was most afraid of, and discovering through this experience that I could look fear in the face and survive. Eileen sent me home positive and hopeful with a relaxation tape to listen to. There was no mention of God, but this was fine from my point of view. I believed God was there in the room with us.

My mother was very negative about my visit to Eileen in general and especially negative about the relaxation tape. I played it the next night in my bedroom, listening to the soft hypnotic voice, trying to follow its calm instructions. But downstairs in the kitchen the sound of the voice as it penetrated the floorboards was having quite the opposite of its intended effect on my mother who became increasingly fraught. (Earphones were not then ubiquitous, and it simply didn't occur to me to use them.) Afterwards, mum made quite clear that visiting Eileen would do me no good whatsoever and that I should cancel my next appointment. My father said nothing to disagree with her.

And so it was that not for the first time and certainly not for the last I unwisely sacrificed my own interests to avoid disturbing my mother and shattering her illusions. I wrote to Eileen, telling her I'd found our session together very helpful and thanking her for it, but explaining that I now felt there was no need for a return visit. I enclosed an article I'd written illustrating from my own experience how Christian faith can sustain you through emotional and mental turmoil. This was, I'm sure, a perceptive and honest piece, and it was perfectly true that I felt at times sustained and comforted by my faith, however wavering it might be. However in writing to Eileen I was turning my back on the beneficial support, insights and therapy which I would have received from her.

*

In the summer of 1980, I bought a book, *Conversion* by A. J. Krailsheimer. It was a study of the conversion stories of several notable Christians – from St Paul to Thomas Merton, and analysed the commonalities and dissimilarities in their experiences. This was a significant purchase. It was not by a writer within the Brethren or the evangelical fold. Moreover, Krailsheimer's book was published by SCM press whose output I had hitherto viewed with deep suspicion. My purchase of it showed a willingness, indeed a desire to think critically about the development of my own faith.

*

During my time as librarian at Airdrie Academy I was sitting in the school hall during a prize-giving ceremony. The Chaplain, a local Church of Scotland minister, led the gathering in the Lord's Prayer. Over the years I had absorbed a certain disdain for the public use of the Lord's Prayer. It was meant, I had gathered, to be a template for extempore prayer not a liturgy to be slavishly repeated by those who did not understand the reality of praying. Some Brethren people would pointedly remain silent if they were part of a congregation which was asked to repeat the Prayer.

But that afternoon I uttered the familiar words with the others and they brought me joy.

'How odd,' I thought, 'that God should be more in evidence to me here in school than down the road at Ebenezer Hall!'

*

A Wednesday evening in winter, just after seven. I was standing outside the front door of our house in Airdrie debating with myself whether to go to the mid-week church meeting. I didn't want to go. Too many memories of sitting through prayer meetings with a sense of heaviness, despairing the lack of connection, questioning why God was silent, suspecting the cause was something amiss in my own life. I would pray audibly because it was expected of me – and just occasionally ideas and words would flow with a sense of 'givenness'. But often, I'd drive home dejected.

On the other hand I presumed the others who attended had a more positive experience and I recalled those stories of people absenting themselves from a prayer meeting on the very day 'God came down in rich blessing'. Perhaps I should go. It would be expected of me. My presence might encourage others. But I suspected that I would still feel on the outside even if God came down in blessing.

I stayed at home. It was as well to be miserable in the comfort of your bedroom.

But I never doubted God's existence, nor the sincerity of fellow Christians. The problem was clearly mine – my experience of God did not match any of the templates which had been offered me.

*

I heard of the Religious Experience Research Unit which the marine biologist Alister Hardy had set up in 1969 to gather accounts of religious experiences, and to publish research based on this evidence. I read his book *The Spiritual Nature of Man: a Study of Contemporary Religious Experience* published in 1979. My impression however was that the 'experiences' Hardy documented were mostly what I deemed to be 'unusual', including clairvoyance, telepathy and out-of-body sensations. I was looking instead for a reflection on 'normal' or 'everyday' experiences of God such as the people I knew described ('Wasn't that wonderful?') and for understanding of why different individuals 'experience' the numinous to varying degrees. Hardy did not help me with this but again what is significant is that I was prepared to look for insight from out-with what I had learned to label as the 'evangelical subculture'.

*

In the early 1980s, I published several articles in the Brethren periodical *The Harvester* and one in the more conservative *Believers' Magazine* besides a couple of workmanlike short stories in the *Christian Herald*.

Several of *The Harvester* articles found present-day lessons in the Old Testament prophecy of Haggai. I had no great understanding of the work's cultural background and relied for basic understanding of the text on a Commentary published by Brethren scholars, but my work was detailed, enthusiastic, practical, at times moving, and always very 'biblical': every point I made was substantiated by a scriptural reference.

Here are some examples of my 'voice' in these articles – similar in style to the sermons I occasionally delivered:

> We are reminded that moving in Christian circles, and hectic engagement in Christian work are no substitute for a close walk with God – indeed if we are not in his will, our fellowship will be less than satisfactory, our activity as fulfilling as a treadmill. As Christians, we must ensure that our work is done for God, and not merely for ourselves to make us feel more 'spiritual' than we actually are.

> We should stop sulking through life whining 'Why doesn't God bless me?' and admit that we don't deserve blessing. And to reach rock bottom and confess that is to discover that our problems are in themselves a blessing – permitted by God to retune our spiritual antennae to his wave-band. And that discovery leads us in turn to praise him for his outreaching love, and to return to him in gratitude.

My God was still masculine. And this, from an article on *Walking with God* in the *Believers' Magazine*, where I am discussing the Old Testament patriarchs:

> We might find ourselves saying 'It was all right for them! They had this tremendous faith. I'd be a much better Christian if only I could always see the way ahead; if only I were always conscious of God's presence.' But to have such effortless certainty would be sight, not faith, and the muscles of our faith, unexercised, would grow weak. It is, rather, that despite the doubts and difficulties as we

press forward, putting our faith firmly on God's promises and past performance in fulfilling them, we become conscious of his presence and help and reality in our lives.

This style of Bible teaching reflected the 'expository' style of ministry I was familiar with from evangelical preachers and writers – notably John R. W. Stott – if not from the majority of Brethren speakers.

The Harvester also published a couple of articles discussing aspects of Christian experience – again, with multiple biblical references. There was an article on *The Christian Workaholic*, which addressed the tendency for Christians to miss out on joy through over-focussing on achievements and the quest for recognition, and through evaluating other people according to their usefulness or status. The ultimate cure I prescribed for this workaholism was an understanding that we are precious to God *as we are,* and a willingness to let that understanding shape our lives.

And there was *When the Morning Comes,* an article addressing difficulties, doubts and depression in the life of the Christian – this may have been the article I sent to Eileen at Monklands Hospital. I finished with a call to realise that, even when we are in 'the bitter cage of some experience,' God 'is with us, even in the darkness'. I concluded:

> *Len Magee has a song with the simple refrain 'And then the morning comes'. 'Weeping may endure for a night, but joy cometh in the morning' (Psalm 30:5 AV) The little mornings of the Christian experience are foreshadowings of a Morning to be when with the breaking of day shadows flee forever.*

I am struck by the confidence and certainty in these pieces written at a time when I was often struggling. My words falsely imply that I felt at home in the tradition from which I had come whose concepts and vocabulary were second nature to me. I'm sure that part of my motivation for writing was to seek approval and fulfilment within that tradition. But I wrote with sincerity and believed every word I wrote while experiencing little. So much is there – the loveliness of knowing oneself accepted and loved by God, the presence of God as a felt reality, the fact that the door to God opens to the extent by which we recognise our need of God, but I saw these from a distance. Perhaps I thought that in writing of them I could draw them closer.

I wonder whether I wrote because in the brief minutes of reflecting and writing I was carried forward to that distant place, and momentarily tasted there the reality which my words palely intuited.

*

One day Alan Ferguson a pupil at Airdrie Academy who sometimes attended the Christian Union came to see me in the library.

'Why don't you come to the Baptist Church?' he asked me.

And I said yes.

I told my parents about the invitation but assured them that this was just a one-off. I had no intention of leaving Ebenezer Hall.

That Sunday evening I met Alan on the church steps. We sat together very near the back.

The minister Liam Goligher was preaching on one of the 'letters to the churches' in the book of Revelation. I found his approach stimulating.

There was coffee after the service and I was welcomed.

Within a very few weeks I was attending Airdrie Baptist Church permanently.

The reason for the move was partly my appreciation of Liam's preaching and his more intellectually refined approach to the Bible; partly my theological concerns about Ebenezer where a speaker reflecting the old Brethren 'dispensational' view of history had not been challenged by the leadership; partly the warmth I experienced from Liam and others in the church. Here was a place where my parents and grandparents were not known, where I was accepted for myself.

And so Alan's invitation was a turning point.

*

Claire was inescapable.

She was a member of the English staff at Airdrie. I met her at departmental meetings and at Christian Union. She'd be there with her classes in the library leaning against the brick pillar warming her bum at the radiator. I couldn't escape from her face, her voice, her name, her pupils, her handwriting. I was forever finding excuses to go to her classroom. It was to Claire that I took the 15-year-old girl who told me she was contemplating suicide. I was invited to preach at her church and throughout my sermon I was conscious of her presence, not far from the back of the church, eyes fixed on me.

I asked her out.

She turned me down kindly enough, but in a rather patronising way, I thought, as though I were a younger brother caught out in some minor wrongdoing.

I was devastated.

The next day I escaped from the house with a notebook, and parked in a deserted industrial estate. It was Saturday, April 3rd 1982 – I remember the date because on the car radio I had playing the live broadcast from the House of Commons, the first sitting of the House on a Saturday for 25 years, when they were debating the Falkland crisis.

Sitting in the car I threw all my thwarted creative energies into writing a dramatisation for choral speaking to be used at the Christian Union weekend we were planning at Kilcreggan. A few days later, I took the duplicated scripts to Claire in her classroom. An offering.

*

On the Saturday evening at Kilcreggan, late, we held a barbeque on the beach. Claire brought a portable radio cassette player and her Abba tapes. As the fire burned low and darkness fell, our soundtrack was *Waterloo* and *Supertrouper* and *Take a Chance on Me*. I saw her a little way off from the rest of us walking along the twilight sand deep in empathic conversation with a third-year pupil. At that moment I ached at her loveliness, her compassion, her remoteness from me.

*

I reflected in a note written later shortly afterwards on my thoughts about relationships and marriage after my disappointment with Claire. It began 'I think I will look back on last Sunday (April 25ᵗʰ) as an important turning-point in terms of my attitude as a Christian towards girls and marriage.'

My thinking was shaped by the thoughts on marriage of the Christian missionary martyr Jim Elliot as recorded in his wife Elizabeth's book *Shadow of the Almighty*. I saw myself having two options with regard to Claire – 'relinquishment, giving over my feelings towards her to God,' or 'thanking God for her inescapability, and seeing it as an opportunity of getting her to change her mind'.

> *In no way did I regret having spoken to her – even amid my hurt I knew that when you expose yourself to people, to love them or to help them, then you are opening yourself to possible hurt. But it's far better to thus open yourself, and risk hurt than to stay clammed up and inward looking. In any case, in life lessons very often come through hurting.*

All along, I wrote, I knew that relinquishment was the right option, though during the Easter holidays I allowed myself to hope that Claire might change her mind. But on Sunday, 25ᵗʰ April, I relinquished her to God, and also 'handed over to God my whole future, and decided that, if God wanted me to be single, then I would be ready to walk, not alone, but with Him'. I wanted this relinquishment to be total – not made in the hope that if I showed my maturity in this way God might surprise me by changing Claire's mind – and genuine –

not simply a balm applied to ease my heart-wounds. I acknowledged the problems such relinquishment involved – the deep sexual desires which were present even as I believed that fulfilment should be found in Christ alone.

I noted that this relinquishment significantly changed my outlook:

Towards Claire. Before I was highly possessive, and jealous of things she was doing which I had no part in. Now I can commit her to God and ask him to bless her in all she does.

Towards my parents. A tremendous sense of liberation and freedom. Gone is the idea that I need a wife if I'm to be happy in life, and leave the parental home. I'm perfectly ready now to live on my own. The freedom I once only felt at missions etc is now a possibility in daily life.

Towards myself. A new sense of fulfilment, and self-reliance in Christ. I realise that up until now I've been sitting around waiting for a girl to come along before starting to carve out an independent lifestyle for myself. I realise now that I can start to be myself from this moment onwards.

Towards God. A greater sense of reliance, trust, and thanksgiving.

Towards other girls. An openness, and ability to have relationships without constant thoughts of 'Is she the one?'

Finally I acknowledged that having these insights in fact paradoxically put me in a better position to be married. 'May I know, to use the image Jim Elliot borrowed from Genesis, the sleep of faith until God, if it is his will, presents me with the Eve of his choice.'

*

Thus I was modelling myself on a vision of ideal Christian manhood which somehow involved a subjugated sexuality while at the same time viewing women almost as a commodity, a route to fulfilment. Despite my pious hopes, the writing of this was to an extent simply applying comfort to my soul. I don't doubt the sincerity of my words, but I know for a fact that I did not relinquish Claire – later I visited her in her home, made a pilgrimage to her mother's grave after all the mourners had departed, and even had a meal with her at my parents' home a few years later. I know that after Claire turned me down, I was drawn to another of the Christian Union staff at the Academy, but didn't make a move through fear that this would be seen as needy and besides she was a little older than I was. I know that I still asked 'Is this the one?'

And yet writing that document allowed ideas of which I had not previously been conscious to surface. Or perhaps one lovely idea: 'I realise now that I can start to be myself from this moment onwards.'

*

In September 1983, I went with some friends from the church to see a performance of *Macbeth* at the Theatre Royal in Glasgow. We ate at a Chinese restaurant, and then took our seats in the gods, where we watched the performance unfold far beneath us. I had never seen a Shakespeare play live before, and was mesmerised by the beauty of the language, and the joy of sharing the experience with others.

A couple of days later, I extracted the volume containing *Macbeth* from my mother's three-volume, slip-cased, collected Shakespeare – part of her Dux prize from Airdrie Academy – and took it with me to St Andrews. My parents were on holiday at Rufflets Hotel, and had invited me to join them for the Glasgow holiday weekend. It would I thought be a good, relaxed environment in which to tell them of my decision to purchase a flat and move out.

On the drive up, Boy George was singing Culture Club's *Karma Chameleon*. The car broke down, and I summoned the AA. Eventually I arrived.

Later I was sitting in the lobby reading *Macbeth*, and finding it not so captivating on the page as it had seemed on the stage. My parents joined me. My mother seemed concerned that I had borrowed her book without consent. I told them in a quiet, calm, reasonable way that I had decided to move out. My purpose wasn't to be critical or vindictive. I probably said something about it being easier to be my own person if I had my own space.

My father said little but was profoundly upset. I didn't understand his reaction and he wouldn't enlighten me. In fact my parents said little to me over the remainder of the weekend.

I accompanied them miserably to church the next morning and then we crossed South Street to the Pancake Place for lunch where we had to feign normality since someone I knew was also eating there.

My parents spent the Sunday afternoon in their bedroom at the hotel, I in mine. 'Your father is so upset,' my mother said accusingly. *Macbeth* was no comfort. I was tempted to phone Liam Goligher back in Airdrie for solace, but I knew the call would show on the hotel bill.

The next day I left for home praying that the car would start.

Karma Chameleon was still playing on the radio.

*

I began looking in Estate Agents' windows: the whole process of buying a place seemed daunting. Nothing more was said about my parents' reaction at St Andrews, but I didn't feel able to discuss my plans with them.

'I thought you were moving out!' my mother said to me a few weeks later. The heavy sarcasm in her voice served only to make me more determined.

I arranged a mortgage, contacted a solicitor, visited a flat in Dunnet Avenue, Glenmavis and bought it for £17,500, £500 of which was for a rather decrepit shelving unit which I later disposed of and should have refused to pay for. But it suited my needs perfectly; the couple selling it were teachers at the school and I knew them. I only saw it after dark which meant that I didn't notice the pylons marching across the field behind. I presented this *fait accompli* to my parents and they could only accept it.

Off to Argos at the Sauchiehall Centre in Glasgow to buy iron and ironing board and clothes horse and basin and toilet-roll holder and everything I'd need. I made the mistake of requesting too many items to carry easily up the steps to the car park.

Would they let me leave some of them behind the counter?

But this wasn't possible. Meekly, I struggled to the car: a slow process, as I was forever dropping things and having to retrieve them.

The Saturday before I was due to move in, I went shopping in Airdrie, and bought a dining room suite, a washer/dryer, fridge and microwave. With naïve optimism, I expected to be able to arrange for the delivery of these items the following Friday and they promised to do their best.

*

I got the keys on a Thursday night, and took my parents to see the flat. We went to B&Q on the way, and they bought me some cloths and cleaning materials. In the weeks which followed, they purchased a new carpet and arranged for my front room to be re-decorated.

'Don't worry,' my father said, when I pointed out the mortgage agreement was due to expire in 2008. It seemed so far ahead.

I spent all day at the flat on the Friday, anxious, awaiting deliveries, sitting on the floor until the suite arrived. It was after five before everything was there.

Saturday morning, 17th December 1983, I hired a Transit, and with the help of some friends from the Baptist Church, moved my possessions from my parents' house.

I had tea with them, and then left for my very first night in my own place.

*

I was very nervous. Would it be OK, I asked my parents, if I gave them a ring each morning for a few days – it would just give me confidence.

But no, they didn't want this.

*

The dark chill of December mirrored my soul.

My colleagues and I went out for Christmas lunch and the brightness of the seasonal table mocked my mood.

*

I was at my parents' house for Christmas Day. On Boxing Day, Liam and Christine Goligher invited me to the manse, where I shared the day with them and their family, free to be myself. We ate, and laughed, and in the afternoon watched *The Scarlet Pimpernel* on STV.

Before I went home, the Golighers' young son David slapped a round orange sticker on my shirt, bearing the words 'God loves you'.

When I returned to the flat I fixed it to the lamp beside my bed where it remained until I moved out nine years later, a constant reminder.

SEVENTEEN

FAITH IN ACTION

In Airdrie Baptist Church I was greeted with love, acceptance and friendship. Joining the church also gave me endless opportunities to be busy. I attended both services each Sunday and the weekly Wednesday evening prayer meeting. I drew comfort from a song we sang there often, about God being a 'hiding place,' an utterly trustworthy place of refuge to which we could have recourse in times of fear. I belonged to a home group, and prepared weekly Bible study notes for the Youth Fellowship. I led what was called a 'Growth Group' for people who were new to Christian faith, who came round to my flat weekly to work through *Discipleship* a book by David Watson. When we reached the chapter on *Communion* I raised theological eyebrows by organising bread and wine for us to share together in my living room.

I managed the church bookstall, so efficiently (or so relentlessly) that one year at least we sold £2000 worth of material. I'd visit the Gospel Literature Outreach bookshop in Motherwell each Saturday even in the worst of weather to collect stock. I'd be at the church forty minutes before the morning service on Sunday to set out my wares. I often opened the front door and greeted people as they arrived. In the evening I would be the last person to leave.

I can see that all this activity however worthy was a means of dulling or hiding from my pain and perhaps a way of seeking relief from it. This activity was a substitute not so much for faith as for the inner calm which faith failed to deliver. Going to church seemed at times like going to the office: a list of duties awaited me. I even wrote memos to the leaders rather than simply speaking to them.

*

One Saturday morning at the bookshop. I had struggled over icy roads and deep snow to get there. The staff seem surprised to see me.

As I often did, I bought a cup of coffee and a Danish pastry, and sat reading a Christian magazine. One article spoke truths about God which as I read set my soul on fire, almost by-passing my mind. In those moments I knew I was loved, I was more confident of my ability to endure and survive. The afterglow of that experience lingered through the remainder of the day.

*

I became involved in Monklands Evangelical Council which was comprised of ministers from different churches in the area who organised regular inter-church events. One of my tasks was to provide a bookstall at these gatherings.

I remember an event in the church hall at Caldercruix on a cold winter evening. At the end of the event I stood behind the book table hoping that someone would come over to talk to me. But everyone was anxious to return to the warmth of their homes.

Eventually, I packed away my stock and carried the boxes through the snowy car-park. I drove miserably back to Glenmavis through the blizzard. The flat when I reached it was cold and dark and lonely.

*

I remember attending a Monklands Evangelical Council prayer meeting in one of the more austere Presbyterian church buildings in Airdrie. We were sitting in front of the pulpit, about eight of us. Our eyes were closed, and people spoke to God at considerable length and with considerable eloquence, praying for salvation for the people of the Monklands.

I sat, puzzled. Why was I not feeling this passion for the district, this 'passion for souls' which these men were apparently experiencing? Why had I no desire to pray in this way? In any case, was anything ever achieved through prayer?

Dutifully, I took my turn. I knew the phrases to use. Perhaps, I thought, speaking them out would bring conviction to my wavering soul, but it was a tired, doubtful optimism.

*

I was asked to go with a group of people from the Church to preach at a service in Skelmorlie. William, who arranged this, was to collect me at the church building. I prepared my talk but I was anxious that I would need to go to the toilet on the way. I drank little that day. Reaching the church a little before William came, I wanted to make sure my bladder was empty but had left the church key at home. I went down the outside stairs leading to the boiler room, and standing there, half-concealed, I brought to light a few drops of yellow fluid.

Skelmorlie went well. At the end I was tired and dehydrated. In the car on the way back, someone said to me 'You've got that down to a fine art!'

I didn't know whether to be pleased.

A sermon, I knew, should not be artifice, but a gift from God, a God-breathed thing.

*

I was sitting on the balcony at Airdrie Baptist Church. Liam Goligher was preaching from Jesus' parable about a 'prodigal son' who demanded his share of the inheritance and went from the family farm to a far-off place where he squandered his wealth and was reduced to penury. In desperation, he resolved to return home and throw himself on his father's mercy.

The father however was wise in the ways of young men, and no doubt aware of the economic conditions in the land where his son had settled. He was fairly certain that sometime the familiar figure would come slowly homewards. And so, day after day he stood outside the farm scanning the point where road met horizon, waiting.

Eventually, this patience was rewarded. In the distance, he saw a lone traveller, walking dejectedly towards him. Could it be his son? He watched as the figure drew closer. Hope turned to certainty. He began running, faster and faster towards the approaching son, his heart thudding with effort. Yes, taking to your heels was considered shockingly undignified behaviour in a man of standing in the Jewish community, but in love and joy and longing he threw decorum to the wind.

I was very familiar with the wording of this story in the Authorised (King James) Version of the Bible, but not with the way it is told in the New International Version which we were using that night in church. The AV describes the father's action on reaching his son in this way – he 'ran, and fell on his neck, and kissed him'. (Luke 15:20 AV) I had always, from childhood onwards read this (perhaps foolishly) as a technical description of an outlandish oriental mode of greeting which involved the father lying prostrate on the dusty road, his own neck touching the ground, before standing up and kissing his son. But the NIV describes in these words what actually happened in Jesus' story: 'But while he was still a long way off, his father saw him and was filled with compassion for him; he ran to his son, threw his arms around him and kissed him'. And as I heard those words read that Sunday a tide of warmth and certainty flowed deep in me.

It was though I had been in an emotionally distant country, with no awareness of God's love for me, assuming from the divine silence that the Lord had no concern for me. I realised that all the time God had been longing to meet me with the same impassioned yearning as the father in the story, and that if I were prepared to move Godwards, God was well able to show me how very much he loved me. I hardly needed to think this through, because the words from Jesus' story, or God speaking to me through, or coming to me in those words brought a joy which made questions unnecessary.

This memorable evening was one of very few occasions when I have been blessed through attendance at a church service.

*

At Airdrie Baptist Church we had begun a Friday-night outreach similar to the one I had been involved in at Ebenezer Hall. The thought of this – approaching people and initiating conversations about faith – was very scary, but I forced myself to do it.

This, after all, was what evangelicals did. One evening only a few of us met, and I as the oldest person present took the decision that we wouldn't go out on the streets. But even as the words were leaving my mouth I knew I had spoken not because we were few, but because I lacked courage. If we only gone out trusting God, I thought, people's lives might have been touched.

*

I was sitting in a school staff-room one lunchtime reading a study by John R. W. Stott of the New Testament book of Ephesians called *God's New Society*, 'What are you reading?' one of the teachers asked. 'Oh, it's a book on Ephesians in the Bible,' I replied with quick embarrassment in a tone which implied 'I'm sure you didn't really want to know this, and I'm not really prepared to talk more about it'. As soon as I had spoken I felt diminished, for I knew I could have encouraged my questioner and been more open about what I was reading and why.

*

I spoke to Liam about my inclination to be re-baptized. He listened attentively and was in theory comfortable about doing this, but he advised me not to proceed. Even though my faith had been defective that Sunday back in 1968 the person baptising me had done so in good faith, he assured me. Baptism, he continued, is not so much what *you* do, as what is done *to* you on behalf of the church. You are taken and immersed in water as a sign to yourself as well as to those watching that you have been spiritually cleansed and immersed in Christ and that you have in a spiritual sense died and risen again, sharing in the benefits of Christ's death and resurrection.

So, Liam argued, perhaps my baptism had, by virtue of the faith of the person baptising me and of the people in the congregation, in some way led to the future fulfilment of what it symbolised. I could see that he was also concerned about how our church as a whole and especially the leadership would perceive my re-baptism if we were to go ahead. There would, he felt, be consternation. Once again not seeing the way ahead, I dropped my request for re-baptism.

*

In the spring of 1986, I visited my friends John and Caroline Brand in London – John was the pastor of Kentish Town Evangelical Church. I drove south just a few days after the nuclear disaster at Chernobyl in the Soviet Union, when there was a suspicion that the rain clouds scudding overhead were seeded with radioactive particles.

I enjoyed myself immensely. Camden, Swiss Cottage, Hyde Park, Oxford Street – I felt I'd set foot in a quasi-mythical landscape. I saw Tower Bridge and Buckingham Palace and the London Stock Exchange for the first time through the rain-spattered windscreen of the Brand's car; we went to the park on a sunny Sunday afternoon and found it bustling with meticulously-clad orthodox Jews; I watched TV with the Brands and their two young sons, and we howled with laughter at *The Cosby Show* (then untouched by later revelations of Cosby's abuse). 'I'd have thought you'd have known the answers to all those questions!' John said with a grin after I'd revealed my lack of knowledge when he organised a Bible quiz for a group of folk from his church.

There was a church meeting in the downstairs room at the Brands' house. The space was full, and I sat on the floor in a corner. Suddenly, I became aware of an irruption of joy and warmth, accompanied by a powerful sense that God was addressing me, saying 'I am calling you to feed my people'. I instantly interpreted this as a call to the Christian ministry and I remained joyfully convinced of this throughout the rest of my time in London, though I did not mention my thoughts to John and Caroline.

*

As I drove north, I began to have doubts. Me? A minister? When I found leading services and speaking from the pulpit so difficult? But this was just part of the challenge, I told myself. If God wanted me to become a pastor then God would change me and equip me, helping me to overcome my fears. In the face of this impeccable spiritual logic, I buried my doubts, and in fact this was easy to do in the afterglow of the original, powerful certainty. The next Friday night, Caroline phoned me at home, putting on an artificial accent and pretending to be a researcher from *The Cosby Show*, seeking audience reaction to that night's episode.

*

I contacted the Baptist Union of Scotland and spoke with the 'Superintendent,' the Rev Eric Watson whose role included supporting and counseling Scottish Baptist pastors and candidates for the ministry. Eric was sensitive and kind, but instead of giving me an unqualified confirmation of my calling, he asked me some searching questions – enquiring for example, how I would handle a situation where I held different views on a particular issue from the members of my congregation. I had the impression that my response was not quite what he wanted to hear. Nevertheless, he encouraged me to explore further the possibility of training for the ministry.

I bought a textbook on New Testament Greek, and began learning the Greek alphabet, but already I was torn between on the one hand what had seemed a genuine and powerful sense of calling, and on the other a recognition of my own weakness and shortcomings. One morning I was standing in the foyer of a primary school in Airdrie waiting to meet the head teacher whom I was to advise on setting up a school library. I felt apprehensive about the prospect of sitting speaking to her and I remember thinking that if this was so hard for me how would I handle a job which would involve me regularly in one-to-one interviews, quite apart from the ordeal of speaking in public every Sunday. I could never cope – but once again I reassured myself that if God had called me, God would enable me. Feeling unfit for the role I'd been called to was surely simply a challenge to my faith, a test of my perseverance and determination. One day soon my tension must ease.

The Baptist Union wrote asking me to arrange a medical assessment of my suitability for the ministry by a doctor who was a member of Kirkintilloch Baptist Church. This prospect added to my anxiety – would he detect my shameful secret, my high level of tension, and would this stand against me?

*

Before I made this appointment, I was to preach one Sunday at Hamilton Baptist Church and as the day approached I was filled with terror. As the church secretary and I prayed before the service I was panic–wracked, despite 5mg of Valium, unsure whether I'd be able to survive the hour ahead. On the pulpit there was a small sign in old-fashioned lettering, visible only to the person leading the service, quoting words from the book of Acts – 'Sir, we would see Jesus'. (John 12:21 AV) What kind of crucifixion would they see that morning, I wondered?

I don't know how I made it through the service. I was in perpetual fear that I'd collapse in panic, or burst into an uncontrollable tirade of gibberish and obscenity. Word after word, sentence after sentence, I tried desperately to focus on the present moment, simply to survive, second by second. It did not, I imagine, make for particularly edifying listening.

In the evening I, and the congregation, were back for more. I was preaching about the Christian understanding of suffering, particularly of depression. About half-way through the service I realised I might actually make it to the end without collapsing, and my mood lightened fractionally.

I concluded the sermon by quoting the opening lines of Hopkins' masterpiece *The Wreck of the Deutschland*, which had meant so much to me as a student. After the experience of unmaking at the hand of God, the poet exclaims in wonder 'dost thou touch me afresh? Over again I feel thy finger and find thee'.

I suggested to the congregation that despite the intensity of our pain and darkness the time will come when God will say 'Enough!', and once again we will experience God's healing intervention. I don't think I felt the divine finger that night at Hamilton. There was simply relief that I had survived. But hope was there no matter how apparently irrational, that one day the sky would be clear, God's touch tangible.

That evening I faced the fact that God was not going to change me, and that whatever was signified by my experience as I sat on the carpet in John and Caroline's house, it was not a call to the ministry. I gave my £40 fee for the day to Liam Goligher. I reckoned he needed it more than I did.

EIGHTEEN

BIG PEOPLE
CRY TOO

Assisted by my colleague George Tweedie who drove the mobile library van to the school, I fixed the cast-iron fireplace to the shelves; put the coal scuttle in place and ensured that the crêpe paper flames in the hearth were realistically crumpled. I stood the mannequin upright on her shoogly base, dressed in Victorian finery ('She keeps falling for me,' I quipped to the kids when the clothed figure overbalanced). I hung up the framed sampler and unpacked boxes of ornaments, brushes and combs, books, clothes, greetings cards and kitchen implements.

It was the mid-1980s. My job, based at the Education Resource Centre in Hamilton's Auchingramont Road had become largely focussed on visiting Primary Schools with travelling learning exhibitions. After we had set up, small groups of pupils joined me on board for 45 minute sessions, while George retreated to the school's medical room to do the library assistant work he had taken with him.

These were stressful days. Would I make it to the end of each session without breaking down in panic? Would I harm the children in some way? I told myself these thoughts were driven by fear, not by any evil impulse. I assured myself that my fear of being suicidal did not actually reflect suicidal intent, and that when the words 'kill, kill, kill' whirled repeatedly through my brain, they were driven by dread of losing control, not by malicious intent. But often my assurances did not assure.

One particular morning, I leaned my head in despair against a shelf, and muttered dramatically (never losing even *in extremis* my love for words and the cadence of language) 'They are asking me to give more than I have got to give.'

Somehow I made it through the day. After work, I drove to my parents' house (they were now living in Crossford in the Clyde Valley) where I burst into tears.

In time these 'learning exhibitions' would become something I enjoyed. More colleagues were drafted in to help. The boss replaced the old mobile library with a purpose-built classroom on a bus chassis, with power points, display boards, AV equipment and the BBC Micro Computer which was then state of the art in schools.

*

I line-managed George, the man who drove me around Lanarkshire, for nine years from 1983 until 1992 but this counted for little from his point of view. In George's mind, it was his vehicle, he was the main man.

George was unique, a one-off, certainly the most infuriating individual I have ever had to work closely with. While I believe he was at heart a man of considerable goodwill he could be opinionated and stubborn and was severely challenged in the area of interpersonal skills.

One the road, George talked endlessly and passionately to his captive audience of one, chiefly about Scotland and Scottish Gaelic. As a young man he had emigrated to Australia but returned to Hamilton in 1967 when Winnie Ewing was (successfully) contesting the Hamilton by-election on behalf of the Scottish National Party.

George was an ardent nationalist, and having seen the election won by Ewing he stayed on in Scotland, finding a job driving lorries on the M74 Glasgow to Carlisle construction project.

To work with George was to be regaled with uninvited readings of his poems which were mainly on Scottish themes. He loved words, and used them with passion, but none of his oeuvre quite worked for me as pieces of writing. He had signed the typescript of each with a bold flourish – 'Tweeddale'.

*

My early days as 'Primary School Library Advisor' before we began the learning exhibitions were grim, although I did have an office of my own – the room which had formerly belonged to the Mr Walker with whom I had had the contretemps over an evening shift at Newarthill Library. My job involved spending a day by arrangement at one of the 220 Primary Schools in Strathclyde's Lanark Division. The mobile library was equipped with a display of appropriate materials for teachers and pupils.

The theory was that the head teacher at each school would arrange for their colleagues to visit the mobile library individually or in small groups to inspect the range of stock available, and potentially to borrow a few items. While they were with me, I would discuss with them the role of the Education Resource Service and how it could support their teaching. At some schools I also spent some time with the head teacher giving advice on the organisation of resources within the school.

In practice most teachers had little desire to come on board. Many of them came on sufferance, surly-faced, with little interest in the services I represented. They'd look round the stock I was carrying in a desultory way, and borrow a few items before heading back to the classroom. Then I'd have a long patient wait until the next teacher arrived. In winter the van was ice-cold – the feeble heating system couldn't be left running for long when the engine was turned off without draining the batteries. Occasionally, I was not even invited into the school for coffee. My recollection of this job is of grim, slow days with zero sense of achievement.

But life on the road with George was always an adventure. Often, seeing something discarded by the road-side, he'd stop the van and climb out so that he could inspect it closely to ascertain if it was of any use to him – if it looked promising, it would join us in the cab. One afternoon, George turned off the engine at the top of a long, steep stretch of road and coasted downhill. 'What are you doing?' I asked. 'Just checking that the wheels are OK,' he replied nonchalantly. Sometimes George would use the van (strictly against regulations, of course) for his own purposes – apparently he had done this frequently when he was in the process of building his own bungalow. I remember the day he insisted that we drive into Lesmahagow to collect from the joiners a new front door, which he carefully laid on bricks in the middle of the van floor. Then there was the afternoon he discovered that staff at a school we were visiting were throwing out a folding bed from the medical room. Could he have it, he asked? The bed joined us on board. Later in the day, we delivered it to a relative of George's in Hamilton to replace a child's mattress which, he told me confidentially, 'was soaked in peepee'.

I remember once sitting on the mobile as George bent over in front of me to pick something up, and realising that there was a rip in the backside of his black uniform trousers, and furthermore that he wasn't wearing anything underneath. A quick visit to the school office secured a needle and thread which George used to make good the damage.

He was most reluctant to be told what route to take when we were heading for a school. He seemed resistant to the idea of returning home the same way we had taken on our outward journey, and he certainly had some form of phobia centred on motorways, which he would take long detours to avoid. I remember one day when we were leaving to go to a school rather later than we should have been, I gave George strict instructions to go by the shortest route, and specified what that route was. He became very cross as I sat beside him in the cab explaining this, and eventually he slipped the van into gear and shot off in completely the wrong direction. He refused to stop and I succeeded in escaping and walking back to the Resource Centre only when he was forced to pull up at a red traffic light. Shortly afterwards, George and van arrived back at base, the former looking rather sheepish. I told him that we were going to set off again, and this time we were going my way.

*

When not on the road with George, I supported my colleagues in the Primary School Resource section but I often found this dispiriting. We were inundated with requests from schools for resources, so many of which we were unable to fulfil; there was no efficient stock management system, so that a significant proportion of material borrowed was never returned.

I had a frequent dream. The Education Resource Centre had been destroyed by fire. I was standing in piles of rubble in the charred remains of the Primary floor, looking up past the blackened outer walls and the gaunt lift shaft to blue sky above.

There was another recurrent dream. I'm going up a staircase. Suddenly I notice that the ceiling is descending, or the stairs rising, or both, so that I have to force my way forward. Eventually, the gap is so narrow that it constricts me, and I'm forced to stop, trapped.

Yet another regular dream. I'm in a public toilet, but the cubicles all have low walls and no doors, so that when I sit down, I am visible to all.

*

George Tweedie was in some respects a tragic figure. He had been devoted to his mother, and missed her terribly. Most of the rooms in the bungalow were fairly chaotic, and there was a thick layer of grime on the wallpaper – George burned over-large chunks of wood sawn from railway sleepers in his grate, and clouds of smoke billowed through the living room. He told me he kept a weapon beneath his bed to grab if the house was attacked by intruders while he slept. And he turned off the electricity at the mains each time he left his house on the grounds that it took a small amount of power – for which he would be charged – to keep the meter running when the current was switched on. One room in the house, the dining room, was uncluttered. The table was set as if for a meal for four, and over it was a clear, plastic film tucked in at the edges. a shrine to his mum.

George was stubborn, opinionated and exasperating, but as I grew in confidence so I became more accepting of him, viewed his eccentricities as almost lovable, and in time developed a certain cautious fondness for him. However I recognise that during the years we worked together I failed both to empathise with him as fully as I might have done, and to challenge some of his unacceptable behaviours. Had I been wiser then, more comfortable in my own skin I could have given George much more than I did.

*

After a six-week strike in the early Spring of 1987, School Librarians throughout Strathclyde Region were awarded a regrading up to the pay grade of my post. Because my job was anomalous, there being no equivalent in the other Divisions of the Region, there was no pressure to regrade my post. The Union, having obtained their primary objective, were not helpful. I lost my seniority, and had to vacate my office, and join my colleagues down in the Primary Department. I accepted this change with a good grace largely inspired by fatalism.

*

I went to the theatre in Glasgow with a couple of colleagues to see *Hamlet*. We were in a short row of seats immediately above the stage on which an extremely energetic Prince of Denmark sweated his angst. The stage design was minimalist, dominated by a huge, gently-inclined ramp.

Some time after the performance began, when we'd already begun dipping into the box of chocolates we'd brought with us, my heart began racing for no apparent reason. The episode was triggered not so much by empathy with the disturbed Hamlet, or distress at his words as by the dramatic lighting effects and the pervasive atmosphere of tense, raw emotion. I gulped deep breaths, struggling to control the pounding in my chest, while a still objective part of my brain clinically monitored my pulse rate – well over three hundred a minute it seemed.

I expected to die where I was sitting, and simply accepted this as a fact. I could have got up and run, but there was, ultimately, nowhere to run to. Somehow, I survived to the end of the performance, said good-night to my colleagues, and collapsed into my car weak and trembling.

*

I listened to very little music during the 1980s. When I was visiting friends, I found background music at meals disturbing – especially melancholy music in a minor key, which drew my spirits lower and triggered a sharp anxiety. Focus, John. Focus. One forkful after another. Slowly! And listen. Listen to the conversation. Engage. Focus!

*

Throughout the mid-1980s, apart from church and work, I focussed my attention on working on the PhD thesis, finding solace in mental escape to late Victorian Edinburgh's New Town. I crunched numbers using the Sinclair ZX81 computer which mum gave dad as a Christmas present – you loaded software from a tape in your audio cassette recorder, and displayed output on your TV screen. I remember sitting on the floor in my parents' house in Crossford typing out page after page, focussing intently on the words and the sentences to hold at bay the barrage of suicidal thoughts.

I had my viva in the spring of 1987. I was more concerned about its location – the office of Blaise Cronin, then head of the Department of Information Science – than about the grilling I received from the external examiner. Since my time at the University of Strathclyde, the Department had moved from the 7th to the 13th floor of the Livingstone Tower and I felt profound disquiet at venturing that high. I feared constantly, that the windows were summoning me to throw myself into the abyss.

I sat, eyes focussed on the examiner. He asked for a few minor changes, and then passed the thesis. 'You can now call yourself Dr Dempster,' he told me, shaking my hand.

I smiled weakly, with no sense of elation or achievement. It was simply the next step, though I was mildly distressed at changes being necessary. I was more conscious of how far beneath us Queen Street lay.

I graduated on 10th July 1987.

*

I stayed with my parents for a few days after arriving on their doorstep in tears. I saw a local GP, Eric Paterson, whom I had known when I was a teenager. Because I was concerned by my thoughts of suicide, he arranged for me to have a home visit from a psychiatrist which took place remarkably quickly. Possibly this was a typical response to all patients with suicidal ideation, but the rapid response was more likely due to my father's position.

The psychiatrist came and sat beside me on the couch in my parents' front room and listened carefully as I described what I was feeling, interacting warmly with genuine interest and concern. His patient, empathic presence was in itself a healing reassurance. I described my sense of smallness and vulnerability when out walking, on the edge of the world's crust, on the shore of the vastness of space, and my fear that I might fall off into nothingness. I was rather enjoying having an audience. My listener mentioned a well-known psychiatrist who had described similar symptoms, and I was somewhat heartened. The psychiatrist concluded that I was no risk to myself and, reassured for a time I was deeply grateful for his help.

Dr Paterson's other intervention was not so beneficial. He signed me off work for three weeks. This, frankly, was not the right decision. What I needed was help and encouragement so that I could cope with my job, rather than time away from it. My work was not the main issue, simply a contributory factor, and three weeks of introspection at home without the healing therapy and the sense of purpose and satisfaction which working gave me on the better days could only make my outlook increasingly negative.

Back in Airdrie, I visited W.H. Smith and bought an omnibus volume of the James Herriot vet stories, and the first of Anthony Trollope's *Barchester Chronicles*. I went home, lay down on the couch, and read and read. I managed to lose myself in these marvellous escapist narratives, except at points where the raw pain of life invaded the stories, heightening my anxiety.

*

Then and in the coming years I sometimes found specifically Christian books helpful both for the hope they awakened and for the realisation they gave me that I was not alone. I was encouraged by popular works from Christian psychologists, such as David Seamands' *Healing for Damaged Emotions* which reminded me that I was of infinite value to a God who loved me. I believed God was making some of the ideas in these books healingly alive to me. Martyn Lloyd-Jones' *Spiritual Depression* also helped – I was particularly struck by the chapter entitled *Men as Trees Walking*, which describes Jesus' unique healing of a blind man, unique in that the healing took place in two stages. First, the man was given a blurred, imprecise vision so that people seemed to him to be like walking trees, and then after a further intervention from Jesus, he was able to see perfectly. This enabled me to synthesise both the fact that I had been conscious of divine intervention in my life and yet at the same time was aware of so much dross, so much work-in-progress, so much I wanted to be but was not yet.

I was comforted by the stories of other Christians who suffered as I was suffering, notably J.B. Phillips, the Anglican priest who translated the New Testament and parts of the Old Testament into modern English. His experience of severe depression is described in his biography *The Price of Success* and is the main theme of *The Wounded Healer*, a collection of his letters to people who wrote to him for help and guidance. I was inspired by the concept of wounded people having by the very fact of their woundedness the power to bring to other sufferers the healing touch of empathy and comfort. It was certainly true in my case that my personal acquaintance with mental suffering enabled me to draw near both in person and from the pulpit to others who were traversing the same dark valley. And it was encouraging to remember that all of us wounded healers were walking in the footsteps of the one who was the paradigm of wounded healers, Jesus himself.

*

I also found solace in 'living by mantra' – allowing myself to be sustained and encouraged by verses from the Bible and by other inspiring words.

'There is nothing to fear except fear itself.' I'd repeat Franklin Delano Roosevelt's words to myself when oppressed by anxiety. If God was with me, and if my end was in God's hands as much as my beginning had been, and if God was infinitely more powerful than any other spiritual force then, I argued, it was absolutely true that the only thing to be afraid of was the fear which further distanced me from any sense of divine presence. Yet at times my deepest fear was of what I might do to myself, and I found it difficult to include that fear among those I could exchange for peace in the presence of God. For I was not confident that God would intervene to prevent me from harming myself if I was sufficiently determined.

'It's as though I'm looking at life through dark, tinted spectacles,' I'd mutter regularly, reminding myself that my perspective on reality was seriously askew. I might be seeing darkness and hopelessness; I might have a sense of detachment from what I was doing and from events going on around me, but these perceptions, I reminded myself endlessly were merely illusions generated by malfunctioning brain chemistry. Reality was different. Reality was light and joy and immediacy, and I must live as I knew the world to be rather than as I saw it through the filter of damaged emotions. By reminding myself constantly of this I survived through many days, but it is a stressful way to live.

Which is why, perhaps, another of my daily sustaining graces was a line from a hymn which I frequently repeated to myself as I drove to work – 'Strength for today, and bright hope for tomorrow'. It was an expression of trust that God was with me, that God would provide the courage, energy and resilience I required to get me through the day and face its challenges. It was also an expression of hope that a day was coming – maybe not tomorrow, or the day after tomorrow, maybe not even next week or next month – but coming, sometime, when once again joy would break through.

This same hope for the future combined with a realisation that the waywardness of my emotions was cyclical in nature is evident in another of my mantras – 'I have been here before, and I will be here again' – whispered in the middle of a particularly painful day. It was an acknowledgement that things weren't going well, but also a recollection that previous, similar experiences had passed, giving way to a breaking in of light. If I could only hold on, the pain would lessen this time also.

When I was struggling to focus, or feeling afraid, or both I would repeat the old prayer, over and over, seeking calm as others had done down the centuries in its familiar syllables: 'Lord Jesus Christ, have mercy on me.'

*

One afternoon I had an appointment at the hospital after work to have an ear infection treated. Anxious and low, I felt like driving past the hospital gates and heading for home.

In the doctor's room, I was impressed by his tenderness, his genuine interest in my wellbeing, his gentle touch. The needs of my ear were attended to. I said 'goodbye' and headed for home. I wished someone would show a similar compassion and gentleness towards my broken spirit.

*

When I returned to work after being signed off, Margaret Sked called me into her office, and enquired sympathetically how I was.

'Have you ever considered becoming a minister?' she enquired.

*

Every Friday morning at coffee break, the Escape Committee, of which I was an enthusiastic member, poured over the *Glasgow Herald* Jobs section plotting to win freedom from the Education Resource Centre. This yearning for freedom was a non-religious aspect of my quest for the one touch which would change everything. Even though I was by now more fully engaged in the exhibition work at the Resource Centre, and hence feeling more fulfiled, I still longed for something more.

I wrote to Colin Sinclair, Scripture Union's new General Secretary, asking whether there were any bookshop vacancies. Wisely, he replied that in life it is usually better to go forward, rather than back. The American Christian publishers Word were looking for an editorial person in the UK, based in Milton Keynes: I considered applying. I sought, and was interviewed for two local history posts, one in the Edinburgh Room at Edinburgh's Central Library, the other in the local Monklands Library Service. I was particularly hopeful in the case of the second of these applications. The idea of working in local history was appealing, and by then I had considerable experience in using historical records in an educational context. Immediately after the interview, I went off on holiday.

It was July 1988, the week of the Piper Alpha oil-rig disaster. I was at Dunblane, staying at Scottish Churches house, on a week-long holiday led by Canon Kenyon Wright which involved touring locations associated with the Scottish saints. It was another attempt on my part to connect more deeply with God, but I found the pace exhausting. In the course of five days we visited Dunfermline, Whithorn, Glasgow, Iona, and Dunblane Cathedral itself.

Three things struck me – the stillness of Compline in the Chapel behind Scottish Churches House as we shared wafers and wine; the apparent willingness of the others on the tour to believe the stories of the saints, regardless of how far-fetched they seemed – drawing spiritual sustenance from these myths seemed more important than confronting their mythic origins; the surprise of the older lady taken aback by my suggestion that St Paul's words were inspired by God, rather than being simply the human words, sometimes mistaken, of an inspired man.

On the Saturday I drove home, knowing that a letter from Monklands District Council would be waiting on the doormat.

I ripped it open.

'I regret to inform you…'

I was extremely disappointed.

But I was encouraged around that time when an inspector of schools, having watched me at work, described me as 'a skilful educator'.

*

Visits to my parents at holiday weekends were always depressing. The festive season was the worst of all. I'd drive down to Crossford after work on Christmas Eve, struggling to be positive, but contrasting the joyful 'home for Christmas' clichés with my mood. On my arrival, we'd have a meal, but I'd feel tense and awkward, and there would be no real communication.

At 11pm, we'd walk round to the Christmas Eve service at the local church – often, as I recall, through frost and snow. We crunched through Christmas card streets, past Christmas card cottages, to a Christmas card service in the old building. The contrast between the images of joy and the pain and emotional distance I was experiencing was crushing. On Christmas Day we'd visit family friends. I felt awkward, and on edge, as though I were a participant in someone else's story.

One year I gave my parents a recording of *My Fair Lady*: we played it. Mum enjoyed the music. 'Let's make watching it a family tradition every Christmas,' she said.

The pain of it! 'Family traditions' signal love and joy and openness. 'Family traditions' signal taking a symbol from the present into the future, and I longed for a new, different future of freedom.

On the three working days between Christmas and New Year I'd drive up to the Resource Centre in Hamilton. Those were grim days; travelling from one insecure place to another; spending hours helping unpack and shelve endless boxes of material returned from primary schools and assembling resource packs for the new term from stock which seldom seemed adequate. Cassette tapes of Christmas songs would be playing: they were intended to be uplifting, but in fact they ratcheted up my tension and deepened my sadness. And then after work, back to Crossford to face the continuing challenge of concealing my pain.

In all those Christmases, I only recall one moment of joy, when I watched a film version of *The Secret Garden*. Somehow, the open door, and the blossoming of beauty reached out and touched me.

I'd go home on the 2nd January; in the morning I'd visit the village shop in Crossford and buy milk and potatoes and perishable foods, heavy with sadness. I'd drive to Airdrie after lunch. Ahead of me stretched an interminable afternoon, and an interminable evening. I'd watch films on television until it was time to go to bed.

There would be healing in the routine as I returned to work on 3rd January. I'd count the days since the winter solstice knowing that the nights were shortening and that spring would come.

A sense of joy one day when I reached the house at 4.45pm after work and found there was still some light in the sky.

Each year, I had the same illusion that things would be better, come the spring.

*

There were occasions when I was almost engulfed in a suicidal hopelessness. I particularly remember one evening when I was alone in the flat watching the film *Manon of the Sources*, the sequel to *Jean de Florette*, set in rural France in the 1930s. My own sadness fed hungrily on the tragic melancholy of this beautifully photographed movie, and I felt the fingers of despair tightening their grip on me. The positive spirit of resistance and hope which enabled me to survive was at its weakest that evening.

*

Against this background, I was very grateful for the loyalty of friends who listened and encouraged, convincing me that I was valuable and that they saw good in me at times when I saw nothing good in myself. Liam and Christine Goligher often asked me round. I'd sit at the bench table in the kitchen with their kids, eating banana bread, drinking black coffee and feeling one of the family.

After the Golighers moved to Kirkintilloch in 1987, I occasionally visited them there too. I was needy: though I entered into conversation about everyday things, I yearned to talk about the sense of emptiness within. At times I articulated this, though sparingly, for I did not wish to be a burdensome guest. But on those visits any words spoken into the darkness however lovingly were immediately sucked down into the vortex, out of sight. No amount of affirmation could fill the deep chasm.

Tom and Elspeth in Bo'ness were also loving, welcoming, affirming. They invited me to take the services at their church one Sunday, and the invitation was frequently repeated – as much for my benefit, I'm sure, as for their congregation's. Elspeth introduced me to the writings of Henri Nouwen, a new name to me, one whose insights into the struggles of faith I much appreciated.

One bright, sunny Bank Holiday Monday Elspeth phoned to ask if I'd like to go out with her and the children for the afternoon. We drove to Aberdour on the north side of the Forth Estuary, explored the town, visited the shops where the kids bought sweets and cheap plastic 'made in China' toys and then went back to their house and sat watching *Little Lord Fauntleroy* on TV, and I felt so at home in the grace of their acceptance.

I sometimes wished, however, that my friends were able to do more for me, or rather that the love they were showing could penetrate more deeply and healingly, for while at one level I was appreciative of their care, another deeper level often went unilluminated by the light of their love.

Alistair and Louise Young were also supportive friends – especially one Boxing Day. I was staying with my parents over the holidays. I was more positive than usual at the end of Christmas Day, sufficiently encouraged at the quality of communication I was having with my parents to try talking to them at a deeper level. I wanted to discuss some of the stuff which had been said in the past, and which had upset me. Notably, I wanted to share my incomprehension at their extreme reaction when I told them that I was thinking of buying a place of my own and leaving home. Since then, we'd never sat down and talked about that terrible weekend, and I wanted to explore their feelings about what had happened, and to explain mine. But they would have none of it. As far as mum and dad were concerned, the past was past, and it was unhelpful to revisit it. That, and other unexplored issues and unfinished business hovered between us.

I experienced a painful rejection, having once again opened up a small gateway in the defensive wall I'd constructed to protect myself from my parents. I slammed the door shut, and bricked it up and concealed the fact that it had ever existed by vigorously plastering over the brickwork. I had to get away, and on Boxing Day, immediately after breakfast, I escaped and headed back to Airdrie. As I approached Chapelhall I thought of Alistair and Louise, and presented myself on their doorstep at what must have seemed a ridiculously early hour. But they flung open the door, didn't register one iota of surprise when they saw me standing there, and invited me in and I soon began weeping in sheer relief at warmth of their love. ('It's all right,' I smiled tearily at their nine-year-old who was looking concerned. 'Big people cry too.') I spent the whole day with the Youngs, doing ordinary Christmas things – crawling around on the floor with the kids as we played with the Scalextric set they'd got for Christmas, and going to B&Q for paint.

NINETEEN

SEEKING SOMETHING MORE

I was still longing perpetually for the one transforming spiritual encounter which I believed would lead to complete emotional healing, the 'Baptism in the Spirit'. I presumed God was withholding this gift from me on the grounds of my lack of faith, or lack of persistent seeking.

Liam Goligher arranged a weekend visit to Airdrie by a team of people from a church in the English Home Counties, led by their pastor the Rev Alex Fraser. By this time charismatic experience and the exercise of charismatic gifts were becoming more common in the evangelical community, but there was little understanding of these things at the Airdrie church and the congregation had not been properly prepared for the English team's charismatic style of ministry.

In the course of the weekend we heard people praising God in rhythmic outpourings of unintelligible syllables. We watched some of those who went forward for personal prayer falling backwards into the waiting arms of one of the team members, having, it was claimed, been deeply impacted by God's power. Those who had been 'slain in the Sprit' in this way would be gently laid on the carpet in a trance-like

CHOOSING JOY

state until they became aware once again of their surroundings – they would then testify to the sense of love and peace which had enveloped them as they lay there.

One of the visitors described how she had received the treasure of God's Spirit after first wondering whether there was indeed a further gift to be received subsequent to one's initial coming to God, and then engaging in a quest for this divine invasion. One evening, while bathing, she was overcome with a sense of the joy of God's presence. The gift had been given.

At the end of the visitors' final service on the Sunday evening the usual invitation was issued and I made my way to the front of the church bearing my customary burden of depression and emotional deadness, seeking the dramatic touch which would change everything. One of the visiting team members came and sat in the pew beside me. I spoke a little with him, outlining the things which troubled me. He put his arm on my shoulder and prayed for me: specifically, he prayed against the 'spirit of suicide'.

I said 'thank-you', and walked numbly through to the church hall where I joined the queue for coffee and biscuits. I had experienced nothing besides a deepening of my painful longing, and a surging fear of the self-destructive demon to which my helper in the pew had alluded. Had his mild words been enough to disarm its malicious power?

One of the older church members, John McNeill comforted me as I washed the last of my custard cream down with black coffee. 'You're all right,' he said in effect. 'We love you the way you are.' That weekend, it was those simple sentences which blessed me.

Still hungry for God I sat in my flat early on the Monday morning reading one of evangelical Anglican Colin Urquhart's books which had been recommended by the team. I opened it at the chapter on receiving the Holy Spirit and meticulously followed the steps it outlined. I knelt on the carpet, my elbows on a dining-room chair, beseeching this Father-like God who withholds no good gifts from his children to give me the one gift I longed for more than any other. I prayed expectantly but I had no sense of having been heard, no sense of the power and presence which Urquhart confidently led me to expect. Eventually I closed the book and chucked it on the table. Clearly I must be a singularly imperfect son when such a very generous Father felt he had to withhold the gift from me.

I preserved intact my faith in the goodness of God by magnifying my own unworthiness. I did not realise at the time that this pattern of seeking and not finding exactly replicated my desperate teenage quest for a first encounter with God.

*

One year I attended Spring Harvest, a multi-site evangelical Christian festival. The activity-packed few days offered a rolling programme of workshops and seminars culminating each evening in a large-scale 'Celebration'.

Together with a colleague, Alex Fraser was leading a series of seminars on the Holy Spirit. I knew this would culminate in another opportunity to seek the Spirit's presence in a deeper way. This was my chance. Surely I reasoned, I would not once again let God down by my lack of ardour or sincerity. Surely this time, in a context where God's presence was so tangible to so many, the gift which God so much wanted to give me and which I so much wanted to receive would at last be mine.

The final Holy Spirit seminar was held very late at night. I waited impatiently as the speakers covered the ground with which I was so familiar on 'how to receive the Holy Spirit'. And then the moment came as I'd known it would when those who wished to receive the gift were asked to stand. I was the first on my feet. Those who had risen were not invited to come to the front of the room for individual prayer – instead, one of the leaders prayed publicly for us all and then the seminar was over.

'Wasn't that *wonderful*?' said a woman standing near me, her face bright with joy. Where had I heard that before? 'Oh yes it was, wasn't it?' I lied, forcing a smile. For once again I felt only emptiness and disappointment. Once again it did not occur to me to blame God for failing to come through, or the seminar speakers for not alerting those who stood at their invitation to the fact that not all those on their feet would necessarily feel any different after the prayer.

The fault must be mine. Somehow, I'd failed, I'd screwed up again, I'd let God down. I approached Alex Fraser and asked if I could have a word with him. I suppose he was tired at the end of a long day, but rather than spending time with me there and then he invited me to meet him in the speaker's lounge the next morning.

*

At the agreed time, there he was sitting in a chair at a low table drinking coffee. I joined him briefly in that very public environment and told him something of my hunger for God, and my frustration at God's inaction. He may have prayed for me briefly (though I have no recollection of this) and then he suggested that I read the book *Something More* (1974) by Catherine Marshall, in which she describes her increasing openness to the Holy Spirit. I had already read this book, without it having any deep impact on me.

Perhaps Alex Fraser was trying to help me see that for some people encountering the Spirit is a gradual quest, a journey rather than a crisis, but I feel he failed me. It can't be easy dealing with those who present themselves as the casualties of your ministry, but I would have appreciated gentle, engaged probing; challenging words, perhaps; a warm hug. As it was, I went away nursing my sadness. I bought another copy of *Something More* and began re-reading it, but I didn't connect with Marshall's experience, and after a few chapters I gave up.

*

Back in Airdrie, I had occasion to visit a Church of Scotland minister and his wife, both of whom were charismatic in their theology. I described to them my experience at Spring Harvest. 'Would you like us to pray with you?' they asked, and I invited them to go ahead. I sat in a chair and they stood one on either side of me, their hands on my head and shoulders, and prayed. I felt nothing, but I was grateful for their concern. Afterwards the minister's wife said to me 'I felt my fingers tingling as we prayed. The Holy Spirit is in you.'

I found this comment slightly zany, and yet was encouraged by it too.

*

I'm surprised how positive I was in my Christmas letter to friends at the end of 1987. After giving all the news, I acknowledged that it was 'so much a record of things done outwardly, when what really matters is the inner life, the walk with God, the peace, integration and harmony without which all the outer activities are mere futile strivings'. And I concluded 'I must say that in general this has been a very joyful year, and I am deeply grateful to God for his love and blessings to me, and for the joy of being part of a living church.'

I do not think I was being entirely honest – many sorrows were hidden behind that 'in general'. My recollection – or perhaps the story I tell myself – is of glimpses of joy rather than any prolonged sense of its arrival. But perhaps there was more joy than I allow myself to remember.

*

A sheet of paper records a moment of clarity on 18th April 1987 in which I wrote five statements of faith as they were real to me at the moment of writing:

God loves me as I am with no strings attached. I do not need to work either to earn, or to retain his love.

To love is to give. One aspect of denying self involves genuinely making room in one's life for others, giving oneself for others either on an individual level or to help improve society. I don't say 'Teach me how to evangelise' but rather 'Teach me how to love' and all else will flow from that..... I must ask God to reveal to me the needs of those I meet, and to show me how I can help them.

I must be flexible, especially in my use of time. So often, I feel time-thirled: part of the problem is that I am so locked into my routine.... Thus I have no time for others, no time to be creative, to do new things. Time must be my servant and not my master...

I need fear no one, for I am secure in God's love, and can walk free.

Things become possible when we believe they are. This may be true at a basic psychological level. It is certainly true on a spiritual level, because our belief in God removes the blockages to God's working. If we look at a problem, and think it is intractable, it will be; if we believe there is a solution, and methodically and prayerfully seek it, it will be revealed. We need to dream dreams. Cathedrals have been built, great pieces of music written because men [sic] attempted the impossible, believing that it could be done.

*

I read *The Normal Christian Birth* (1989) a book by a Baptist Bible teacher David Pawson. He argued that many people live unsuccessful Christian lives because something has gone wrong in the process of their coming to faith, or else some key stage has been omitted. If that is true, Pawson reasoned, then the only way to enjoy the full blessing God wants to give us is to go back and resolve the problem. As I read, I once again felt the conviction that I should be re-baptised. It was I think not so much a quiet sense that this was something I had to do, but an almost superstitious compulsion that this step would unlock the great gift I was still seeking.

Once again I spoke to Liam Goligher about re-baptism. This time he was prepared to baptise me – in the Kirkintilloch church where because I was not known the ceremony would not provoke the same degree of controversy it would have done in Airdrie.

On my first visit to Kirkintilloch, Liam gave me a tour of his new church, and we had refreshments in the coffee shop. And as we sat there, I had an extraordinary sense of peace and wholeness. It came as a gift, unmediated, it seemed. The light shone brightly, but briefly; then there was the long afterglow; and beyond that the memory of it nourished me. It was a kind of baptism.

I never followed up on Liam's offer to baptize me because I came to see it was more important for me to seize the future than trying to fix the past. For despite my perplexing and unsuccessful attempts to encounter God in a deeper way there was an intermittent growth towards something closer to wholeness, a realisation that 'This is life! Live it! Don't squander the present by perpetually seeking some gift you believe will change your future.'

*

Throughout my thirties, I was slowly, and very belatedly learning to relate to women. There was the young student midwife I got to know at church, bright, musical and very pretty. I invited her to a prom concert, but she declined – there was a significant other in her life, currently working in Africa. I remained close to the couple, and attended their wedding.

There was the woman I fell in love with absolutely at first sight the day she walked into church. We talked, and I felt completely at one with her. I was still working at Airdrie Academy at the time, and in the subsequent week I looked her up her former school record and felt closer to her having an address and phone number on a slip of paper in my pocket.

The next Sunday, I was primed to ask her out. I couldn't wait for the sermon to end.

She must I think have discerned the words which filled me before I had a chance to voice them. She was committed to someone else, she told me, someone who was not a Christian believer. All the advice in the circles I moved in then was not to marry out-with the faith. I was tempted to seek to change her mind by persuasion, but I recognised that the honesty and integrity of her commitment to this young man was deeper and lovelier than any dogmatic principle. That evening I found myself relinquishing her while wryly acknowledging that she was not mine to relinquish.

It was hard, later, to sit in the pew and watch her lips mouth 'I do!'

*

There was the young woman I was introduced to by a well-meaning mutual friend, shortly after another relationship had come to an end.

I knew she was not for me and yet I took her to dinner at the Popinjay Hotel at Rosebank in the Clyde Valley. After the meal, we walked in darkness down to the river beneath a frosty moon.

My lips found hers and lingered though my heart was elsewhere.

*

Coalburn Primary School playground. Lunch time. I was standing in the snow with a colleague: we were visiting the school with a learning exhibition, and were chatting to children on their break.

It seemed to me that we were more than a team; a couple, rather.

On days when I was at the Resource Centre and she was out on the road with George Tweedie, I sensed that something was missing in the workplace environment, some spark of life.

The heartsleap when the mobile classroom swung back into the car park, George at the wheel, and I saw her sitting there in the passenger seat! Everyone noticed my jubilation.

We were standing in my former office one afternoon after a busy and productive day. Evening was falling as we looked across at the Episcopal Church next door. As we stood there, longing was about to press 'send' on a declaration of love.

But I said nothing. The moment passed.

*

I'm very grateful to Liz, who also belonged to Airdrie Baptist Church, though she lived in Glasgow where she was working as a nurse.

One Saturday afternoon in the spring of 1987, she arrived at my door with a lasagne which she said was spare, and some cream-cakes. I made coffee.

Our first date was to a bistro in Airdrie called *Somesuchplace*. Afterwards went for a walk in Strathclyde Park. She let me take her hand.

That night, I arrived back in the car park beside my flat just after sunset. A neighbour was calling for her cat. 'Puss! Puss! Puss!' and in that moment of crepuscular serenity I realized that nothing would ever be the same again.

*

We spent time together, Liz and I and went for walks – to Chatelherault in Hamilton; to the West Sands at St Andrews. I learned things I had not known. As we ambled along the windswept beach she took my hesitant hand in hers and placed it firmly on her breast.

'Let's go to the Keswick Convention for the weekend,' she said one Friday in July. We drove down to the Lakes, and Liz took the lead in locating accommodation. 'We want two single rooms,' she said confidently at the Visitor Centre.

Surprisingly, a couple of singles were available, in the one house.

Later, we sat beside Derwentwater in her car while she made coffee with her portable kettle which you plugged into the car battery. We sat, looking out over the sparkling water.

'Now, you're not to come into my room,' Liz said, after we were back in the guest house. I was surprised and mildly hurt that she felt it necessary to say this.

We went to the Convention meetings. On the Sunday evening, we sang Frank Houghton's hymn about missionary evangelism, *Facing a Task Unfinished*:

With none to heed their crying
For life and love and light,
Unnumbered souls are dying
And pass into the night.

I could see these words meant a great deal to Liz, but as always such spiritual zeal was a passion I did not shere.

Later that night, we drove north, Liz at the wheel, my hand resting casually on her warm thigh.

*

One Saturday in August I had arranged to meet Liz in Glasgow and she was late. When she arrived, it seemed to me that her excuse was trivial and that she could easily have been there in time. This brought to the surface doubts which I had been suppressing. There in Buchanan Street, I saw quite clearly that we were temperamentally unsuited for one another.

We went ahead with the plans for the day. I took Liz down to Largs, and we walked in the sunshine along the path leading to the Pencil, the monument celebrating the Battle in 1263. Afterwards we had ice cream in Nardinis, sitting in the wicker chairs well-remembered from childhood. But I knew it was over.

*

The next morning, sitting in the pew beside Liz after the service, I told her I thought we should break up.

But my thoughts after that first date were correct. Nothing would ever be the same again. I had experienced a deep friendship with a woman; I had known for the second time in my life what it is to love and to be loved.

*

I am also grateful to Fiona Colquhoun who succeeded me as school librarian at Airdrie Academy. With Fiona, who was a Roman Catholic but often attended Airdrie Baptist Church with me, I had a good, honest, down-to-earth, mutually supportive, non-romantic friendship. I appreciated the long Sunday afternoons when we relaxed over Indiana Jones films before going out to the evening service.

*

In the summer of 1989, I booked myself on a holiday in Wales for Christian single people. Friends living in Wigan in the north of England invited me to stay overnight with them on the way. As the date drew closer I felt increasingly less positive about my ability to cope, until I was struggling daily in a mist of anxious lethargy.

I was due to leave from work on the Friday at lunch time. The night before I dreamed that a gang of thugs set my feet in concrete and tossed me casually into the deep end of a swimming pool.

Gloomy and tense, I headed south from Hamilton. The traffic on the motorway was heavy; there were frequent delays. Anxiety filled my bladder frequently – I worried that I would not make it in time to the next toilet.

Eventually I arrived in Wigan, where I was warmly welcomed. Throughout the evening, I struggled to hold back the panic, attempting to converse without disclosing my inner turmoil. Eventually I escaped upstairs, and went to bed in the little room over the front door, but I slept badly, feeling completely inadequate for the fortnight ahead. Sometime during the night, I made the decision to abandon my trip and head back north.

I was up early, and I remember sitting on the edge of the bed waiting until it was a reasonable time to go down for breakfast, and leafing through one of the books in the room – John Betjeman's children's story about the adventures of his teddy, *Archie and the Strict Baptists*.

I shared breakfast with my hosts and waved goodbye to them, saying nothing about my decision to return home, and when they invited me to drop in and stay over with them on my way back north, I lied that I'd keep this kind invitation in mind. At the motorway interchange, I took the slip-road heading in the direction of Scotland with a great sense of relief. When I reached my parents' house in the middle of the afternoon I had a delicious sense of having arrived at a secure place.

It wasn't like that of course, because the insecurity lay within, and back at home on the Monday morning, facing the two empty weeks of annual leave which lay ahead I was once again in the grip of a familiar dread.

*

My father was concerned when I abandoned my Welsh holiday: he was perturbed by what my GP, Dr James Duthie had told me – that I would simply have to learn to accept, and to live within the limitations imposed by my condition. James had described to me the distinction as he understood it between reactive and endogenous depressions – the former being triggered by some life event or series of events, the latter arising from chemical imbalance in the brain. You could, he said, more easily walk away from reactive depression once the underlying cause had been dealt with; endogenous depression was not only potentially always with you, but also much harder to treat.

In his judgement, my depression was of the endogenous variety. I'm not sure how accurate this was – mental health experts disagree on whether you can, in fact, so easily distinguish between the reactive and the endogenous. You could argue that my depression was a reaction to my anxiety, but in fact you could never identify which came first, the anxiety or the depression – each fed destructively off the other. However, at the time I found James' analysis helpful, in that it enabled me to concentrate on coping with the symptoms rather than probing for a cause.

In the 1980s the relationship between attachment issues in babyhood and later experiences of anxiety and depression was not realized. And so at that point I lacked the comfort with came later through discoveries suggesting that my anxiety was most likely the result of something which happened to me, rather than to something innate in my physical identity.

My father felt I was unnecessarily surrounding myself with barriers I thought I'd never be able to cross because of the limitations I believed my condition imposed on me. He rightly saw this as an unhealthy development, and remembering how encouraged I'd been by my previous encounter with a psychiatrist, arranged for me to have a private consultation with another professional who was known to be a Christian.

On a bright summer morning my father drove me through Glasgow to Ross Hall Hospital. For forty-five minutes I answered the psychiatrist's questions, baring my soul, unwrapping my fears and presenting them to him, eager to help him help me by giving as accurate and honest a description of my symptoms as I could. He listened impassively. Eventually, the torrent of sentences dried up and I paused. There was nothing more to say.

I sat back, and waited for the words of understanding and empathy, for the encouragement which I was sure would enable me to go forward with hope. But there was nothing. Not a word. He would write to James Duthie, he said. The consultation was over. I left the room feeling violated. One by one I had shared the precious, repugnant treasures of my darkness, but I had been given no light in return.

*

When his letter arrived at the surgery in Airdrie, James read it to me – it simply confirmed what he doubtlessly knew already, that the patient was suffering from 'chronic anxiety and neurotic depression' and that this was 'very hard to treat'. It concluded by recommending medication which James wasn't comfortable about prescribing. It had, he told me, been superseded by more effective drugs, and in fact could be dangerous when combined with certain foods. The letter was filed away and never referred to again. Eventually the £50 bill for the Ross Hall consultation arrived, and I paid it grudgingly.

Dr Duthie prescribed Anafranil (Clomipramine), one of the family of drugs which maintains in the brain a higher level of the chemical serotonin than would otherwise be present. As in the case of all such treatments, he explained, it would be about two weeks after beginning the course of pills before I'd begin to feel the benefits of them.

I will never forget the Saturday morning fifteen days later. I had gone to the Motherwell bookshop, and was standing at the counter waiting to sign a cheque. I realised that whereas normally my hand would be so tense that, afraid I wouldn't be able to sign my name legibly, I'd produce a hurried, tortuous scrawl, today there was a sense of calm, a tide of peace flowing into a dark empty cavern. I smiled, and wrote my name on the cheque slowly, with the characteristic straight line terminating in a dot beneath my signature. To celebrate this joyful blessing, I went to a nearby café, and had coffee and a jammy scone, tranquil and relaxed for the first time for many years.

That a small dose of medication could work such a profound change in outlook seemed miraculous. I was too glad at this lifting of my spirits to question whether I should have been given access to that particular treatment much earlier. It would be very far from true to say that since that day I have not experienced times of sadness and anxiety, but these have never again been so physically consuming. The change was due in part to the medication and in part to increasing self-knowledge and openness to the spiritual.

*

In my Christmas letter for 1989 I noted: 'I'm delighted that my attitude is now much more positive and calm. I have a much greater sense of God's presence and love, and I think a much greater awareness of self, and self-acceptance.'

A dream, inspired I think by a feature in one of the kids' comics I read as a child, where the artist's pencil and rubber actually featured in the strip, visibly changing the reality the character experienced. I am in a room, with blank newsprint-white walls, kneeling painting the floor, concentrating hard on the task. I look up, and realise that I've started at the wrong place. Behind me, there's a corner; between me and the door a thick covering of sticky, brown paint. I pause, and begin to panic. But then I remember the possibilities. I stand up, and taking a pencil from my pocket draw on the wall behind me the outline of a door, and hinges, and a handle. I turn the handle; the door opens; I walk out of the room into another world. I'm in deep countryside; the sun is shining through the trees; there are leaves and foliage in every conceivable shade of green; birds are singing, and not far away a stream gurgles. Lightness in my heart, I take my first, tentative steps.

PART 3

PART 2

TWENTY

DARING TO DISAGREE

In the autumn of the year I abandoned my singles holiday in Wales, my parents invited me to join them for a few days at the Kirroughtree House Hotel in Newton Stewart.

It was one of those establishments with pretensions to grandeur where you were expected to dress up for dinner, and forewarned by my mother I duly took along a suit. During the first course on my first night at the hotel I grew uncomfortably hot and removed my jacket.

'Put that back *on* John,' said my mother, severely.

'But it's too warm!'

She would not be placated.

I did not yield, and the jacket remained over the back of my chair for the duration of the meal.

My mother scowled at me.

Afterwards, another long evening, alone in a hotel room.

*

One afternoon, we drove to the Galloway House Gardens at Garlieston. I appreciated its beauty and tranquillity. I had recently been reading

Listening to God, by Joyce Huggett, which emphasises that God is always communicating with us, speaking for example in the beauty of nature. I said something along these lines in a simple, honest attempt to initiate meaningful conversation with my parents.

'That's pantheism, John,' said my mother, closing down the exchange before it had begun.

When the time came I drove out of the manicured grounds of Kirroughtree House and headed homewards with relief.

*

That same autumn, I visited my parents one afternoon at Crossford, and as usual my mother was very vocal in expressing her opinions. It seemed she would still not rest content until I was in every respect a son created in her image.

As I walked down the drive towards my car with dad afterwards I said to him with deep feeling, 'That woman is a bloody pain'. I never, outwardly at least, used such colourful words and I glanced at my father to gauge his reaction. He neither disagreed with me, nor seemed shocked. But what a liberating joy to vent those words: 'That woman is a *bloody* pain!'

*

By the early 1990s, though there were still times of stress and tension, I was calmed by the medication and my work at the Resource Centre was often joyful. I researched and wrote an accompanying booklet for a learning exhibition on the Scottish Immigrants to the Red River Settlement in Canada; planned and helped deliver quincentennial interactive sessions on the 1492 voyage of Christopher Columbus; wrote a summary history of education in Lanarkshire to accompany an exhibition; prepared notes for curriculum-centred educational visits to the Melrose area.

One of our most satisfying exhibitions from my point of view was aimed at pre-school children. Called *My Favourite Things* and conceived by Margaret Sked, it included textiles and artefacts from different locations and eras. We included an elephant from India, about one metre tall, covered with fabric, coloured segments, beads and tiny metal mirrors. With groups of children, we explored colour and texture; searched for different shapes; counted squares and triangles; listened to songs. We finished with a story, after which each child, if they wished, could sit on the elephant.

This was often sheer delight – there was a particular loveliness in seeing the world through a young child's eyes and heart.

*

A colleague took the lead in implementing computer technology at the Resource Centre. Stephen Grant acquired computers for us, but in my time we never managed to begin cataloguing stock, and electronically controlling its circulation.

Stephen left a computer running with the Windows analogue clock on the screen. As he hoped, I was mightily impressed, given my limited knowledge of programming in DOS. How had he done that, I wondered? And so, for the first time, I was introduced to the world of Bill Gates.

CD-ROMS of encyclopaedias, newspaper archives, and other library catalogues began to transform our ways of working. They said it would all become available eventually on-line, and that downloading information would be quicker than accessing it from a CD. To me, that seemed a dream too far.

Someone enthusiastically demonstrated an early version of email: white text, green background. That'll never catch on, I thought. Much too slow and cumbersome.

Our graphic designer purchased very early Apple Mac computers. From the start I realized the potential of being able to word-process documents and produce camera-ready copy.

*

Margaret Sked moved to a new post in Glasgow. I was asked to speak at her presentation from Education Resource Centre staff. By then secure in my relationship with Margaret, I had the confidence to tease her gently. 'You know Margaret,' I said, grinning. 'Sometimes you work us pretty hard, and some have been heard to mutter "Does that woman not realise we have a life outside work?" and occasionally even "Does that *bloody* woman not realise….."'

*

It seemed to me that the evangelical faith acted like my mother, seeking to squeeze me into the mould of its expectations, reluctant to validate me as I was. Here too I began the long slow process of daring to disagree with others, at least inwardly.

I was showing around the Resource Centre some visitors who mentioned their Christian faith. We talked about God and I said how refreshing it was, in my limited personal experience, that God constantly communicated with us in so many ways. It's significant that I felt free to voice this opinion, but I was surprised by their reaction.

'No, God only speaks through the Bible. That's the only place to hear his words.'

I grunted, but I was thinking 'How strange to muzzle the God you are so eager to hear from.'

*

The Resource Centre housed a large collection of artefacts purchased to support aspects of the Primary and Secondary curricula which we loaned out to schools, and also used in the learning exhibitions. There were North American Indian objects – birch-bark canoes, decoy ducks, clothing, masks; fabrics from India and the Silk Road;

traditional Scottish furniture and agricultural implements; there was even a brush collection, comprised of brushes of different sizes, purposes and materials.

I was often asked to give a children's talk at church, and on the Friday I would wander round the shelves looking at each of the objects in stock asking 'What story are you telling me?' In the end I would choose one, and take it to display to the congregation on Sunday. One week it was a jigsaw puzzle: I spoke about each of us having a place in God's dreams, and about finding our place and remaining connected with the adjacent pieces. Another week it was a Victorian oil lamp with its message of light in dark places.

I came to believe that in 'listening' to the artefacts, I was actually praying and that the ideas and words which came to mind were planted by God.

At home I tried to pray and read the Bible – to have what evangelicals traditionally labelled a 'quiet time', but this was often a duty in which I could not fully engage as my mind was drawn to other things. I came to wonder whether the 'quiet time' as I imagined it should be was actually an obstacle to me, a barrier to listening in stillness to God at the centre of everyday life.

I rarely had any sense of God 'speaking' at church; but at times, when I was stretched out comfortably on my sofa reading, a word or an idea would resonate deeply and spark understanding, joy and energy. What I had read became real to me emotionally. After a short while, the immediacy of that experience would fade: for a day there might be the familiar afterglow, and then simply a memory. I would re-read the chapter or passage but the enchantment would be gone. I would continue further into the book, but often while my mind was instructed my spirit remained untouched.

However, if I waited patiently, there would in time be another book, another article, another line from a poem. I regarded these moments of clarity as God-given gifts.

*

Communion was held weekly at Airdrie Baptist Church as an add-on at the end of the morning or evening service. Those who wished to partake would wait behind; the minister would lead, accompanied by two deacons. Thanks to God would be given by one of the deacons for the bread, after which a silver plate would pass from person to person, each helping themselves to one of the cubes of white loaf it contained. After the other deacon had given thanks for the wine, silver trays with minute individual glasses of fruit juice would be circulated. Week after week I participated. I was fully aware that bread and wine represented the body and blood of Jesus, and that my body's absorbing of these 'elements' (as we called them) symbolised a spiritual oneness with Christ, yet still as in earlier churches I felt absolutely nothing except sadness at the absence of positive religious feelings. I assumed that all of those standing around me, heads reverently bowed, were profoundly nourished by the ceremony.

I remembered the song my mother had sung when I was very young:

> We're feeding on the living bread,
> We're drinking at the fountain head
> And who so drinketh, Jesus said,
> Shall never thirst again
> What, never thirst again?
> No never thirst again,
> What, never thirst again?
> No never thirst again,
> And who so drinketh, Jesus said,
> Shall never thirst again

One morning, leading communion, I asked if the congregation knew this song: they did, and we sang it together. The haunting tune, my mother's voice remembered, the old familiar words, had a beauty in them. Yet why did the blessings of bread and wine not touch my spirit?

*

I was once invited by one of the deacons to the Missionary Prayer Meeting held in his house. I went along, and spent a dispiriting evening with a very passionate and loving group of people. They cared about missionary work. They cared about seeing folk on other continents becoming Christian believers. They believed their prayers would be heard and answered by a listening God. I would have loved to share their passion. But I knew that nothing in me was sparked to life at the thought of missionary work; and I sensed a deep scepticism about whether these prayers would make any difference. I left the house saddened that I was not as these people were.

*

At church we saw a short video produced by the Billy Graham Evangelistic Association demonstrating how to share the Christian faith with others. It featured couples and individuals inviting neighbours and colleagues into their homes, getting to know them, and finding ways of turning the conversation to questions of faith and the spirit. It then demonstrated talking them through the story of sin and sacrifice, guilt and forgiveness in Christ. I found it difficult to watch – it seemed to me to be a manipulative practice, building links with people in order to change their minds to your way of thinking.

Three of us from work were at a wedding, including a colleague whose husband had recently passed away after a battle with cancer. She and I had had discussions about Christianity before, largely arguments over issues such as woman's rights and homosexuality as I defended the conservative position as defined by evangelical leader John Stott in his book *Issues Facing Christians Today*. That afternoon we were sitting outside in the sunshine; she was talking about her loss, and I tried to speak into the situation as a person of faith. At the time I felt I was being compassionate, but I fear much of what I said was about hell. I thought I was speaking in Jesus' name.

One day I took Michael Green's *Jesus Spells Freedom* with me on the mobile library. All my conditioning told me that I should be sharing the gospel with George Tweedie. I found it hard to speak, and in the end I simply thrust the book into his hands saying he might find it interesting. He declined to take it. On another occasion I spent a whole day struggling with an obsessive sense that I should invite George along to an evangelistic event at our church. In the end I stayed silent, and cursed myself. There is irony in my offering someone an assurance that 'Jesus spells freedom' when I myself was clearly anything but free, the prisoner of 'oughts' and of other people's expectations.

*

As a child, there was an air of mystery about the 'deacons' court' to which my father devoted an evening each month. I envisaged stern, be-wigged judges. The word 'court' had been dropped by the time I was appointed a deacon at Airdrie Baptist Church, where the role combined practical responsibilities with support for the pastor and care for the congregation. I had stood for election in the mid-1980s, motivated both by a sense of obligation and I suspect a desire for status. I did not feel comfortable in the role.

I found to my perplexity that I felt no passion about the items on the agenda, no sense of purpose or satisfaction in visiting members of the congregation. I was particularly unhappy about visiting people who wanted to join the church and interviewing them in the company of another church member, asking questions about their faith story. We would then report this back to a church meeting where the members would vote on admitting the new person to membership. I was perplexed at my discomfort with this process.

Before long, I resigned from the diaconate.

*

When the church was without a minister, I was appointed to be one of twelve people on the 'vacancy committee' whose task was to identify a suitable replacement and recommend that person to the church. We reached a point where eleven of us were enthusiastic about one candidate. I was the twelfth. I was becoming conscious of the challenges and questions with which the Bible presents its readers and I was dimly aware that from my perspective the candidate seemed oblivious to these issues. He was a gentle caring man, but I found him too conservative, too unquestioning in his approach to the Bible.

What was the point I felt, of one person deviating from the view of the majority? In any case I would have found it hard to put the reasons for my disquiet into words, even if I had been brave enough to do so. The new minister was recommended unanimously by the vacancy committee and subsequently accepted by the church.

*

With my friend George Cringles, I attended a Reformed Conference held at Stirling University's MacRobert Centre. One of the Bible expositions was on the New Testament book of Jude. I was surprised by the aversion I felt towards the speaker's approach – he seemed to me to be ranting with such vehemence and certainty, but I sensed an artificiality in what he was saying, a mismatch between the words on his lips and the reality in his deep self.

*

But at that point I did not have the confidence to fully own these whispers of disquiet. I told myself it was my reaction which was wrong, and I despaired. Was the fact that I was thinking these things evidence of something diabolical within me? Were my negative thoughts such as those about the Evangelism film planted in me by the devil?

Dare I disagree? Surely the mother of evangelicalism knew best?

*

When Billy Graham was preaching at Parkhead football stadium in Glasgow in 1991, I was responsible for arranging transport and entry tickets for people in the Baptist Church and in the wider community who wanted to attend. I had no intention of going to the meetings myself, as I was afraid I would find their intensity discouraging and intimidating. Evening after evening I waved the buses off outside the church and then went home. But on the last night of the mission on impulse I joined the others.

Arriving at Parkhead I made my way past the hot-dog stands and up the steep steps into the stadium and found somewhere to stand. It was raining. The choir and speakers on the platform which had been erected on the pitch were small, distant figures. There was no charisma or emotionalism in the proceedings. Billy Graham spoke, but I was conscious only of the damp cold.

And yet when the appeal was made for those who wanted to commit their lives to Christ to go forward, I watched the iconic image of people, first just a handful and then a growing stream and then a crowd walking across the turf towards the podium, putting up umbrellas to shelter them from the downpour. Drawn it seemed by a powerful conviction which they recognised as the voice of God, they were seeking to be washed in a torrent of divine grace. A husband and wife from Airdrie who had travelled with us on the bus went forward in this way, and as a result of what happened that night their lives changed direction permanently.

TWENTY-ONE

CHOOSING LOVE

In the summer of 1990 after being on Anafranil for ten months I felt sufficiently positive and calm to visit family friends Norman and Margaret McGrail in Brussells By then, Norman was working as Strathclyde Regional Council's representative at the European Community.

I was very apprehensive about going abroad for the first time and especially about flying. My flight was due to leave from Glasgow Airport in the early evening. That morning my OCD checks that the front door was definitely locked took three times as long as usual.

I spent an anxious day at work before driving to the city and leaving my car with friends who lived not far from the airport. Once the plane was in the air, and we were high above a North Sea bathed in summer evening sunlight, and I saw for the first time ever the topside of the clouds, and the pilot gave us the latest score from that evening's World Cup match, I began to thoroughly enjoy the experience. Later, as we stood in a pool of lamplight in the Rue Albert Elisabeth while Norman found the house key in his pocket, I looked down at my black Revelation case sitting in shadow on the pavement. It was difficult to believe that that morning it had been in another world, on the carpet of the flat in Glenmavis.

Being abroad was liberating though I was still nervous. Walking in to the city centre with Margaret, remembering the trauma the last time I stayed with them I was anxious I'd be caught short far from a toilet. Over the next few days I did the usual tourist things. I explored the Erasmus museum in Brussells and travelled by train to visit renaissance publisher Christophe Plantin's house in Antwerp, but I didn't stay long feeling drawn back to the security of the McGrails' house. And I quickly gave up trying to use my execrable French in shops, instead simply speaking in the ubiquitously understood English. One evening in the Grand Place Norman and I stood outside a bar looking in as a musician performed on a double bass. When Norman asked 'Would you like to go inside?', I shook my head hesitantly, and then forever regretted it. On the positive side I remember sitting in Margaret and Norman's house listening live to the original three tenors concert held on the eve of the World Cup Final.

On the evening of my arrival in Brussels we sat up very late talking. It had been years since I'd spent time with them and I told them the whole story about myself and my struggles with faith and emotion, and about the problems I was having communicating with my parents. They listened closely and non-judgmentally with the occasional sympathetic interjection. Above all they treated me like an adult and this was new to me. I don't remember them saying much when I had finished, but their supportive presence combined with the sense of independence which was my reward for finally making it out of the UK to bring into focus a growing realisation that I could, and indeed must take responsibility for my own life.

Margaret and Norman dropped me off at the airport for my flight home. Standing in the crowd, smiling, they waved at me as I went into Departures. I waved back and then headed for the gate. I never saw them again, but during those few Brussells days they were an incalculable blessing to me.

*

Back home in my flat, I wrote a list of nine resolutions for the future. These included:

'*Need for a closer walk with God, vision of his majesty, trust in his Word.*' Influenced by the McGrails' genuineness I was still aspiring to become and to feel thoroughly evangelical.

'*Need to take responsibility for my own life, not racing ahead of God but facing up to my need to make decisions and take choices*'. I had been waiting for the magical guidance which would unveil the future, but had now realised that the future was in my hands, in partnership with a God who would gently prompt through everyday circumstances and inner whisperings.

Most significant of my resolutions, in terms of direct consequences was this: '*Marriage. I think I should try a Christian Introduction Agency*'. It was this decision, again reflecting the new insight that God's guidance is not passively received but actively sought which led directly to my marriage two years later.

*

I edited my PhD thesis into a form suitable for book publication. Since T. & T. Clark was no longer privately owned, the book could not be published under their imprint, but Ramsay Clark agreed to pay two thirds of the cost of publishing it with The Pentland Press who issued works at the author's expense, while I paid the remaining one third. Some of the more recent archives of the firm, by no means as comprehensive as those from the 19th century housed in the National Library of Scotland were still in Ramsay's hands, and I borrowed these to update the firm's story until the 1980s. We printed and bound 400 copies, and priced the book at £45. Published in 1992, it was not a rapid seller, but it was well reviewed in specialist journals, and copies were purchased by key libraries with publishing history collections.

I was also commissioned to write a series of articles for the *Dictionary of Scottish Church History and Theology*, notably one on the history of Christian Publishing in Scotland. The editors kept asking for more, including short pieces on most of Scotland's religious periodicals. I spent a day researching and photocopying in the bowels of New College Library at Edinburgh University, but I grew stressed with the pressure of writing to deadline. Eventually, I bundled up my research notes and send them to the editor, asking him to find someone else! But he did not follow this up, and so the coverage in the *Dictionary* was not as comprehensive as it might have been, although it did include a general article from me on Scottish religious periodical publishing.

I wrote other academic papers, and began to be in contact with academics in the field of publishing history who were developing the *Edinburgh History of the Book in Scotland*. Ramsay Clark put me in touch with someone from the venerable Edinburgh Bookseller's Society, which was formed in 1776. The Society's archives had been deposited in the National Library, and they offered me £1000 to research and write a history of the organisation. I accepted, and subsequently went to Edinburgh on my day off to inspect the archive. Realising how much time it would take to undertake the necessary research as well as my day job, I handed the minute books back to the librarian, and headed rather sadly for home.

Back in Airdrie I met a friend and drove him up the Clyde Valley to Lanark where we had tea. I knew I had a choice: I could opt for academic life, and immerse myself in the history of publishing, or I could make marriage and family my goal. It might have been possible to have both, but I sensed I was seeking through historical work recognition and satisfaction which it ultimately could not deliver. And so that afternoon talking to David in Lanark's Woodpecker Restaurant I decided that my academic researches were over.

*

Shortly after my return from Brussells, I signed up with New Day, a Christian introduction agency widely advertised in the Christian press. You completed a form (this was of course before there was wide access to the internet) giving information about yourself and indicating the type of person you hoped to meet. There was no need with this particular agency to get your application form signed by one of your church leaders who could vouch for your genuineness – this I think I would have found too embarrassing.

In due course Sue Sexton at New Day would phone – I think 'New Day' was a one-woman operation, or ministry. 'Call me back,' she'd say, to save her phone bill. You'd ring her and she'd give you details of someone she thought you might like to meet. It was clear that in making these pairings Sue first contacted the woman, describing the potential date and asking if she were happy to have her name and contact details passed to him. If the woman responded positively, Sue would then phone the man, and it was his responsibility to set up a meeting.

Over the space of about a year, I was given three names from Sue – one woman was from Edinburgh, about ten years older than I was: we agreed to meet, but the more I thought about it the more I realised that I didn't want to rule out the possibility of having children and so with great embarrassment I cancelled our rendezvous. One woman came from Harrogate. We chatted once or twice on the phone, and agreed to meet somewhere between Airdrie and Yorkshire. But somehow the line from the south went cold.

Then in June 1991 Sue phoned again. 'I've got someone for you with a nice Scottish name,' she announced. 'She's from Inverness. Lorna Anderson.' I had to try Lorna's number several times before managing to contact her. We chatted about ourselves, our work (Lorna was a Care Worker at Cameron House, a Church of Scotland-run residential home for elderly people living with dementia) and about the churches we attended. Lorna belonged to a Brethren church – Culloden Gospel Hall – which she had been part of since a Christian conversion when she was 16. Our shared Brethren experience gave us much to talk about. She was on the point of going on holiday to visit friends in Dublin but we agreed to speak again on her return.

When I made contact again some weeks later – having received an encouraging post-card from Ireland – we arranged to meet on 31st July 1991 in Pitlochry in Perthshire, roughly half-way between Inverness and Airdrie. There was a war memorial surrounded by park benches half-way along the main street, Lorna told me. She would meet me there.

And so that Wednesday morning I drove north to Pitlochry in ridiculously good time, and stationed myself on a seat at the appointed place where apprehensively and yet with surprising calmness I read *The Times* in bright summer sunlight. I hadn't paid much attention to what I was wearing that morning, but fortunately my appearance must have passed muster, for had it not Lorna might (or so she tells me) have simply kept walking.

I looked up as she approached. 'You must be Lorna,' I smiled.

We greeted one another and then found somewhere to eat. As I faced her across the table Lorna's eyes seemed liquid, bright and alive. Afterwards, we walked round Loch Faskally, close to the town. As we approached the waterside I said rather rashly 'May I hold your hand?'

Later, hand in hand, we walked out towards Moulin and sat on a seat overlooking Pitlochry, and talked and talked. In the early evening I waved goodbye to her outside Fishers Hotel as she climbed into the bus which would take her back north, and then returned light-footedly to my car.

*

Lorna sent me cassette tapes of Christian worship music and I played them constantly on my way to and from work. The soundtrack of my life over the next year, they brought Lorna close.

I sent flowers to her via Interflora at her work address ('Cameron House, Culduthel Road, Inverness' – even the street name, I thought, had a wild romantic feel to it). I later learned that Lorna was embarrassed by the arrival of the unanticipated bouquet, but she accepted it with good grace.

We wrote frequently. I spent three days with Lorna in Inverness at the beginning of September. We were both gauche and hesitant. I expected when I reached her door in Inshes Wood that we would be continuing where we had left off a month before at Pitlochry, but in fact it was more like beginning again. We had a meal and walked beside the River Ness in the twilight; the next day I took her to Hugh Miller's cottage in Cromarty and we walked up the Fairy Glen while I calculated whether an alfresco kiss would be too risky.

'All I want to do is to be with you, and do the things you do, and visit the people you visit,' I said, which was sweet, but short-sighted. We came to realise that a relationship works best when each of the partners is truly themselves.

We shared our stories. I told Lorna about my proneness to depression and anxiety, concerned as to how she would respond. 'It makes me love you even more,' she said.

At the start of October we both attended a residential Bible Conference at Kilcreggan, at the same centre the Airdrie Academy Christian Union had used nine years before. I had decided that while at Kilgreggan I would ask Lorna to marry me but the problem lay in finding a suitable opportunity. Finally, on the Saturday evening we escaped from the conference centre, and walked in the friendly darkness down towards the shore where last I had stood watching Claire walking with Abba. There, I asked Lorna to be my wife, and she said 'Yes!' without any hesitation.

I'd told my parents about New Day and Lorna before my first trip to Inverness sitting having lunch with them at Fraser's store in Glasgow's Buchanan Street. I knew that regardless of how they responded it was a glad message to share. At that stage they were both positive but to my disappointment and pain when I later introduced Lorna to them, my mother was not as welcoming of her as I had hoped. Against this background we made all the arrangements for the wedding ourselves.

There were those who tried to discourage us: on Lorna's side, some wondered if she would be comfortable with someone who belonged to a Baptist Church; while one of my friends, without having met Lorna warned me that in a relationship 'One person always loves more, and the other gets hurt'. I was also taken to task for my willingness to leave Airdrie Baptist Church as I was planning to do and with Lorna attend a church in Airdrie which was more Brethren-like in its style of worship. But we survived.

We were married on 12 September 1992, in Culloden Gospel Hall, at a service conducted by David Wiper, husband of Lorna's close friend Betty who had been a mother to her. Liam Goligher was best man. I was 40, Lorna 13 years younger.

My knowledge of romantic honeymoon destinations being rather restricted, I'd booked a few days at the Green Park Hotel in Pitlochry close to where I'd taken Lorna's hand on our first walk round Loch Faskally. It seemed full of elderly people and reminded my new wife of Cameron House.

*

Lorna had resigned from her job and found a new post at another care home in Hamilton. But in July 1992 I saw advertised a vacant post with Highland Regional Council Libraries as Education Services Librarian based in Inverness.

I applied for this new post which involved developing services to adult learners. After careful research, I detailed my extensive experience in educational librarianship, and related it to the innovative strategy of opening up learning opportunities to adults by the provision of 'open learning packs' in public libraries. I was called for an interview, which took place just two days before our wedding, and was appointed.

We had to rapidly amend our plans, and by the middle of October after a month in Glenmavis we were back in Inverness, where we've remained ever since.

*

Although Lorna and I each took the initiative in signing up to New Day Introductions and although I applied for the post in Inverness and worked hard to ensure I was fully prepared for the interview, we nevertheless sensed that this significant change in our lives had not occurred simply by chance, nor had we by our own efforts made it happen. We believed rather that after the years of waiting God had given us a new beginning together.

This book charts my personal journey; Lorna has had her own journey from childhood to maturity, a difficult and ultimately very lovely story which is not mine to tell. But though our journeys have been different, we travelled in love. We have been brought in the end to a very similar place and that has been a great joy to us.

TWENTY-TWO

THEOLOGY IN THE LABOUR ROOM

'Three bare bear bums past the belly button.'

After I'd applied a generous smear of Sudocream (or 'bum balm' as I described it) to the cleansed and fragrant baby's bottom, this was the formula devised after extensive trial and error which I used to ensure that the nappy was secured with just the right amount of tension. I calculated the best position to attach the Velcro fixing strips by counting the bears pictured on the border of the nappy in relation to the naval just above it. Besides, there was music in the alliteration, and a just a hint of naughtiness.

Lorna and I have two daughters, Rebecca born in late December 1993 and Bethany who arrived early in January 1996. Lorna was not amused when I walked into the delivery room before Rebecca's birth with a Bible and a pile of theology books, hoping to work on a sermon as labour progressed. I didn't make the same mistake next time round.

Newly born, Rebecca was wrapped in a towel and handed to me. I held her, muttering inanely 'Welcome to the world'. I felt no great rush of emotion at either of the girls' births, but remained matter-of-fact. I was however glad we had two girls, having the mistaken idea that since I am not remotely macho my modelling of masculinity to sons would have been deficient.

We brought Rebecca home on 31ˢᵗ December. That January in my memory is full of living-room bath times, curtains tightly drawn against the night, the fragrance of Johnson's baby powder, the music of Michael Card's cradle songs playing repeatedly, love and laughter.

*

I'd struggled to keep upright during our wedding service which was elongated by the length of the sermon – having torn something in my back, I was doped up with pain-killers. This problem recurred particularly in my early years at Highland Libraries – it was not unusual for me to lie flat on my back on the floor for a few minutes to try to ease the discomfort.

There was a chiropractor in Cawdor, Lorna told me, and took me along. I had never had such treatment before and was suspicious that though the practitioner's basic task was skilful manipulation, nevertheless there might be an occult dimension to his practice. My evangelical background had engendered a suspicion of anything out-with the mainstream. I went because I needed help, but with deep suspicion, which was heightened, rather than diminished when I saw the cross hanging on his consulting room wall.

As he plied his trade I inaudibly muttered over and over 'Lord Jesus Christ, have mercy on me,' seeking to surround myself with a protective screen of Spirit. The chiropractor noticing my obvious tension, commented that I was a singularly unresponsive patient.

This didn't, however, prevent him from vigorously manipulating my bones and muscles. The air was filled with yelps of pain – somewhat over-dramatic, as Lorna pointed out severely when I joined her in the waiting room where she had been sitting, listening with mounting embarrassment.

*

My new job in Inverness was never dull. On 19th October 1992, I reported to my manager Peter Reynolds, the Senior Reference Librarian in Highland Libraries Central Services Unit. We worked from 9am to 5pm at a leisurely pace with an hour for lunch – time to read, or go home to watch the lunchtime edition of *Neighbours*. At 3.30pm everything stopped for coffee break. There was still a rigid demarcation between librarians and library assistants: the staff room was recognised as the assistants' territory – the rest of us, joined by the Principal Librarian, sat round a table in the open plan office. Talking about work was forbidden. We ate biscuits slightly past their use-by date, provided in great quantities by the cataloguer, Miss Robertson who always had an eye open for offers at the supermarket. (Everyone called her Miss Robertson, but I had the daring to call her Isobel, which I think she appreciated.) It was, from the perspective of a quarter of a century later, another world, a calmer more civilized place. For a short time, the Library Service was adequately staffed and funded.

Though there was a database of stock holdings managed using software written by the Council's IT Department, libraries were not on-line, and the work was labour-intensive – the location of stock was manually changed item-by-item on the database by central staff as books were sent, via the Unit, from one of around fifty libraries and mobiles to another. An up-to-date print of the catalogue was produced periodically in microfiche format, and copies sent to all branches. Computers were available for reading reference works on CD-ROM, but much to my frustration we did not have PCs on our desks. I had to sweet-talk the receptionist to persuade her to let me write reports on her Amstrad PCW.

I loved life in Inverness – living and working in the same town brought innocent pleasure. One day I would be hosting an exhibition of business-related learning packs at Inverness and Nairn Enterprise's office in Bridge Street, the next having coffee and cake with my family in the tea shop across the road, with the Director of Education at the next table. This unity of place was satisfying.

I have always found driving stressful, and there was anxiety too while venturing out of contact, over miles of wilderness. I had a recurrent fear of having a heart attack and in my final moments writing a plaintive farewell to my beloved wife and children. But there was also pleasure in travelling round the Highlands: navigating the library service's old yellow Peugeot along a tranquil Loch Ness-side on a bright autumn morning at 8.45am, the only vehicle on the road; watching the North Sea far below over the bonnet as I gingerly negotiated the Berriedale Braes on my way home from Wick; queuing for the ferry to Skye at Kyle of Lochalsh before the bridge was built.

*

I arranged for users of Mallaig Swimming Pool to have access to a range of library books on healthy living which they could borrow at the pool. Delivering this stock in the Peugeot van I took with me our dog, a wayward Yorkie called Rhanna.

The foul smell assailing my nostrils round about Corpach puzzled me until I realised that Rhanna, or rather Rhanna's unhelpful deposit on the passenger seat was its source. My first request on arrival was for a bucket of water and disinfectant. Rhanna blamed my driving.

*

One day's trip took me from Inverness to Kinlochbervie in the west then along the north coast via Bettyhill and Thurso before heading south, covering much of what is now known as the North Coast 500 route.

My key role was the purchase and promotion of learning packs produced by the Open University, the Open College and other providers. Many of my library colleagues viewed these activities as not being 'core' to the library service and I suspected that they viewed my post, and my budget as diverting resources from the 'real business' of providing books.

I therefore found myself more at home with the members of the Highland Adult Learner's Group – representatives of all the different agencies in the Highlands which offered learning opportunities to adults. We ran joint events, and I edited a booklet showcasing learning opportunities for adults in the area. For a time I chaired the Group. I was always frustrated, however, that I did not see the way to building an accreditation route so that someone could be awarded a qualification locally for work done using a learning pack from the library.

I got to know the Learning Group members well – we completed a Strathclyde University Adult Guidance Certificate course together, with all the personal sharing which this involved. The course taught me even more about being at home with myself and with other people than it did about supporting learners. These colleagues were passionate about the power of education to change lives whereas I still considered that the deep level of change they were referring to could only be achieved through the power of God: I had not yet begun to see the link between the two.

I interpreted my role of promoting learning through public libraries in the very broadest sense. Hence the trip to Mallaig with Rhanna. I persuaded a couple of the Local Enterprise Companies to give me PCs and monitors, installed the software from floppy discs, and delivered them to some of the larger libraries for members of the public to use for word processing. These machines had only 40MB of hard disc space, and ran Windows 3.1, and issues of viruses and data protection did not at first enter my head.

One year in the mid-90s I heard the word 'internet' for the first time. I saw it once in a newspaper article – and then, suddenly, the word was everywhere. Peter Reynolds and I purchased a modem and linked it to a computer. It fizzed and crackled, and then connected us. I was able to access the catalogue of an American library, run a search, and pull back the results. To me what has since become commonplace was a miracle.

I also focused on health education, and partnered with local agencies including the Chest Heart and Stroke Association to further health promotion. Users of some libraries were given the chance of having their blood-pressure read. I volunteered to go first at Culloden Library – and promptly fainted!

By this time, the Principal Librarian had taken early retirement. Senior managers at the Council's HQ got to hear of my 'outreach activities' for which twenty years later I would have been praised and one of them concluded that I should be 'reigned in'. 'You have done what you came to do,' he told me, matter-of-factly – his voice flat, devoid of either praise or of malice.

Peter Reynolds and I prepared a robust document defending my position, but by then a new Principal Librarian was in post, and all the talk was of 're-organisation'.

*

I don't know what prompted the move to rename as Evangelical Churches those Gospel Halls which were more open to change. The aim may have been to signal that very openness; possibly too there was a suspicion that in a changing society the words 'Gospel Hall' were meaningless, or worse bore negative connotatations. But although Celt Street Gospel Hall in Inverness, where Lorna and I were members from 1993 until 1999 had become an Evangelical Church its style was almost identical to that of Allander Hall of childhood memory. We were welcomed; it was a place of love.

Central to the church's week was the 'morning meeting' at which as in my childhood men but not women were free to pray, speak, and 'give out' hymns – in the 1990s as in the 1950s the *Believers' Hymn Book* was used. I was not at that point aware of Lorna's growing frustration at the exclusion of women from aspects of the worship and ministry of the church, and regrettably I had not yet realized how contrary this was to the spirit of Christianity.

I enjoyed the freedom of the morning meetings. I was ambivalent about preaching sermons: often in preparing I'd sense that some thoughts were coming to me with a sense of 'givenness', but still the actual delivery was terrifying and often only possible with the assistance of Valium. Afterwards, I'd be left with conflicting emotions – an unseemly pride, a hungering for humility, and an urgent need to be alone to recharge spent batteries.

'I like it when someone knows when to stop, and doesn't continue talking to fill the time,' someone said to me after I'd finished preaching at 7.25pm instead of the expected 7.30. I smiled in reply, not sure whether this was in fact the compliment it seemed at first sight. In reality, I had been so tense that I galloped through my material and had nothing more to say.

The morning meetings were different. The theory was that the course of this worship was directed not simply by human intention but by the prompting of the Holy Spirit. I am sure we often got it wrong and drove the service forward with our own thinking, unprompted by the Spirit. Thus we might consciously or unconsciously replicate remembered patterns of thought and song, or share things we had reflected on previously, in our desire to speak shutting ourselves off from the Spirit's whisper. But I certainly found that in many morning meetings sequences of ideas, or pictures, or associations, or insights into Bible verses came to mind in a fresh and vibrant way, and gently insisted that I give them voice. To some extent this was the fruit of my own psychology, but I believed, and still believe that the creative wind of God was blowing. When we later moved on from the Brethren, it was the morning meetings and that sense of 'givenness' and grace which I missed.

Every few Sundays I would look after the crèche which consisted of our two girls and few other young children. We'd play with toys, read stories, have juice, while all the time the slow soundtrack of morning devotion reverberated, scarcely audible, on the other side of the wooden partition.

For a while Lorna and I led the small Youth Group and probably I learned more than the teenagers. Once I was asked to speak on evolution and creation: I read extensively and concluded that there was no conflict between the two. I shared this view with apprehension, suspecting that my listeners came from staunchly creationist families, but there was no disagreement with what I had to say. On another occasion I thought the young people would benefit from a talk on the wonder of inception, gestation and birth illustrated by the vivid photos in a Dorling Kindersley book. I spoke to blank, bored eyes. They knew the script better than me. I had made the mistake of assuming that these 1990s Brethren youths were similar to the gauche 1960s Baptist teenager I knew best.

I was asked to preach the first sermon of a series at the evening 'Bible Hour' on the life of Joseph the Old Testament patriarch, Joseph of technicolor dreamcoat fame.

The text I was assigned from Genesis (see Genesis 37:1-10) included the passage where young Joseph has a couple of dreams which seem to foretell that at some point in the future his elder brothers will bow down before him. To deal with this material with integrity I knew I would have to examine the gift of seeing the future in historical and contemporary contexts, examining in particular the phenomenon of 'second sight' – the ability to catch glimpses of things still to come – which was particularly prevalent in the Scottish Highlands. I researched this, particularly focussing on Elizabeth Sutherland's book on the subject *Ravens and Black Rain: the Story of Highland Second Sight*.

I discovered that in history some of those having this ability regarded it as a gift from God and it seemed to me that the way they exercised this gift and the situations in which it was used confirmed that in their cases at least it did indeed come from God. And so a major emphasis of my study on the life of the young Joseph was on second sight, or 'prophecy' – to use the more appropriate New Testament term – as a gift from God, and I attempted to apply this to contemporary Christian life.

This was a new approach to many in the audience. After I had finished speaking, someone came up to me and said, stony-faced with disapproval 'It was Joseph I came to hear about!'

I was growing concerned about what seemed to me to be the selectiveness of Celt Street's agenda, its reluctance to deal with cultural issues and face up to the questions which a thoughtful Christian looking at everyday life would inevitably raise.

*

In the months before leaving Airdrie I had contributed a few short reflections to a *Food for Thought* series in the *Airdrie Advertiser*. Shortly after we were settled in Inverness I wrote to the *Highland News* enclosing some cuttings, and asking if the editor would appreciate a weekly 400-word piece on a Christian theme.

Nick Hunter called me up at work, and said 'Yes, let's try it for a few weeks'.

The first piece, which Nick headlined *Christian Viewpoint* appeared in the issue dated 24th April 1993. I promised that the column would be 'very personal':

I'll be passing on things I've heard or read in the Bible which have encouraged or challenged me, taking occasional glances at current local or national issues, and sharing my own successes and failures as a follower of Jesus. I believe when you're talking about these things it's important to be real, and not to pretend to be further in to God than you actually are.

Over the years the column has remained true to these principles, reflecting honestly on my own journey, finding parables in everyday life, engaging with culture, reflecting a broad ecumenism, and responding (often inadequately) to stories in the news.

Nick's 'few weeks' has extended to nearly thirty years.

*

I came across the psychologist Carl Jung's concept of synchronicity – meaningful combinations of events which have no discernible causal relationship. You think of someone, and moments later receive a phone call from that person; you sense a prompting to visit a friend, and find yourself arriving at just the right moment to help them. I knew that Christians see these meaningful co-incidences as expressions of God's grace and guidance, but up until then it had not occurred to me that similar synchronicities, often life-enhancing are a common human experience regardless of people's beliefs. I realised that to credit God with examples of synchronicity in a Christian context, is to see God as the source of all life-enhancing synchronicities. God was much bigger, much more indiscriminately gracious than I had imagined.

*

Another sermon I gave at Celt Street was about the work of the Holy Spirit. As well as dealing with the familiar topic of the Spirit's input into each Christian's life, I wanted to begin by considering the Spirit's activities out-with the Church. (Only later would I realise that the best pronoun to use for this expression of God, so often encountered in gentleness, sensitivity and whisper is 'her'.) I believed that the Holy Spirit was at work in the world and in peoples' lives, eloquent in the beauties of creation, inspiring creativity and prompting folk towards goodness and truth and joy, despite the fact that they may have not consciously engaged in the quest for God. I confidently opened Berkhof's *Systematic Theology* to see what he had to say, and was disconcerted to discover that his pages made little comment on the subject of the Holy Spirit's activity in the world. The Bible, I felt, was not silent on the subject of God's work in the world: the issue must have been off the theologian's interpretive radar.

*

As we were chatting after a church home group I asked a fellow-member of the church whom I knew thought through things deeply, 'What do you think about the divine inspiration of the Bible? I know God did not dictate the Bible word for word, and that editors and authors expressed their own judgement in writing. But does inspiration mean that every word is where it is because God wants it to be there?'

'Something like that,' was all he said.

*

The elders at Celt Street had decided to run a series of the *Christianity Explored* course (which was similar to another introduction to Christian faith, the better known *Alpha Course*, but did not have the same emphasis on encountering the Holy Spirit). We were asked to visit houses in the vicinity of the church inviting people to attend. Still I felt uncomfortable with this approach. Was it unbelief on my part, or simply shyness? Was it a sense that religious beliefs are personal and that attempting to share them in a doorstep context is an intrusion? Was I still cringing at sin-focussed evangelism and shrinking from anything resembling it?

*

A family visiting Inverness from elsewhere in Europe came to a coffee morning we held at Celt Street. I got into conversation with the father about Jesus. He told me that, to him, Jesus was an example of a fully-evolved human being – humanity at its full potential.

'Yes!' I said with enthusiasm.

*

The Brethren elders of my childhood nodded their heads with a grim sadness when anyone mentioned. *Father and Son*. This classic memoir published in 1907 by 'man of letters' Edmund Gosse is still in print. Gosse was born almost a century before me in 1849, twenty years into Victoria's reign. *Father and Son* tells the story of his mother's death from cancer when he was a young child, and his upbringing in the Christian Brethren by his father, the naturalist and committed evangelical Philip Gosse. I read *Father and Son* for the first time in the mid-1990s and followed it up with Ann Thwaite's biography of its author.

I'm struck by how little Brethren worship had changed in the century which separates us. Our meeting hall when I was a child was similar to his place of worship in Devon – a corrugated iron building. The saints still gathered round the table for simple worship on Sunday mornings. There was the same teaching about fleeing from worldliness in all its forms, and about the soon-coming of Jesus – and wasn't the daily news full of signs that this must imminently take place?

My childhood had much in common with young Edmund's and yet when it comes to spiritually-related suffering, I believe mine was greater than his. When Gosse was 10 he was baptised and welcomed into the church his father led, though he claims that in a deep part of himself he always held out against Christianity. If he was conscious of hypocrisy it did not seem to trouble him whereas in my case I spent my teenage years crushed by guilt.

Despite the similarities, there was a fundamental difference between Edmund Gosse's inner journey and mine. As a child, Gosse, aware of his 'dedication' to the Lord by his parents, felt 'like a small and solitary bird caught….in a glittering cage'. He continues: 'I saw myself imprisoned for ever in the religious system which had caught me.' Even at the age of 16, he tells us, 'I was still but a bird fluttering in the network of my Father's will, and incapable of the smallest independent action.' If Gosse was struggling to get out of a system he felt was controlling him and plotting out his life ahead I was the opposite. As a young person I felt excluded from the joyous and purposeful reality of the faith I saw in others around me and struggled to get in.

Gosse had a robust personality, a strong sense of self. I on the other hand had little personal resilience. Ground down by guilt it seemed to me that the sole place I could be accepted and survive was within the only Christianity I recognised as authentic, the Christianity modelled by the significant people in my life.

Yet here I was in middle-age still feeling on the outside despite my faith and encounters with God, still struggling at times to be accepted and to survive.

*

In 1996, after Bethany's birth, my parents moved north from Lanarkshire to Inverness to be close to us. My mother was already showing signs of dementia, but was unable, or unwilling to acknowledge this and my father did not challenge her. Unwavering love for mum was his main focus. He would do anything to smooth her pathway, but love submerged wisdom: things which should have been said were left unspoken. Hence, mum never had the assessment which might have led to her having a better quality of life in her final years. Her symptoms were treated with antidepressants, but there was no attempt to discover and name her true condition. Once she was admitted to Raigmore Hospital having had difficulty swallowing; but she signed herself out in the middle of the night and with sadness I collected her and took her home.

Mum loved the role of 'granny' but was unable to talk to the girls at their level. When one of them began a conversation about what she had been doing, rather than engaging with the child, mum would pour out memories from her own early years, baffling our two. She allowed them to take advantage of her by smearing her face with makeup, and furiously combing her hair, which of course they enjoyed. There were hugs, but mum was unable to be the affirming rock of love which children need in a grandparent.

She remained strongly opinionated, but as always there was no way of having deep, reflective conversation with either of my parents. My father would always support my mum's viewpoint. Almost all of his conversation was at a superficial level: it frustrated me that he was unwilling, or unable to dig deeper, but I accepted that I would never have the deep exchanges about the past which I yearned for, and that I must simply love my parents as best as I could as they were in the present.

Other than attending church on Sunday, visiting us, and shopping, my parents, though only in their mid-70s did not much engage with the local community. But everyone who knew my father – in church, in shops, in the cul-de-sac where my parents lived – spoke highly of his graciousness.

I circulated my newspaper column to some friends before publication, including my father who forwarded it to a friend in Lanarkshire. On one occasion, I wrote of the emotional struggles I had earlier in life, but was not in any way critical of my parents. My father (accidentally, I hope) copied me in to this forwarded mail. And he said to the friend 'You can see what trouble we had in those days' or words to that effect. This saddened me, but I greeted it with a wry shrug, and said nothing. But something in me now, understanding the attachment issues which make my life challenging wants to draw him to me and whisper with compassion and forgiveness 'You see what trouble I had – with YOU pair!'

*

Lorna and I had helped to publicise a concert by a Christian singer, Bill Drake at the Culloden Academy auditorium. It was a lively concert and the performer invited, indeed expected members of the audience to stand up and celebrate in time to the music, waving their arms enthusiastically.

I rose, but could not with any sense of integrity physically express the rhythm of the music. Lorna glowered at me, and I made a half-hearted effort to join in.

But I was coming to realise that by nature I am an introvert. The term was new to me: hitherto, I had thought something was wrong with me – why did I find being in enthusiastic groups of people exhausting, craving to be alone and to re-charge in the healing space of quietness and reflection?

I learned that whereas extroverts draw energy from group situations, introverts find theirs depleted in similar contexts. I realised that this distinction had been insufficiently recognised in churches, where many of the activities presume extroversion, leaving those of us who are introverted feeling deficient, on the edge.

As an introvert, there is a sense of disquiet when someone appears walking on the pavement towards you, or crosses the road to your side, or when you have to sit beside someone on a bus. A sense of space invaded. It's a challenge – to be open, and smile, and say hello, and welcome any comments made in response. But the disquiet in such circumstances is deep-seated, ingrained.

*

I remember praying quite frequently 'Father, I know you want me to speak to someone about your love today. Please give me an opportunity to do this, help me to recognise this opportunity for what it is, and to take it fearlessly.' And I would come to the end of a busy day, and there had been no such opportunity at least as far as I had been aware. And I felt a sense of despair. Why was God silent?

And yet there would be other occasions, when I'd be planning to write something, and didn't quite know what line to take; or when I had a problem at work and needed information to resolve it. 'Please show me,' I would pray, and often (but not always) I would find what I was looking for, whether it was an idea rising up within me with clarity, or a book or website which answered my query.

*

That morning on my way from the bus stop to the office, I walked past Inverness Library with a rising sense of excitement. Later that day, I might be Area Libraries Officer, based there.

The 1998 Highland Libraries reorganisation aimed to put local management in place in each of the Council's geographical areas, which had for some years been administered from Inverness. Several of the subject-specific librarian jobs – including my own – were dispensed with in order to create new Area Library Officer posts. There would be no redundancies, but we would have to apply for the new posts.

Lorna and I were very keen not to have to move from Inverness, so I applied for each of the jobs based there, or in close proximity. I compared myself unfavourably with my colleagues, with their passion for libraries and for the transformative power of books. Whatever was true back in Carluke in the mid-1970s, I knew that now I was no longer a committed mainstream librarian. However it was easy in preparing for the interview to imagine myself in the role, sitting in an office in Inverness Library with my name on the door.

The interviews were held late morning, but for some reason the results were not announced until the very end of the day. Lorna and the children collected me from Library Support Unit at 4pm; I dropped her off at the care home where she worked and went back to the office with Rebecca and Bethany. I sat them on the floor on a story-mat and I read a book with them until the summons came.

I drove the girls home for tea afterwards, heavy-hearted. One interview down, and no job. The librarian already based in Inverness Library got the post – as indeed she deserved. It had been presumptious of me to imagine myself in her place.

In the event, I ended up as Senior Librarian Systems Support, with responsibility for overseeing and developing the Talis Library Management system. 'Talisman', I called myself,

In 1998, there were five Highland Libraries on-line. In the next few years, working with Fujitsu who were contracted to run the Highland Council infrastructure, I led the technical operation to bring all 40

Highland Libraries plus school libraries on-line; we implemented an off-line system for mobile libraries; and launched a live public catalogue and reservation system. I loved the methodical nature of this work; the fact that I was supporting both colleagues and members of the public. From having a role 'on the edge', not fully appreciated by other library colleagues, I now was positioned at the very centre of the service. No longer was my lack of passion for traditional librarianship a concern.

It became clear to me that this was a role in which I could be authentically myself, and flourish. I know, looking back that I was fortunate not to be appointed to the Inverness Area Library Officer post. I saw the touch of God in this whole process and I felt blessed and very grateful.

*

A group of people within Celt Street Evangelical Church, Lorna and me included, began to feel growing dissatisfaction. It seemed to us that some of our fellow-members were content to perpetuate the ways of doing church established by their parents and grandparents, believing that the only way to please God was to do things as they had always been done.

Those who were dissatisfied, while recognising that the traditionalists found reassurance and security in preserving past ways, had come to believe that a creative God was calling us as a church to be open to the divine in a new and deeper way, to be prepared to take risks, to change some of our practices not for the sake of change, but in response to a divine prompting. Those in favour of new ways were inspired by books such as those by Jack Deere, including his *Surprised by the Voice of God*, which emphasised that it had always been God's practice to speak directly to people through their everyday circumstances as well as through the Bible, and *Surprised by the Power of the Spirit*, which argues that Christians should expect God to be supernaturally active in their lives through the Holy Spirit.

The evangelical church worldwide was divided in the mid-1990s by reactions to the 'Toronto blessing' phenomenon, which began in January 1994. Worshippers at the Toronto Airport Vineyard Church had a deep encounter with the Spirit of God which resulted in their experiencing joy, freedom and sometimes physical healing, and in their expressing worship in laughing, leaping, dancing and 'roaring'. What had happened at the church stimulated great interest among Christians internationally, and thousands travelled to Toronto to experience the on-going phenomenon for themselves. Local manifestations of a similar 'blessing' were reported from around the world. Was this a display of demonic power as some argued or a genuine manifestation of the Holy Spirit?

*

I went along with some friends from Celt Street to a meeting in Dingwall at which a representative of the Toronto church was speaking. I watched as a number of those present were 'slain in the Spirit' as I had seen others affected in Airdrie in the 1980s. Afterwards, as my Airdrie Baptist Church friends had done, they spoke of the joy which had swept through them as they lay on the floor overwhelmed by a sense of God's love.

I shrugged wryly as I stood at the back of Dingwall Town Hall watching all this going on. As usual, I was untouched by it. But despite my own lack of any particular sense of encounter with God either on that occasion or through Jack Deere's books, I was happy to position myself with those arguing for openness in the way things were done in the Celt Street church.

There were many meetings over this issue, but it's the last one I particularly recall, a brief session at which those who remained as elders announced that nothing was going to change. I left the church, and walked in the bright spring evening sunlight across the Ness islands. It's an intensely beautiful corner of the city: the Islands are covered with great trees rising beside the River Ness as it purposefully glides down to the Firth. I allowed the sun's warmth and the gentle gurgling of the water to ease my tension before going home and saying to Lorna what I knew she was already thinking: 'We've got to leave.'

TWENTY-THREE

'YES' MOMENTS

This is more a chapter of ideas than of stories, if you'll pardon me.

I continued to have doubts about the reliability of the books I bought on my last day at Scripture Union which I once thought contained 'all the theology I'd ever need'. Especially after what I'd learned in preparing sermons for Celt Street I was questioning the whole concept of systematising theology. Was this attempt to capture beliefs about God from the biblical text and categorise them in dense prose legitimate? Or was it akin to netting butterflies, pinning them in a display cabinet and watching as that which when alive was vividly colourful became drab and dusty in lifelessness?

Once awakened such thoughts cannot be unthought. On my positive days I welcomed them; when I was more negative they triggered guilt. Forty years of incessant inner programming insisted that the approach to interpreting the Bible I had grown up with was the only faithful way of handling it. My understanding of God and of faith was so closely tied to this particular interpretive viewpoint that I felt if I could no longer hold with intellectual integrity to this perspective – and on my wiser days, when I allowed myself to be real, I longed for integrity – then what lay ahead for me was atheism, or at best agnosticism. I had never been trained either in my teenage years or later to discuss different views of the Bible, respecting those who thought differently. I believed there was one package of core Christian essentials which you accepted in its totality or not at all.

*

I remember standing at the bus stop in Oldtown Road in Inverness at 7.40am one grey morning in the late 1990s wrestling with the implications of God's absence, as all I had ever tried to believe crumbled to dust. Was life on earth simply an exquisite, mocking cosmic absurdity? Was the great story which had come alive for me as I studied the writings of Martyn Lloyd-Jones, the great story in which I had invested so many years, so much energy, simply a delusion?

I hoped that if this conclusion kept pressing upon me so that it became irresistible I would be able to find the courage to be real, the courage to walk away no matter the cost from the faith to which I had clung so hopefully for so long, finally admitting with Edmund Gosse that it had failed me. I was afraid that somehow, to avoid the pain of nothingness, I might manage to bury the doubts and take refuge in the shell of my former faith, persuading myself against all the evidence of my deepest knowing that I still believed.

I questioned the merits of attempting to build a coherent picture of truth about God from a book (the Bible) written over many centuries. Over this period insights into what God might be like had evolved in line with the receptiveness of generations of hearers: they received from God what they were ready to hear. Were statements from different parts of the Bible to be given equal weight or did some, inasmuch as words ever can, provide a more accurate picture of God than others?

My questions about the Bible as I had understood it grew. I was concerned about the violence and vindictiveness of God as portrayed in some passages. I was especially perturbed by the story of Abraham's willingness to sacrifice Isaac, when he would have known that child sacrifice was abhorrent to God. Even if Abraham believed God would provide a substitute, surely, I argued, no father would choose to put their son through such an abusive experience?

I was concerned by the theological sleight of hand which seemed necessary to harmonise some contradictory Biblical passages. I recognised that how you interpreted a passage of Scripture was influenced by your pre-suppositions. Evangelicals might reach one conclusion, other Christians a different, though equally viable one. I felt reluctant to suspend my disbelief at some of the Old Testament supernatural stories which in any other ancient document would be assumed to be mythical.

I was perplexed by the black and white nature of much evangelical teaching on biblical ethics, with no room for the 'greys' which I often saw in everyday life. I was particularly concerned at biblically-based opposition to gay partnerships: how could God not smile on true love and commitment in whatever context it was found? I reflected on the writings on the subject by the American Christian Tony Campolo and Roy Clements, a pastor from Cambridge who resigned from his charge when he 'came out' as gay in 1999 and found myself with a particular passion, (what evangelicals would call 'a burden') to defend and stand with gay people in a Christian context.

*

I continued asking questions about the Bible. On holiday in Carlisle one summer, I picked up a copy of a book by Professor I. Howard Marshall of Aberdeen University's department of Divinity and Religious Studies on *The Inspiration and Authority of Scripture*. This work reminded me that there were scholars who knowing intimately the process by which the documents in the Bible came to be written and assembled, were still able to believe that it was a unique God-given book. Marshall's work discussed the issue of inerrancy which was troubling me and yet I finished it with a sense of dissatisfaction. I had,

I suppose, hoped to be utterly persuaded by the evidence that the Bible had divine origins, but it seemed there could be no absolute proof. Factors such as the coherence of the Bible's overall story and the giving and fulfilment of prophecy suggested a strong likelihood of divine involvement in its composition but being certain of the uniqueness of the book appeared to be a matter of making a faith choice on the basis of personal conviction.

Much as I appreciated the work of Marshall, and of younger evangelical academics such as Alister McGrath and N.T. Wright, I did not want to believe in the uniqueness of the Bible simply because other people did, and told me that I should too, but because I was convinced myself. And at times it seemed that the evidence, and my own experience, failed to convince. I was perplexed by the fact that the Bible was so obviously a human book and grew almost afraid to open it in case I came across something else which undermined, to my way of thinking, the traditional story of its givenness.

*

I read several books by Christians on the subject of doubting hoping they would help resolve my difficulties, but to my dismay they dealt with doubts about specific aspects of the Christian faith (such as 'How can God permit suffering?') and about the individual's personal connection with the faith ('How can I be sure God loves *me*?', 'Can I lose my faith?') and not with the doubts about fundamental tenets of Christian faith with which I was struggling as I asked 'Is God there?' and 'Can I trust the Bible?'

I had read many years before of the crisis of faith over the question of the Bible's uniqueness which Billy Graham had passed through while he was a young man. He described this again in his 2006 volume *The Journey: How to Live by Faith in an Uncertain World*. It was 1949, and he was preparing for a city-wide outreach in Los Angeles. A fellow-evangelist whom Graham 'respected greatly' had begun to express doubts about the Bible urging him 'to change [his] belief that the Bible is the inspired Word of God,' telling him that 'people no longer accept the Bible as being inspired the way you do. Your faith is too simple.'

In a cabin in the mountains east of Los Angeles. Billy Graham revisited the Bible's own teaching about its divine origins. The prophets, he reminded himself, 'clearly believed they were speaking God's Word'. Archaeological discoveries had repeatedly confirmed the Bible's historical accuracy. And Jesus himself clearly regarded the Old Testament as the Word of God. Graham concluded 'Shouldn't I have the same view of Scripture as my Lord?'

Finally he went for a walk in the moonlit forest and kneeling down with his Bible on a tree-stump in front of him he prayed. 'O Lord there are many things in this book I don't understand. There are many problems in it for which I have no solution, but Father, by faith I am going to accept this as Thy Word. From this moment on I am going to trust the Bible as the Word of God.' And he comments 'When I got up from my knees, I sensed God's presence in a way I hadn't felt for months. Not all my questions were answered, but I knew a major spiritual battle had been fought – and won. I never doubted the Bible's divine inspiration again, and immediately my preaching took on a new confidence.'

I wished I could do as Billy Graham had done, allowing my doubts to be washed away by faith. But I simply could not with a good conscience accept the Bible as inerrant as I assumed from his description of his experience that he had done. I attempted to deal with these doubts by repressing them until finally I had to accept that I was quite simply not the uncomplicated evangelical I longed to be.

I turned to books written by Richard Holloway, at that time the Episcopal Bishop of Edinburgh in which on the basis of his own struggles he explored the theme of the believer's doubts. I particularly enjoyed Dancing on the Edge – the title resonated with me, reminding me of my own occasional epiphanies of clarity and joy among the uncertainties when the journey's landscape was instantly transformed and serenity broke through. And yet Holloway's books did not in the end satisfy me either, because it seemed to me that he questioned and questioned until there was nothing left except questions. Was this really the only way to go? Nevertheless I sensed that despite all his questions this man was a true fellow-traveller: the path I was taking was similar to his.

*

That I was able to move forward was due to books I came across which validated my questioning, and showed me that I was not alone and might in fact, be on the right track.

I came across an older book in a second hand bookshop in Inverness, a work by Raymond Abba entitled *The Inspiration and Authority of the Bible*. Abba was clearly a man of deep personal faith and I was glad to have him as a guide. He showed me that it is possible for us to approach the Bible with our critical senses alert. He showed me that it can be seen both as a human book (with the potential for human errors) and also as a unique gift to us from a God who was both actively involved in its composition, and who encounters us as we read it.

Another 'Yes!' moment came when I read an article by Dr Anne Townsend in 1998. It was referenced in *Gone But Not Forgotten* a UK research report into people's reasons for stopping attending church. The article, published in *The Tablet* on 9 November 1996 described Dr Townsend's painful journey away from her evangelical roots. Her words resonated with me and finding her London telephone number in the *Medical Directory* I phoned her partly to express my appreciation of what she had written but largely, I suspect out of a deep need for guidance and direction.

Like the good counsellor she was, Anne didn't tell me what to do but did send copies of three of her books, including *Faith without Pretending*, which I read with avid interest. This volume, and the article in *The Tablet* describe her growing sense that there was a mismatch between the person she tried to be outwardly as she struggled to conform to evangelical expectations and the person she knew she truly was.

She began questioning the evangelical position on the inerrancy of the Bible. She wrestled with traditional views of the goodness of God, particularly in the light of the death in the 1970s of five close friends (3 of them carrying full-term babies) and seven of their pre-school children in a tragic accident near Manoram Hospital in Thailand. She realised that it was not always as easy as she'd thought to make the right choice when facing moral dilemmas. She describes her growing sense of tension between the line she was expected to take as Director of Care Trust and her own personal convictions.

Pressure at work, the stress of this sense of hypocrisy, the drivenness of trying to do more for God than any one individual possibly could combined with a familial depressive tendency and unresolved issues from the past brought her to the point where she felt she had been 'abandoned by the God in whose service [she] had spent [her] life'. She broke down, and attempted suicide.

Faith without pretending describes the slow process of healing through reading, reflecting and seeking help from a counsellor and a spiritual director to the point where she discovered that God accepted her as she was, and that consequently she did not have to be as other people expected her to be. For the first time she was enabled to connect with herself, to experience the joy of being God's one-and-only Anne Townsend. She learned to abandon the defective images of God which had scarred her thinking, and to discover in new ways the God who loves and affirms life, to move beyond symbols of God to the vast reality which they signpost. In the process she found she had to 'defect' from the evangelicalism which had hitherto shaped her thinking. In her *Tablet* article she describes her gratitude at having left 'the spiritual "playpen" in which I barricaded myself away for a large part of my life'. She writes:

I now realise from many people who have contacted me in recent years that I am but one of hundreds of former evangelical Christians from the more fundamentalist end of evangelicalism who have recently accepted the terror, isolation and guilt of moving away from their former religious pathways. Now we journey through new territory – barren deserts and lush, formerly forbidden green pastures. We have discovered in a deeper way how our Shepherd leads us.

Reading Anne Townsend's account of her own release from pain was liberating and affirming: I certainly knew something of 'terror, isolation and guilt'. But I was puzzled, too. She came to realise, she tells us in *Faith Without Pretending* that her faith did not 'depend absolutely' on her being able to accept that the translation of the Bible she owned was 'totally and comprehensively flawless'. 'Ultimately,' she continues 'my faith rested on the massive, rock-solid security of Jesus Christ.'

It was all very well, I thought, for Anne Townsend to suggest that ultimately our foundation as Christians lies in the perfection of Jesus and not in the perfection of the Bible. But how other than through the pages of the Bible do we form an impression of who Jesus is? If you begin to question its unshakable accuracy, how can you be sure that your mental picture of Jesus has any grounding in reality? How can you be sure that your faith is built on something solid? How can you know that the Shepherd whose voice you are following is the authentic God?

*

Another 'Yes!" moment came as I walked round our kitchen excitedly reading Dave Tomlinson's book *The Post Evangelical* which once again confirmed that there were others like me who were uncomfortable with the intimidating certainties of an evangelicalism which seemed to leave no room for those with doubts and questions. 'Far too often,' Tomlinson writes, 'doubt is portrayed simply as an enemy rather than as a potential friend; as something mature Christians should not suffer from, rather than as a vital means of Christians becoming mature.'

Tomlinson believes that the inner journeys of those Christians whom he describes as 'post evangelical' were shaped by the late 20th century cultural shift towards postmodernism. Tomlinson's book was, I think my first introduction to the concept of postmodernism and of all he wrote two things in particular connected with me.

The first was his description of a move away from the modernistic approach to faith which stressed the intellectual grasp of belief and spoke in the scientific language of certainty, towards a view of Christianity which left more space for intuitive responses to God. And the second was his description of 'paradigm shifts'. A 'paradigm' is a way of interpreting reality which is taken for granted by the members of a particular group – their way of seeing. When something happens which can't be explained in terms of this conceptual 'window' they adjust the borders of the paradigm to accommodate the new data. But if they then discover that too many things in their experience can't be comfortably explained by their existing paradigm no matter how much they reconfigure it, they're faced with the disturbing challenge of leaving behind that paradigm and adopting a new take on reality which comfortably accommodates the new observations. The move from one paradigm to another, Tomlinson writes, is often taken as an intuitive leap.

Reading Anne Townsend's work and his confronted me with the inadequacy of the paradigm I was operating with which left no space for my questions about the Bible, and I became uncomfortably, yet joyfully aware that I would need to adopt a new perspective. 'In my view,' says Tomlinson

> *the central issue in this paradigm shift has to do with the nature of truth; it is a move away from the sense of certainty which characterises evangelicalism to an understanding of truth as something more provisional and symbolic, and therefore less able to be put into hard and fast statements.*

The changes which were taking place in me were not as far as I was aware shaped by external cultural values. Rather, they were the result of my examining my own experiences – my longing for a sense of God, my appreciation of the power of intuitive and poetic insight, and my realisation that for me at least, following God didn't always work out in the way my evangelical friends had led me to expect. My heart was more radical than I had realised. I recognised that I had always been a postmodern: only in reading Tomlinson's book did I discover this word which made sense of so much.

*

One morning at work I discovered a volume of extracts from the writings of the Victorian art critic John Ruskin, a discarded library book in a recycling bin in the garage at Central Services Unit. I knew nothing at that point about Ruskin's background, or about his slow retreat from orthodox Christianity, but his description of an episode in his life touched me deeply as I lingered in the chilly cavern reading it.

He describes how, one July Sunday in 1858 while in Turin he attended a Waldensian chapel in the southern suburbs of the city.

> The assembled congregation numbered in all some three or four and twenty, of whom fifteen or sixteen were grey-haired women. Their solitary and clerkless preacher, a somewhat stunted figure in a black coat, with a cracked voice…put his utmost zeal into a consolatory discourse on the wickedness of the wide world, more especially of the plain of Piedmont and the city of Turin, and on the exclusive favour of God, enjoyed by the between nineteen and twenty-four elect members of his congregation….

Ruskin then walked back into Turin 'neither cheered nor greatly alarmed by this doctrine,' and walked into an art gallery 'where Paul Veronese's *Solomon and the Queen of Sheba* glowed in full afternoon light'.

The gallery windows being open, there came in with the warm air, floating swells and falls of military music, from the courtyard before the palace, which seemed to me more devotional, in their perfect art, tune and discipline, than anything I remembered of evangelical hymns. And as the perfect colour and sound gradually asserted their power on me, they seemed finally to fasten in me the old article of Jewish faith, that things done delightfully and rightly, were always done by the help and in the Spirit of God.

For Ruskin, this was a moment of insight, in which his reflections 'through many years' were confirmed and brought to a conclusion. 'There was no sudden conversion possible to me,' he writes, 'either by preacher, picture, or dulcimer. But that day, my evangelical beliefs were put away, to be debated of no more.'

Reading Ruskin's words was another 'Yes!' moment – a moment when deep, half-acknowledged thoughts were both surfaced and validated. They confirmed my suspicion that God was much bigger than I had thought, that God was too colourful to be confined, that God was present and gloriously alive throughout the vibrant creation.

TWENTY-FOUR

FATHERING

The years after the girls were born were intensely busy. For much of the girls' childhood Lorna was working five-hour evening shifts at a nearby care home, and so it was my privilege to supervise tea and bath-time; story and bed; and in later years homework, the battlefield of piano practice. Vivid recollections kaleidoscope:

I'm sitting on the sofa giving Bethany the bottle Lorna has left for her while Rebecca is stretched out on the floor watching *Postman Pat*. Sleepily, I drift in and out of consciousness as baby lips suck vigorously. I'm singing silly songs in the bathroom, and playing the mildly disgusting 'Toe game' which involves me pretending to eat toes every time they appear above the bubbles for a microsecond. I'm reading *Cowboy baby* again, and again, and yet again, assuming a pseudo-Texan drawl.

I'm giving my daughter a hug, and become aware that our contact is being unnecessarily prolonged through my own need of comfort. I edge away gently. Bethany is in our bed on Sunday mornings at 9am while Lorna is showering. 'Scratch my back,' she demands. When my fingers relax as I drift back to sleep, the same words draw me back to consciousness.

The house was always full of children – our two, kids from the neighbourhood, and from the church we were now attending.

I was constantly aware of the privilege of fatherhood, and the privilege too of being entrusted by our friends with their children. To me, single for so long and watching families from the outside it was a wonderful thing, a precious gift I had feared would never be given.

*

More of those memories:

Dad taxi trips to and from Brownies, Good News Club, friends' houses. School runs. Sleepovers. 'Can't you keep the noise down! It's *one o'clock!*' Delivering home at midnight a child whose overnight visit with us was terminally disrupted by homesickness.

'What's the birds' favourite TV programme?' Answer: 'The feather forecast.' This amused our daughters for days and days long after repeating it to them grew tiresome.

The cinema. *Finding Nemo, Monsters Inc., Winnie the Pooh, Shrek.* Later, *Harry Potter.* Popcorn. Singing in the back of the car. Driving my daughter and another child round the block in their night clothes just for fun; driving into town the evening the Christmas lights were turned on so that the girls could gawp at reindeer and Santa Clauses and elves and the Christmas Tree at the Town House and everyday reality transformed, bathed in colour.

Pushing the girls repeatedly on the roundabout on summer evenings – we're at the playground which, with a nod to the equipment it contains, we have dubbed 'The Twirly Park'. I'm standing outside Lochardil Primary School on a winter's night, watching the child I have just dropped off run across the playground, the flashing lights on her trainer heels punctuating the darkness with complex patterns expressing energy, joy, expectation, beauty. I'm sitting in the car on a summer afternoon outside the school watching the girls and their friends familiarizing themselves with the trunk and branches of the friendly tree which has challenged generations of Lochardil pupils.

Stopping beside the River Ness one night and taking the two girls at their request across the bridge to the deserted Ness Islands where they stand in darkness as the waters, laced with pulsing strands of brightness from reflected street lights, run black and deep. Travelling up to Culloden Battlefield in bed-time darkness and listening in the eerie stillness for the march of spectral soldiers; stopping in a layby on the way home to watch the stars and the lights of Inverness and the Kessock Bridge spanning a languid Moray Firth. Collecting Bethany from piano lessons and slinging her bike into the back of my mother's old car which we named Wendy. We'd put an apple core on the roof when I was driving Bethany and a friend to Inverness Harriers, seeing how far we could get down Stratherrick Road before it blew off in the slipstream.

At Bught Park on November 5th. Walking down in our wellies; waiting in turn to cross the bridges linking the Ness Islands in small groups so that the bridge structures, unaccustomed to such sustained traffic, would not be put under undue pressure. The blazing pile of wood; the military-grade thunder of fireworks.

I know that at times I have been an over-indulgent father. But why should I curtail the girls' joy when, for example, they were playing with plastic toys and lashings of mud in the garden as the summer sun sank lower? After they were in bed could I not hose everything clean and put it back in the shed? When adulthood was so testing and unpredictable, why should they lose a second of childhood's joy simply to make an evening easier for me? And it was no hard choice, for their joy enriched me.

I have always equated fatherhood with 'service' defined not as doing for our daughters what they should properly be doing for themselves (though at times I have been guilty of this – 'What did your last servant die of?'; 'He didn't die, dad.') but as walking with them and facilitating at some personal cost their journey to adulthood.

I determined insofar as was consistent with their growing maturity to be real and vulnerable with the girls, seeking not to pretend, not to hide. Bethany complains that this policy of honesty led me to reveal to her at rather too early and age the truth about Santa Claus.

By half-past nine the girls would be in bed and on the cusp of sleep (though I probably had had a struggle with Bethany who craved attention and devised 'the get-away game' as a means of forcibly retaining my presence beside her bed). I'd put on a CD of Pachelbel, Bach and Albinoni, and chill. Soon Lorna would be home.

I never, never lost sight of the privilege of being a father.

*

A woodpigeon coo'd as I parked the car opposite the Library Support Unit as it was now called one Saturday morning. It was a change from the usual avian species frequenting that part of town, not far from the harbour. Each lamppost normally enthroned a proud gull; no car was unmarked at the end of a shift. I had been known to mutter under my breath 'Bloody shitty seagulls!'

In my spirit the gentle call of the pigeon had been forever associated with sadness. I would be staying in a rural hotel with my parents, and hearing this birdsong in the woods, symbolic of a peace and harmoniousness to which I was a stranger, the sadness would deepen.

But this particular day, I was aware only of the loveliness of its tone. Something deep within me called back.

*

The best of my fathering reflects what I saw in my own father's approach. But I had no desire to impose expectations on Rebecca and Bethany as I felt my parents had done in my own childhood. I made it clear, always, that I would be disappointed if they did not persevere, seeking to fulfil their potential, choosing joy. I told them I wanted to let them discover the unique people they are, playing to their strengths and running with the energies which awaken them. I am convinced that a key element of good parenting is getting to know the people who have been entrusted to our care as they get to know themselves, and helping them through challenge and reflection to progress on their journey in self-knowing.

I also reacted to my parent's style of child-rearing in my strong disinclination to put pressure on Rebecca and Bethany to choose Christian faith. As they grew up, they were aware that Lorna and I were believers; we discussed faith with them from time to time. They accompanied us to church and had plenty of fun, but also regrettably saw some of the tensions which can arise when Christians get it wrong. Lorna and I, with all our imperfections, sought to model faith, grace, love and forgiveness to them. We aimed to show them in age-appropriate ways that it's OK to disagree with other Christians, OK to have doubts and questions. I sought to live before them a life of honest faith leaving them free to make their own choices and welcoming every sign of love and self-giving in them.

*

One Tuesday afternoon in September 2001 I was in the hall of Holm Primary School beneath the big bow window overlooking the slopes of Craig Dunain, listening to Stephen Fischbacher and his Fischy Music colleague Suzanne Adams. I had arranged this gifted Christian musician's visit to Inverness. His background like mine had been in Brethrenism. I loved his powerful emotionally honest songs encouraging children's resilience. Stephen's music palpably brought healing to vulnerable young people: he implicitly acknowledged that God is present in every movement of love regardless of the specific beliefs of those through whom it comes.

'You are a star!' The Fischy team led Primary 5 pupils though a series of imaginative songs most of them not specifically Christian emphasising the specialness, the uniqueness of each child. No room here for the grim curse of original sin. 'You are a star, just the way you are!'

We discovered soon afterwards that as we laughed and sang, on the other side of the Atlantic passenger jets were remorselessly targeted at the World Trade Centre.

*

In the following days Stephen and Suzanne were able to bring some peace to children traumatised by images of destruction, encouraging them to reflect on their own personal experiences of cruelty.

You can either 'build up one another,' they reminded their audience, 'build up your sisters and brothers' (here you used your fists to represent building a wall, fist upon fist upon fist) or else you can 'tear down' those around you (you grabbed an imaginary sheet of wallpaper above your head with both hands and ripped it to the ground).

Soon in the playground groups of children were building walls of fists and singing.

'Build up one another.'

*

The song which meant most to me that week was *When People are Cruel*. To the tune *Streets of Laredo*, its theme is the life, death and resurrection of Jesus who faced 'the bullies of Calvary'. Yet he was not daunted because 'he knew where he came from and where he was going'.

The song's implication is that it is precisely because Jesus knew his origin and his destiny that we too may know where we are going and so remain undaunted.

When people are cruel it makes all the difference
To know where you're going and where you've come from

I found this of great comfort in those chaotic days. I was beginning to understand more fully where I had come from; to discern more clearly my possible futures. But knowing where you have come from and where you are going is part of a more fundamental knowing – knowing your identity, knowing who you are.

*

My boss, the Principal Libraries Officer was promoted. I applied for the vacant post and was called for interview along with other candidates, one of whom was also internal.

I researched widely and familiarised myself with the current national library policy documents. The job paid better so I felt duty-bound as a family man to apply and tried to stir up some enthusiasm. But I was denying my deepest insights which would have reminded me that managing staff and change was not one of my strengths, and that I was not in fact passionate about the future of libraries. I now knew in my deep self that Information Technology was my professional calling. But I persuaded myself that faced with the challenge I could grow into the vacant post and do the job.

I walked downstairs from the interview room. The sun cast through a window bright angled squares of light on the yellow emulsioned wall. I met a friend in the corridor and talked, buoyantly.

But back at the office, there was no phone call.

Much later my colleague who had been offered and had accepted the post, arrived. Her face announced the news before her lips opened.

'Congratulations,' I said.

I was wounded yet at the same time deeply relieved.

*

We were at the Braehead Centre in Glasgow with friends from Inverness. I accompanied Bethany and her mate Sally who wanted to explore the shows out the back. They chose to go for a ride in a smallish 'big wheel', paid their money and got on board. But once the wheel picked up speed they were seriously frightened: I could see them shouting and what I should have done was to approach the operator and insist that he stop the ride. But I was reluctant to confront, to intervene. 'It will stop soon,' I told myself, and probably shouted out to them too. Eventually it did, of course. Other than a few bruises they suffered no ill-effects and seemed to bear me no ill-will.

But I knew I had let them down and suspected they knew it too.

*

9th July 2005. I was sitting in bright sunshine in the garden. I was due to preach the next day, and I wondered what I could possibly say in the light of the events in London two days before. 52 people were killed and over 700 injured in terrorist attacks. What could stand against the destructive power of hatred and explosives, lethally combined?

And then I realised what my theme should be. I would speak about another explosion, an explosion which changes the world, the eruption of love which had as its epicentre a hill outside Jerusalem. From there love reverberates, rippling across the world and down through history losing in the process none of its potency, healing and redemptive power.

This idea came with a sense of 'givenness'.

'Thank you, Father!'

*

I locked the empty car in the Glasgow airport car-park and turned away.

'The next time I see you we'll be safely back,' I said yearningly.

The previous night in our grossly over-heated hotel room I'd struggled restlessly to sleep, remembering a recent winter morning when I was in a small plane at Inverness airport. It was still dark outside; we'd left the stand, but the pilot was waiting for clearance to take off. The cabin was dimly lit and my fellow-passengers silent. In the eerie stillness I began to panic – first a knot in my stomach, then a cold tension spreading throughout my body as I struggled to keep my mind calm and focused. I knew that were it not for the physical effects of the antidepressant my heart would be racing uncontrollably.

The memory of this kept me awake that night at the Glasgow Airport hotel. Again I tried to focus my mind, imagining arriving safely with the family at Palma and walking off the plane into the warmth of Mallorca with a sense of jubilation tempered only by thoughts of the return flight in a fortnight. I reminded myself that throughout the flight God would be with me.

*

When we checked in for our flight. Lorna and the girls were assigned three seats together but I was in the row in front in the corridor seat.

When we were on the plane, the woman next to me (her name was Rachel, she said) offered her friend and me a barley sugar. For a while, as we waited to take off, she read a book. But then she turned to me. 'Are you apprehensive about flying?' she asked.

I explained about my anxiety and Rachel confessed in turn that she had found herself unable to face boarding the last two times she had booked flights. On both occasions, she had returned home sadly from the airport. In the meantime, she continued, she had been on a British Airways 'Fear of flying' course, which covered the structure of aircraft, the different noises made by the engines in flight, and strategies for coping with fear. It concluded with a short flight over the English Channel. After all that, she was ready to try again.

*

Rachel turned over the book in her lap to continue reading, and I saw it was by Joyce Meyer who at the time was one of Lorna's favourite Christian authors. After we were airborne and the Clyde Estuary was falling away beneath us, Rachel and I chatted about Meyer's books, and about the churches we belonged to. And then I told her about my thought the previous night that God would be with me on the flight.

'Do you know,' she said, 'the very first words I saw when I opened this book this morning were from the Bible: 'Do not be anxious about anything.'

*

When Rachel was away from her seat her friend turned to me 'Thanks for what you've done for Rachel today.'

But it seemed to me that the God we both believed was with us, demonstrating that the divine presence makes a real practical difference both in and beyond the coping strategies. God had entrusted Rachel and me to one another as traveling companions.

I know I saw our conversation as a gift from God. Seven miles high, my spirit was awash with gratitude.

After three hours the Boeing 757 touched down on the runway at Palma. Rachel turned to me and smiled. 'We're alive!' she said.

*

Standing patiently in a winding queue at Border's Bookshop at the Inverness Retail Park. The next Harry Potter book is being unveiled at midnight and hundreds of children and adults are waiting to get their hands on a copy. Rebecca turns immediately to the final page to see how the story ends.

325

We were on Majorca when the final Harry Potter film was released. Rebecca and I discovered that there was an English language showing at a multiplex in Palma. On release day we got the bus along the coast to the city and took a taxi to the cinema which was off the normal tourist route. None of the staff knew English. 'Let's just go dad,' Rebecca said, probably embarrassed by my attempts to communicate. But someone in the queue knew enough English to help us and we secured tickets. With deep satisfaction, we sat outside drinking Coke until showtime.

*

One of our best family holidays was in 2005 when we spent a summer fortnight in our new Vango tent on the Glororum Caravan Park at Bamburgh in Northumbria. We explored Alnwick Castle and Gardens, including the magical tree house, 'window-shopped till we dropped' at Newcastle's Metro Centre, crossed the causeway to Lindisfarne. I teased the girls about the Grey Starling for which Bamburgh was famous.

It was our first and only family tent holiday and even though the weather was coolish something about the experience stilled and calmed me, as we sat reading by gas lamplight while dusk gathered, and later lay in our sleeping bags listening to the laughter and chat of neighbouring campers slowly dying out as they too drifted off to bed.

Regularly sometime after midnight our younger daughter Bethany who was 9 would need to go to the loo. She would reach a hand urgently through the canvas door of the pod where Lorna and I were sleeping and shake my shoulder or my head and ask me to accompany her to the toilet block. I'd drag myself out of the sleeping bag, find my shoes and anorak in the darkness and unzip the tent.

Bethany and I would make our way together along the sparingly-lit tarmac. As night followed night she got into the habit when she needed to waken me of hissing 'Toilet man!'

For some reason it seemed, (and this is not simply the voice of nostalgia's sad sweetness) that these brief nightly trips were among the most precious moments of parenthood. I savoured every second of them. Hand in hand, we'd walk in sleepy silence through the small-hours chill in the hush that wrapped the campsite in sleep. We could hear the roar of waves breaking on the distant shingle and see the warmly-floodlit façade of Bamburgh Castle across the fields. I would nip into the Gents, and then wait outside the toilet block while my daughter did her business, and then we'd go back to the tent. Bethany and her dad. Together, and it seemed to me profoundly at one.

We'd climb back into our sleeping bags on wobbly inflatable mattresses. Silence. Until the next time.

'Toilet man!'

TWENTY-FIVE

THE FRAGILE SAPLING

A sunny afternoon at Little Garve in Ross-shire. The four of us with the Donald family are sitting on the grassy bank above a dark, rocky pool into which the Black Water dives just below General Caulfield's Bridge. The kids (our two, and Beth and Steve Donald) splash, dive and swim (when they aren't trying to sneak illicit photos of Lorna changing behind a bush).

Max and I sit side by side, saying little. Striving as always for purpose I'm holding a notebook in which I'm drafting a press-release to mark the opening of our new church building.

*

Lorna and I had joined Holm Evangelical Church in Inverness in 1999. Before this I visited their new pastor, Max – the same Max Donald who had offered me a bed for the night as a student had I been prepared to incur parental ire by attending William Brooks's party. I outlined as best as I could the theological issues which were troubling me and explained my uncertainty as to whether someone with as many questions as I had would be welcomed as a member of the church.

Max assured me that people with questions were welcome. He did not however mention that the church had a Statement of Faith which members were expected to affirm.

Max and his wife Ruth had five children – three older sons, and Beth and Steve who were approximately the same age as our daughters. We drew close to the Donald family. Our families visited one another often. I remember Sunday lunches at Jimmy Chung's Chinese Buffet; driving with Max in a futile search for a chip shop in Gairloch after we'd spent an idyllic day at the beach; standing side-by-side with him around the civic bonfire, each of us with a personal Bethany perched happily on our shoulders. The Donalds and Dempster spent Boxing Day together annually: a meal, games, laughter, TV – though underneath it all ran the throb of my seasonal sadness. In 2004 we watched, shocked at the first images of the tsunami in South East Asia relentlessly engulfing the shoreline.

*

Despite what I thought I had learned about over-busyness in churches, I was soon immersed in activity once again with multiple roles as well as writing the weekly newspaper column and occasionally contributing to the *Christian Herald* magazine. I preached frequently, served on a couple of church committees, produced a weekly newsletter and helped with church holiday clubs. Lorna was active too – she found her involvement in the church liberating as her gifts were recognised and used and she was encouraged on her own faith journey.

In retrospect, it was all too much. Those years brought some joy but it was often counterpointed by a song in a minor key. The GP and I experimented with varying dosages of the antidepressant.

When Max strongly recommended to the church an influential book by American pastor Rick Warren, *The Purpose-Driven Life*. I recoiled from the work on account of its title alone. Pressurised as I knew my life was I longed for a way of living which was spontaneous and peaceful and not in any sense 'driven', a way of living where it was enough simply to 'be' with no pressure to achieve.

*

For me church was not in general a good experience. Other than when I was preaching or leading there was little sense of ideas and images coming to me with a sense of 'givenness' as had been the case at the Celt Street morning meetings. It perplexed me that still almost the only church services at which I had any sense of encounter with God were those in which I myself was involved. And it is salutary to listen to a recording of a service I chaired. My long prayer – which I'm sure at the time I felt flowed freely from somewhere deep – seems in retrospect rambling and self-indulgent.

Perhaps because of the introversion which I have come to recognise and to accept, I have never been able to enter into the singing of hymns and worship songs. Generally these leave me unmoved though occasionally a phrase will burn with meaning. Most people seem to find shared song a helpful way of reflecting on and engaging with God, but to me worship songs seem a distraction from the quiet discipline of focussing on the spiritual. The noise of voices and instruments and other people's movements make it impossible for me to home in on the still centre where I believe God speaks. Unable to lose myself in a song and express worship physically I wait patiently until the singing is over. For years, I made a half-hearted attempt at participating, appearing to conform, but I concluded that it was more honest simply to remain silent.

There's something too about the physicality of being at a service – or indeed any kind of public event – which distances me from participation in what is taking place. I am always the observer. I rarely go to classical concerts but can lose myself in music when I am at home in a safe space. Relaxed and comfortable in the kitchen while drying dishes I often improvise crazy songs at the top of my voice and when the texture of a piece of music on Classic fm moves me my arms instinctively reach heavenwards like those of the most enthusiastic charismatic worshipper, saying 'Yes!' to beauty and loveliness and the creative Spirit.

Very very occasionally during a service at church I was aware that something was happening: a stillness descended and there was a faint sense of what I interpreted as the numinous, an intuition that God was present and engaging with other people's lives if not perhaps with mine.

*

One of the most electrifying performances I have ever watched on television was of Valery Gergiev performing the *Pathétique Symphony* with the orchestra of the Mariinsky Theatre. His engagement with the piece was total and I felt Tchaikovsky's pain in what I read as an autobiographical statement – a sensitive, enormously gifted man alienated because of his homosexuality. The rich theme of the final movement, blossoming then struggling to rise again, struggling to sing, yet plunging ever downwards in a terrible poignant beauty until only silence remains. At the conclusion, Gergiev's expressive fingers remain motionless for what seems an age and the silence seems as much part of the music as the notes which preceded it. And then slowly he relaxes. I still feel the pain of this piece but I welcome it now as an unflinching take on humanity's anguish.

*

My questions about the Bible remained unresolved despite my theological reading and coloured my responses to Max's earnest sermons.

Max spoke about God's care for the weak, widows, children. I wrote in the Journal I was now keeping daily:

How does that square with the God who calls for the slaughter of all the inhabitants of Canaanite cities?

On another occasion I agonised:

Max, having preached about Zechariah being temporarily struck dumb because he expressed uncertainty about whether his aged wife would fall pregnant as the angel promised, mentioned that leaders should keep doubts to themselves. But if God acts like that in response to our understandable desire for authentication, where does that leave me? I feel sad, struggling, untouched.

Again, Max preached on 'Behold I set before you an open door,' and applied it exclusively to evangelism. I wrote:

It occurred to me that the whole day is full of open doors – of opportunities to do good, and do your work well, and help and encourage. I don't see that these open doors are any less from God than doors for evangelism. I guess evangelical churches can so emphasise evangelism that they neglect the God who inhabits the ordinary.

I was concerned about my own continuing lack of passion for the evangelistic agenda. I could understand, given orthodox Christian beliefs, the logic in seeking to 'save souls' but I still lacked the passion and confidence which we were told should drive evangelicals to communicate their faith in a challenging and inviting way. I suspected all good Christians should have this passion but it always eluded me and from its absence I drew the logical conclusion.

On yet another occasion Max preached on the lack of faith shown by the majority of the spies sent by Moses to report on conditions in Canaan: as a result of their negativism, the Children of Israel were condemned to wander in the desert for a further 40 years. I responded:

Felt that if I had more faith, I would be out of the desert and into the promised land. The 'promised land' type of Christian in Max's terms is 'on fire for Jesus,' knows setbacks and struggles, but is victorious. I get this picture of a constantly joyous achiever. Yet this model of Christianity Max has in mind – is that the only model? After all, in Christian life there is desert in the promised land. And aren't my glimpses of glory, the daily challenge to be gracious and loving, aren't these expressions of Christian reality as much as seeing folk turning to Christ? If my kind of Christianity is valid, why didn't Max qualify what he said this morning?

*

As the notes of the last worship song died away I would feel a sense of dejection and failure: once again I had been unable to engage with God during the service. Afterwards over coffee I would go up to people and force myself to talk to them, asking God to take my readiness to engage with them as an expression of the love and gratitude to God which I knew was appropriate and yet could neither feel nor demonstrate in any other way. And sometimes through these encounters and the responses of those I spoke to there came a wavering sense that I was valuable and loved.

*

In the mid-2000s Max had a deep experience of the reality of God which revitalised his ministry and gave him a new sense of divine presence in his life. We sat one day over lunch at Dow's Diner: we often met for lunch but I never felt that one-to-one we were completely open, completely at home with one another.

Max told me he prayed and trusted that I too would soon experience God's touch in a deeper way. Torn as I was between on the one hand a sense that I had to follow my own instinctive journey into uncertain territory where the familiar old evangelical landmarks were growing hazy, and on the other a deep longing to belong, to suspend my uncertainty and unbelief, to let the warmth of unquestioning evangelicalism enfold me, I wondered what a deeper encounter with God might bring. Would it draw me forward into new pathways or enable me to live comfortably with the old certainties?

*

Max asked me if I'd be willing to join a Leadership Support Team (LST) which was being formed to give help and backing to the elders. I should have declined both because of my conviction while at Airdrie that church leadership was simply not my calling, and also because I could not honestly sign up to the church's Statement of Faith of which I was now aware and which in briefly summarising the church's view of the Bible used the word 'inerrant', a term with which I was growing increasingly concerned.

'You're not a *liberal*, are you?' Max asked when I explained this to him.

'No of course not!' I replied, the speed of my response an attempt to bury my own uncertainty as much as to reassure Max. I was surprised that he had raised this question of 'liberalism' given that I had been up-front about my questioning attitude before joining the church. It now seemed to me that in Max's mind there was a limit as to which questions could be pursued, and to what extent.

But my quick reply was dishonest. I knew in a deepest self which at that stage was mostly beyond my reach that I was in fact well on the way to liberalism – not a dry, unenchanted liberalism certainly, but one imbued with Spirit

As I considered his invitation to join the Team, Max gave me some books to read on the subject of inerrancy. These simply confirmed in my mind that this doctrine was a mammoth intellectual construct based on the premise that if God inspires something then it must be perfect. I think this is a flawed premise and on this ground alone I should in honesty have declined to join. However wanting to be helpful, glad to be needed and allowing myself to be persuaded that I could in good conscience interpret 'inerrancy' as 'trustworthiness' I agreed. It was a bad mistake.

*

I drove to LST meetings with a heavy heart conscious of the gulf stretching between me and my fellow leaders. I told myself and the others that if I had any role in the group it was as a representative of those in the church who felt 'on the edge' as I did, emotionally, spiritually and psychologically. I felt I had nothing to contribute to the discussions, no strong ideas about how the church should develop. It was comforting to take minutes of meetings thereby making, I felt, at least some contribution.

I decided to step down from leadership at the same time as an elders' election at which Lorna was appointed as the church's first woman elder. I was impressed by the speed with which she adapted to her new role, a task for which her personality and previous experience had prepared her. She had strong convictions about the church's direction of travel and saw what changes must be made to plot that course. Walking free from leadership was a great relief to me and I knew it was the right decision and yet perversely I also felt wounded and sidelined.

*

Subsequently here were serious disagreements in our church. Some of us felt that the leadership was not being sufficiently supportive of Max at a difficult time in his life. Lorna resigned as an elder. Ultimately Max and about thirty others left the church, and in 2009 formed a new congregation, Grace Community Church which met in a local school. I found myself once again thrust into leadership. 'Of necessity,' I told myself.

*

I was in an all-day meeting about the future of the new church dutifully taking the minutes. I participated little in the discussion, conscious as ever of distance from evangelical language and the evangelical agenda, burdened by a dull heaviness.

What I was doing, I told myself, was 'helping my friends do church'. Even if I could not buy into their language and agendas I could surely use what skills I possessed to help them.

Despite this I often led and preached at Grace sincerely and with a sense of 'givenness' about the love of God. I suspect that what I was reacting to so negatively at that meeting was not the evangelical agenda as such but the past events of which it forever reminded me.

*

I parked the car in Burn Road, and stood in the warm summer sunshine looking along the hedge-lined drive. We had a church leadership meeting that evening: I would be taking the minutes as usual. I heard children playing, a dog barking. My eyes lingered on the beauty of the oak tree, the detailed texture of its leaves. Always pushing the buggy uphill, Always the pusher, never the pushee. My deep self cried for freedom.

And then reluctantly I walked up to the front door and rang the bell.

Love welcomed me.

But when I finally emerged night had fallen.

*

In the late afternoon of that day at Little Garve after we'd eaten our picnic we all crossed General Caulfield's Bridge and took a short walk through the trees. We passed a burn, gurgling its way down to the river.

The water was low, and on a minute island of rock and earth a sapling, not yet twenty centimetres in height, was growing optimistically.

I paused, struck by its vulnerability and hope.

Little does it know I reflected sadly that winter will come, the torrent will engulf it.

'Come on, John!' Max called.

I turned, and hurried after him.

TWENTY-SIX

SITTING ON THE FENCE

Another chapter more about ideas than stories. But perhaps the ideas are the story.

During these years as I recorded daily in my Journal it seemed to me that I *was 'endlessly sitting on the fence'. 'See, I go round in circles.' 'Am I trying to be in two camps at once?'* Where, I wondered, was my theological home? And there was another question: *'Sometimes I wonder which is the real me – the neurotic self who appears in these pages, his neurosis feeding off religious beliefs and fears, or the much more together self most people see.'* I wrote often of *'the underlay of sadness,'* on one occasion noting that *'I could give up the struggle and grow old'.* At times, God seemed absent and I'd often blame myself for driving God away, while occasionally wondering more insightfully whether *'In all this am I loading the blame on myself for not seeking earnestly enough rather than on him for not being there?'*

There were more positive experiences, the memory of which sustained me through the hard days when bleakness closed in: *'A sense of joy today in being me.' 'Knelt after breakfast, opened myself up to God; healing grace. Joy.' 'It was a real moment of serendipitous peace – unplanned and joyful.' 'A sense that for all my inner confusion, God loves me.' 'I am deeply blessed. Joy of God's presence.'*

The memory of these days when joy was a gift effortlessly received and not something to be striven for, allowed me on other occasions to 'choose joy' once again. Day after day the first words in my Journal recorded that it had been *a choosing joy day*. The *more together self most people see* was not a thin, hypocritical veil but a deep resolve to live as though I were still experiencing the joy, and there was a peace in so living even though existential uncertainty still churned somewhere deep down.

The neurotic angst recorded in these Journal entries is not unique to the 2000s, but rather colours my adult life as a whole. It is simply that from October 2001 onwards the daily vicissitudes were recorded, and are hence retrievable.

*

Those fundamental issues about the Bible which made me question Max's sermons remained, and found it increasingly difficult to square the evangelical doctrine of Scripture with what I found in its pages. I read more 'progressive' books as I had done in the 1990s (though the word I used then was 'liberal') and tasted freedom and joy and yet I found it difficult most of the time to acknowledge that this questioning, freedom-seeking self was my true self.

I had discovered other books which confirmed and validated the 'Yes' moments I'd experienced previously. Alan Jamieson's *A Churchless Faith*, subtitled *Faith Journeys Beyond the Churches*, was originally published in New Zealand in 2000 and released in the UK in 2002. This volume was the outcome of a research project exploring the views of people who had left evangelical, Pentecostal and charismatic churches not because they had abandoned their faith but because they were questioning the relevance to their own lives of the churches they had been attending.

I was startled and encouraged by the extent to which some of these people's journeys mirrored my own – those who having hitherto accepted all that was taught in their churches now found themselves overflowing with questions. Jamieson describes them as spiritual pilgrims. In the course of their pilgrimage they feel constrained first of all to deconstruct their previous convictions ('I used to believe this, but I am not sure that I now do so.') and then to reconstruct a faith which is authentic and personal, validated by their experiences, so that they can move on, comfortable with their new paradigm. In fact, what they believe at the end of this process may be similar or even identical to what they believed at its start, but now their beliefs spring from deep personal conviction and are no longer simply a giving of assent to what they have been told and expected to believe.

I found particularly encouraging Alan Jamieson's discussion of the stages of spiritual growth first proposed by James Fowler in his book *Stages of Faith – the Psychology of Human Development and the Quest for Meaning*. Although Dave Tomlinson had introduced me (joyously) to the 'paradigm shift' concept I think in my everyday believing I still held that though Christian maturity might deepen with the passage of time this deepening was the result of interpreting reality through a faith-window defined by an unchanging framework of Truth. Jamieson's book confirmed my suspicion that this was not necessarily the case. The window might reconfigure, paradigms shift, though no stage of development is to be seen as inherently 'better' than another.

This spiritual journey is not, Jamieson insists, a 'journey away from pain, doubt and confusion, but the journey through struggle to a new appreciation of God at work'. It leads to 'a phase rich in the mysteries and presence of God, where teaching and Scripture give, and the reality of life interprets'.

This last phrase in particular impressed me. I had always been taught that as a Christian you should interpret your own inner experience and the events of your life in the light of the teaching of Scripture, and that any resistance to that teaching was sinful. Indeed I had frequently been blessed by my 'choosing joy' mantra, believing that what the Bible said was true of me as a Christian whether or not I felt the reality of it at that particular moment. Jamieson's words were helpful because they gave me permission to ask questions, to wrestle with what the Bible seemed to be teaching when it was at variance with what I saw around me in the world and not to accept unquestioningly the answers I was given by tradition and people of influence. Rather I could seek to arrive at answers I myself had tested and proved.

My reluctant embrace of an irresistible call to journeying was further authenticated by Brian Maclaren's *A new kind of Christian*, a fictionalised description of a Christian pastor asking many of the same questions as those which troubled me written by one of the leaders of the Emergent Church movement in the United States.

*

And yet it was hard for me to accept that the journey was valid one. My upbringing and my church background screamed out 'Beware of questioning and unbelief'.

I felt I was a hypocrite – '*outwardly evangelical, inwardly hoping my spirit will catch up with the outward image*.' '*Still I waver – evangelicalism or liberalism, or the no-man's land of belonging nowhere.*' '*Perhaps I need to decide once and for all if I am an evangelical or not.*'

I was frustrated that my theological thinking and experience did not develop in a linear way – rather as I alternated between the evangelical package of beliefs and the more open, questioning, liberal approach the cycle repeated endlessly, driven by neurotic anxiety.

*

I knew very few people who modelled the questioning Christianity I felt at home with, the 'hermeneutic of suspicion'. My anxiety made it harder for me to trust myself. I distrusted my opinions and was convinced at times that God felt even more negatively about me than

I did about myself. I was desperate to mould my spirit into a form I believed God and others would cherish.

And then a sermon or an evangelical book would deliver both what seemed to be a stronger joy and a rebuke for what I saw as my waywardness and the cycle turned yet again. Afraid of leaving the security of what I was told was certain, afraid too of rejection by God and by those around me, I once again drew back from the precipice. '*I feel more in the evangelical camp.*' '*Today, I was blessed, a sense of the attractiveness of clear, Bible-centred belief.*'

I wrote over-optimistically on one occasion:

I have a sense that I have been to the edge and am on the way back, embracing the many good things in evangelicalism while retaining the freedom to think for myself which I have appreciated.

In early 2004, I was significantly encouraged by evangelical leader Michael Green's autobiography *Adventure of Faith*:

I feel a pull in two ways. I've been blessed by drawing back to evangelical thinking in a way that I was never blessed by 'stepping out of the playpen,' in the words of Anne Townsend. She was blessed by stepping beyond evangelicalism. Yet the words and experience of Michael Green have been the means of drawing me into what I believe is closeness to God. It feels (intermittently) delicious. Though intermittent, it's more sustained than anything I've known in recent years. I plan to get up at 6am to spend time seeking. But where does that leave Anne T? Was she wrong? And how do I plan to face up now to problems in the Bible? What I plan to do is to read the Bible and seek to listen to God in it, and see what happens.

But in time as before the questions would grow too powerful to be contained within the garden of 'sound theology', my reading would widen and I would again turn my back on the centre. Thus, some weeks after writing about the impact on me of Michael Green's book, I noted over a few days *'I'm drifting away from evangelical certainty and comfort'*. *'I have lost hold on the evangelical certainty which filled me recently. Don't know whether to say "if Michael Green believes, so do I."' 'I guess I need when I'm like this not to give up, but to draw confidence from other people's certainties.' 'It's just that "I have returned to questioning"* – the tag they apply to folk in one of the strict Jewish communities who leave behind the *certainty of community structure.' 'But I want my own certainties.'*

'Wonder if I am a blind rebel. Should I just accept [conservative] views, or would this just be papering over the cracks of cognitive dissonance,' I wrote. *'"How long do you halt between two opinions?" I want to love God, live for him, serve him. And the evangelical voice in me says "But on whose terms?"'*

'I don't want to make a shipwreck of my faith,' I agonised, *'but I am in danger of so doing. I don't want to close my mind to objections and embrace the evangelical view while blinding myself to the problems with it.'*

What confused me was that both liberalism and the retreat to evangelicalism brought joy. On the few occasions when somebody embraced me in unconditional positive regard, I flourished, feeling joy regardless of my position at the time on the theological spectrum. What was the truest joy, the most consistent, the most authentically founded?

There were moments of clarity: *'Feeling content in belief in God, while having moved beyond strict evangelicalism.'* Times of peace too, and new confidence in my 'complicated evangelical' position: *'I wonder if in "coming away from the edge" [withdrawing to a more conservative position] I've been denying myself as I am. Perhaps I'm meant to live – even dance, in [Richard] Holloway's phrase "on the edge."'*

*

One Christmas Eve, as I watched our elder daughter, I reflected *'In choosing faith, choosing joy, I hope I'm not being like a little girl leaving refreshments for a Santa she knows in her heart won't come'.*

For at times I saw the appeal of atheism or at best agnosticism. I wrote in the Journal: *'I do so want to believe and trust, and yet there is the still, logical voice that says that religion is a human artifice, and that what I should do if I'm honest is to "come out" and turn my back on [Christian faith] I tell myself that I will do this if I am utterly convinced of it, yet I thirst for God'.* I continued:

> *Sometimes I think I am in denial about the failure of the Christian truth to live up to its claims. When God seems far away and prayers go unanswered and I keep telling myself it's true, and counting blessings and seeking encouragement and confirmation in the stories of others. But on the level of experience, the reality of it is pretty patchy. I don't want to live in denial. I want to be courageous enough to turn my back on the faith if it is not real.*

*

One spring day I took our dog Mollie for a walk across the Islands in the River Ness. The evening before, I had watched on-line a presentation on *Science and the God Delusion* given by the evolutionary biologist Richard Dawkins at Eden Court Theatre in the city. I found his arguments against the existence of God cogent and unexpectedly powerful.

As Mollie and I crossed the bridge from one island to another, I realised how easy it would be to believe that there was no God, that the galaxy was, in all its stunning beauty, an amazing miracle of chance. A miracle the more wonderful, more miraculous because of its randomness than would be a miracle of creation.

I felt I was standing at a beckoning doorway and that just one step would take me through a portal on the far side of which lay freedom from all the questions about God and guilt and suffering, all the wounds inflicted by churches. Nothing but a simple, sharp focus on courageously living to the full, relishing the flickering beauty of my brief life and the lives of others, seeking to bless those around me knowing that tragedy was arbitrary and death the story's final word.

As I stood there in the sunshine, surrounded by trees in a million shades of green, the river sparkling at my feet beneath a blue May sky, it seemed that nature had never before had such beauty, such intensity. I remembered the old Christian song:

Heaven above is softer hue
Earth around is sweeter green
Something lives in every hue
Christless eyes have never seen

It was as though the journey from belief offered the same initial heightened sensitivities. And yet I stepped back, and did not enter. What made me turn away wasn't I think conscience or fear of change. It was the thought of Easter Sunday, an open tomb, a risen Jesus. I remembered the strong indications that something decisive happened that particular morning, that death was overcome, that Jesus was alive.

And so, on the Ness islands, Mollie straining at her lead, I chose to continue believing. Perhaps I am wrong. Perhaps after all there is no more to the Easter rising than a powerful symbol, perhaps my yearning for God is no more than a construct of my longing. But that day, I committed myself once again to a life shaped by faith in a living Jesus.

*

It was to be some time before I knew for certain that my calling was to be a dancer on the edge. In the meantime I struggled to understand my emotions. One of my problems with attending church was that I found myself engaged in a battle with lust and negative thoughts and a sense of how inferior I must be not to be blessed as others seemed to be. I wrote in the Journal of *an inner barrage of critical, unbelieving thoughts* and wondered *Where does the constant meteor-storm of doubt, bitterness, imputing bad motives to people, belittling others come from?*

Formerly, I would have attributed such thoughts to the devil and thirty years before had been encouraged by *Christian Warfare*, Martyn Lloyd-Jones volume of sermons. Was this the source of the clamour within me? Or did the negative thinking come from some segment of my selfhood? Or from both sources? By the early 2000s, I had grasped something of Carl Jung's thinking on 'the shadow self', and found this idea helpful. I drew encouragement from reflecting that I could come to God as I was, the good and the bad, knowing that I was completely accepted. This was the message I had not received in early childhood, possibly due to those attachment issues with my mother.

'*Help me,*' I prayed on a clearer-seeing day '*to embrace my whole self as I am, with all my inconsistencies as you embrace me, and help me to rest in you*'. On such days, to befriend the negative stuff recognizing that I and no-one else was its source was to deprive it of much of its power. Later I was to find a deeper source of freedom in recognizing the implications of attachment issues and realizing that 'It's not my fault! Hallelujah, it's not my fault!'

In the autumn of 2006 our church began to use in small groups study material by a US author Neil Anderson published by Freedom in Christ Ministries. Anderson emphasised that freedom from any and all of the multitude of things which bind us inwardly, restraining us and stopping us from fulfilling our full potential as God's children is to be found in Jesus Christ on account of his victory over the spiritual forces of darkness. He was restating what I had previously learned from Lloyd-Jones. I certainly felt myself in need of spiritual liberation.

And yet I noted that the theological context in which Anderson's teaching was presented was very conservative (as indeed were Lloyd-Jones' writings). If I were to experience once again the liberation of which Anderson wrote, would it be necessary I wondered to embrace his theological position in its entirety, to make a positive regression to where I had been twenty years previously, acknowledging that two decade's worth of struggles and awakenings had been a wrong turning? Could I find a sense of belonging and freedom by denying, ignoring, burying, labelling as false and destructive the questions which had challenged my thinking?

I now realise that much of my pain arose from unconscious conflict as I tried to pour my deepest self into an evangelical mould from which I was being called to freedom. *'Feel stressed....partly through cognitive dissonance between what seems to be the Christian norm and what I feel. A bit fractured and on the edge of cracking up.'*

*

But on my clearer seeing days, I knew that *'My spiritual experience is, and always has been, out of sync with the "evangelical norm." Frankly, I went through all the hoops before, and it didn't work.' 'Is there,'* I wondered, *'an authentic spirituality for me?'* I was glad to be *'recovering the thought that it's good and important to be my own person, and not feel I have to fit into other people's moulds'*. I told God *'I'm happy to be loved by you as I am, and I don't need to model myself on other Christians'*.

'I guess all Christian communities seek to squeeze Christians into the mould of their vision....I want to be the person God wants me to be (do I really mean that?) rather than the person Max Donald thinks I should be.' Books helped me as I struggled to be my unique self: *'Read* Churchless Faith *again this evening, and again find it describes where I am at, and authenticates/validates my position.'*

I was encouraged by a sermon I heard on *Christian Maturity* from Jim Robertson, then minister of the Barn Church in Culloden: I expected the predictable list of 'shoulds' and 'oughts' with soul-crushing enjoinders urging more prayer, more Bible reading, more discipline, more worship. But while not denying the importance of these things, the preacher told us that in his view Christian maturity involves becoming the person God intends you to be. This authenticated my journey confirming that I had to be what I was called to be, even if this involved an uncomfortable transition which not everyone would understand.

I was also encouraged by words from Rowan Williams, Archbishop of Canterbury. 'At the day of judgement I will be asked why I wasn't myself.'

*

One Sunday morning, Max preached a traditional evangelical sermon. He told us that the most important question any one could be asked was this – 'Are you saved?' But as I wrote later, highlighting the theological differences between us: '*To me the most important question of all is "Is God there?" – everything else follows from that.*'

Sitting in church, as the sermon continued, I realised that the church's emphasis on experience and activity and their certainties about God and the way God worked had often led me to assume that the fault must be mine. If only, I had been saying, I could find the faith, the disciplines, the genuineness in prayer then I too would become as they are. But though the key I was being offered might open the door for others, in my hands it did not turn.

I felt challenged by that sermon, but not in the way Max had intended. I felt challenged to be authentic, to distance myself from some aspects of the beliefs and experiences held dear by the church, perhaps even to leave it. I felt I had to release myself to be the person I was called to be just as I was learning to release my wife Lorna to be her unique self. In acknowledging this, I instantly felt for a while freer.

'This new freedom brings the great joy of more sustained encounter with a God whose bigness can only be hinted at in the words and symbols which point to God,' I wrote in my *Highland News* column. I felt I had taken the step I knew I had to take and God was still there. I had feared that God only loved you if you were a conservative evangelical, and that if I once stepped beyond the safe, enclosing boundaries of evangelicalism I would somehow put myself beyond his love. Yet having taken this step, I realised that God loved me none the less. I realised that it was indeed possible to experience the liberation of which Martyn Lloyd Jones and Neil Anderson spoke while having significant theological differences with them.

Another day, I wrote with clarity '*My honest story remains one of glimpses in the shadows, of extraordinary co-incidence, but lots of divine silences, a story of wavering faith, not certainty.*' And in another insightful moment I said '*Yet in my deepest self, I think I am resting on Christ*'. This was my true foundation, my true place to stand – the same place where Anne Townsend was standing. My struggles were struggles of faith, not struggles of unbelief.

And yet for a few more years I was torn between evangelical and progressive beliefs as the cycle rolled on relentlessly. It is very hard to step free of a belief system in which your mind has been marinated from its earliest days. For a few more years I sat on the fence, an ex-evangelical disguising myself as that wavering 'complicated evangelical'.

TWENTY-SEVEN

IMPERFECT FAREWELLS

By the early 2000s, my mother was showing increasing signs of the dementia which overshadowed the final years of her life. She still would not accept that anything was amiss: my father still colluded with her in pretending that all was well as she became increasingly confused and irrational.

Eventually I accepted that I would never know this woman of whom while I found her so hard to love, others spoke so well. She would never know me as I wanted to be known. In the spring of 2004 mum was admitted to New Craigs Hospital and early the following year transferred to a nursing home in Inverness. At every stage my father did all he could to ensure that she had the best possible care.

*

My feelings about mum remained ambivalent as my Journal recorded: *'Oh, it's not her fault; but I do dislike/hate her so intensely, and I guess I've just got to acknowledge and own those feelings.' 'I sit and hold her hand. I do not love her.' 'Wish I felt love for her but there's this bit of me that wishes she would hurry up and die.'*

At times, her angst and raging calmed. *'So sweet and lovable. I have never known her so lovable as she is these days, and I am able to kiss her without shrinking from her. Oh, the irony of it, that I can love her and be close to her now when she's so confused, and I couldn't before.'* *'I cuddled her and told her that I loved her, which I hadn't done since I was a child, and I meant it, but I know words come cheap and emotion is easy and what matters is commitment. I love you mum.'* *'I guess tonight I just wanted to take her in my arms as you would a child and kiss her better.'*

One day, she spoke of something she had never mentioned before:

In a moment of lucidity (or was it just another delusion?) she told my father how she was physically abused by her mother, made to lie on the floor and be kicked, how she did not have the love she saw her friends Molly and Kathleen had. Dad said that kids who are abused today have access to help. She said 'I wouldn't have recognised that I needed help.' She claimed this abuse had overshadowed her whole life, and triggered the stress she is currently experiencing.

I acknowledged the desperate sadness of this, and continued *'The story rings true, and softens my heart.'*

From what I now know about attachment theory I can see that since expressions of love to mum from her parents were fragile and unreliable she is very unlikely to have been unconditionally cherished as a baby. And was my grandmother's inability to love the fruit of deficiencies in her own welcome into the world, conceived out of wedlock as she was? And so hurt is passed on down the generations.

More than ever now, I love my mother, understand her, forgive her.

But the night she was admitted to hospital *'The doc asked me what she was like before all this, and I didn't have much to say. I had to acknowledge that I didn't know her very well.'*

*

Not long after mum entered the nursing home her condition began to deteriorate. I visited her dutifully but there was little meaningful communication of any kind. Until Bank Holiday Monday, 2nd May 2005. I went to see mum and later wrote:

She sat on the bed whimpering and I sat beside her and cuddled her for a few minutes, her head against mine as she talked sentences I couldn't interpret in between her moans. The longest period of physical contact I've had with her, I suppose, since I was a child. 'Thank you,' she said, and held my hand. And I loved her.

In that moment of clarity it seemed that the thanks were for far more than simply my presence beside her that day.

I was alone with her when she died early in the morning of May 31st, one hand on her brow as her breathing slowed, simply repeating 'I'm here'.

*

I found my mother's note-book from the decade beginning 1986, before the shadow of dementia encroached. The fragments it contains record a woman's holy longing for God, love for God, worship of God. Possibly they truly reflect her thoughts and feelings; possibly what she aspired to think and feel – I know from experience that we can capture in words what we glimpse as possibility before we have actually reached the place of which we write, and that often many miles lie between where we currently stand and what we envisage

'Lord Jesus, keep me centring my life on You,' she wrote. 'Oh that I might die to self a little more each day that the beauty of Jesus may really show through.'

She quoted Psalm 30:1, traditionally authored by Israel's King David – 'I will exalt you, O Lord, for you lifted me out of the depths' and then reflected 'David was often in "the depths", in dire straits, in danger often. We, too, experience "the depths", perhaps the "depths" of disappointment, of bewilderment, of indecision, or sorrow. Whatever our "depths" the grace of David's Lord is still sufficient.'

On another occasion she wrote:

> Lord, forbid that I lose the blessing and joy of the 'now' by an undue concern for tomorrow. Help me to live a moment at a time with you, rejoicing in your presence and provision, surprised again and again by the abundance of your giving.

> Imagine a path through a wood, part shade, part dappled shade, part sunshine – to each side the Scottish bluebells bloom in rich profusion and [a]way ahead at the end of the path, the sun shines brightly. How like the Christian way! Ahead is sunshine of far greater glory than any earthly sun – unimaginable glory – Son-shine! Such is our goal. Meantime life is a mixture of sun and shade and bluebells, representing the good gifts that God gives us richly to enjoy. But don't let's linger! Let us press on with our eyes on the glory!

And there's a poignant 'grandmother's prayer':

> Lord, thank you for our two small grand-daughters. What joy they bring. But oh Father they are born into an increasingly evil world. Protect them, I pray, and early in life, may they, through the love of older believers, come to love Jesus and know that he loves them. Such was their Granny's experience before ever she heard the words justification, redemption etc. Lord, hear a granny's prayer.

As I read mum's words in these notes I warmed to the writer. I see the source of my love of words, and of my instinctive use of symbols and images to describe spiritual experience. I wish I had known the woman who wrote these pages. I wish I had understood earlier the demons she struggled with and thus been able to express my unequivocal forgiveness.

*

In his closing years I was able to tell my father that I loved him, and I believe he was proud of me although this sentiment was seldom articulated. I admired and respected his grace and integrity. But things which needed saying remained unsaid and I was never as close to him as I would have wished.

Dad was lonely following mum's death. He had few interests outwith the house and by then lacked energy to develop them. He felt neglected by his church and perhaps by me too although I phoned daily, had lunch with him once a week, and we welcomed him round every Sunday afternoon. He appreciated kindness wherever he found it.

He spoke often of God guiding him, and left yellow post-its – on which he had written verses from the Bible and lines from hymns – in strategic places around the house to remind him of God's promises. He mentioned waking at night, alone and perhaps afraid, and words from hymns coming to mind with a sense of 'givenness', sustaining and encouraging him.

Until the autumn of 2010 he retained his zest for life, his inquisitiveness, his sense of wonder.

More than once when my father spoke of driving to Dores Beach near the head of Loch Ness and being uplifted by the beauty of creation, and sensing God's encouragement, I felt resentful. I knew it was a reprehensible response and I gave it no nourishment. But I wondered what made me in moments of negativism or jealousy grudge this gentle, lovely man these touches of joy.

'I didn't know life could be so hard,' he said one day in the early months of 2011. He was 88. 'If the Lord spares me,' he had always said when talking about events in the future. He was, he told me, now ready to die. There was perhaps a hint that the Lord had spared him for rather longer than he would have wished.

My dad was admitted to the Royal Northern infirmary on 10th June suffering lingering infection following a fall but he did not respond to treatment. Father's day, Sunday 19th June was his last day of clarity. Thereafter he was unable to communicate although he acknowledged our presence with a squeeze of the hand.

I remember one day rearranging dad's bed covers when he was restless and having an extraordinary sense that my grandmother Phemie Dempster was somehow with me, within me even – comforting her son through me just as decades before she had stood beside a small fidgety child's bed in Wiston Schoolhouse.

His last day on earth was Sunday 3rd July. The Hospital Chaplain Iain Macritchie visited and prayed for dad, not for healing but for safe journeying through death. 'Iain prayed dad into heaven,' Lorna said, moved.

I sat and held my father's hand telling him I loved him; I prayed, and crazily I sang not some affirming Christian song, but *Ten green bottles*, a favourite from his childhood. I sang every verse until the last bottle had gone.

I was with him when he died.

*

At the funeral, I began my tribute to my father by noting how many people had used the word 'gentleman' to describe him, and concluded with these words:

On Sunday at teatime as the birds sang over the Royal Northern Infirmary and the Ness flowed down to the Firth as it flowed on the day of dad's birth, and dishes clattered cheerfully in the day room and he lay dying, there were no last words of triumph, no radiant eyes seeing a vision of the beyond. Simply shallow, faltering breaths, and then, silence.

So does he live now only in the good he did, and in the memories of those of us left behind? Well, he put his faith in the risen conquering King, death's victor, who promises life beyond the shadowlands. Those of us who knew my father saw in his grace, in his love, in his courage glimpses of the dimension beyond, piercing the shadows. And on Sunday at teatime I believe a door was opened, and a voice whispered 'Come in, sit down, eat'.

Christians believe that as well as being a place of rest and homecoming, the dimension beyond is a place of challenge and opportunity, a place where we become fully ourselves, where there is no darkness, no shadow, where our creative gifts flourish as we build God's kingdom in partnership with the King. And there, even now bearing the memories of his years with us, stands William Hodge Dempster, still rubbing his eyes at the unaccustomed wonder of it, more gentleman than ever.

TWENTY-EIGHT

'I'LL NEVER JOIN A CHURCH AGAIN!'

In March 2010, just before Easter, I met Max Donald by chance one lunch-time in a grey, damp Inverness High Street. We were close to the spot where we once held summer-evening church events with singing and fun and a burger afterwards at McDonalds on the corner. I told Max about a job interview I'd been called to for a post on the Highland Council's ICT Services Team.

By then, Max was facing serious personal problems. Still pastor of Grace Community Church, he was now living apart from his wife Ruth. Over the months, I had been close to him, supporting him, sitting by his side when there were no words to say. He was on his way that afternoon to Marks and Spencers to buy shirts. Max smiled broadly, and I put my arms round his thick navy-blue coat, and hugged him firmly. It was the last time I saw him.

He sent me an encouraging text the next morning, the day of my interview. 'Praying you get the job John. You deserve it.'

Later, in his flat, Max had a fatal heart attack.

What was it I'd thought at Little Garve? 'Winter will come and the torrent will engulf it.'

A fortnight later I preached at the Easter Sunday service at Grace about hope and resurrection.

*

A year later, Lorna and I both felt it was time for us to move on from Grace Community Church. We had been too busy for too long. I was very cynical about churches seeing only the negative aspects of my decades of church experience. It seemed to me that churches sought to police your beliefs and take over your life, sucking you into a vortex of activity; that vested interests in churches strove to maintain the tradition, and the status of people in leadership at all costs; that there was no room for introverts.

None of this was entirely fair. I was forgetting the genuine love shown me in each one of the churches I had been part of and how precious engaging with other Christians had sometimes been. Perhaps I had not yet accepted that no church is perfect since all churches are full of broken people. Or not yet faced the fact that my primary problem was my own neurotic neediness and my inability, most of the time, to feel that I belonged.

But I had had enough. Lorna explored another community of worship in Inverness but I resolved never again to join a church.

*

One night I had a dark dream. I was in a shadowy space, a cellar, a cavern perhaps and was aware of evil presences surrounding me.

'Lord Jesus Christ, have mercy on me,' I prayed in my dream seeking protection, afraid but confident. The immediate darkness receded.

But then I swung round and became aware of another presence in a corner. I approached it. 'Lord Jesus Christ have mercy on me,' I repeated.

Instead of retreating, the darkness sprang forward and engulfed me. I woke, damp with sweat.

I shared this over lunch with the pastor of Lorna's new church.

'Have there been any recurrences of the dream?' he asked me.

Had it recurred, I believe he would have offered to pray with me and for me, for freedom from darkness.

*

One Sunday morning in March 2011 I went to our local church, Hilton Parish Church in Inverness and found a seat at the back. There was a guest preacher, Peter Neilson, a Church of Scotland minister with extensive experience of people 'doing church' in 'alternative' ways.

I don't think I had ever heard in a church service anything like what he said that morning. Peter acknowledged that Christians find their connection with God sustained in different ways. For some the traditional fare of prayers, sermon, hymns and worship songs doesn't nourish.

There are however other ways of connecting with God, he said: he mentioned reflecting on the Bible; silence; appreciating music, art, and the beauty of creation; the regular rhythm of liturgy; images and symbols which signpost, and draw our hearts into unseen realities.

If such things could be said in Hilton Church, then perhaps it was a church which I might learn to call home.

Since then I have been part of Hilton Church though I have never formally joined. The past had left a residual fear of becoming enmeshed, and I wanted my escape route to be clear.

*

I asked the minister at Hilton if there was a discussion group in the church for people who had the issues with traditional church which Peter Neilson had highlighted.

There wasn't, but he suggested I speak to Iain Macritchie who was part of an Inverness Men's Group comprised of people of different faiths and none.

Iain invited me to chat with him in his chaplain's office at New Craigs Hospital. We met on Good Friday 2011, and I found his room more sanctuary than office, with candles, prayer cards, good coffee and a sense of ineffable peace. I told Iain some of my story. He listened attentively, hospitable to what I was saying. He asked sensitive open questions, respecting my space. He lent me a book, Gordon Lynch's *Losing My Religion* with described the author's journey out of evangelicalism.

Later that day I walked homeward along Balloon Road in bright spring sunshine my spirit singing with the joy of Easter. There would, as is inevitable in a neurotic personality be further waves of anxiety, struggle, and lack of certainty but I felt that day as if I had passed a milestone.

*

Iain and I got together regularly in town after work. I remember joining him in Girvan's Coffee Shop on Stephen's Brae, where we sat across from one another at a round table, drinking coffee and talking. One afternoon, the background music included a piece featuring a string orchestra.

Recognising the first few bars, I exclaimed in anticipation 'It's Barber's *Adagio*!'

I looked at Iain: read in his eyes that the piece moved him as much as it did me and felt that somehow in the music we met as one.

*

Occasionally over the years after I was married I had a recurring dream. It featured my old flat in Dunnet Avenue Glenmavis where Lorna and I had lived in for a month after our wedding. I would dream that the flat was still unoccupied and in each repetition something different was wrong with it.....a leaking roof, rotten window-frames, torn wallpaper.

I knew such dreams signified something left undone, something insisting I address it, but I had no idea what this particular dream might symbolise.

TWENTY-NINE

END OF DAYS?

One Saturday afternoon, stretched out on the couch reading *The Times* I noticed a blemish in my right eye's field of vision – a small, circular grey area obscuring the text behind it. I blinked and rubbed my eyes, but the cloud remained. The optician whom I consulted, visibly flustered, referred me to the Opthalmology Clinic at Raigmore Hospital.

It seemed that a 'macular hole' had developed in the affected eye, but I understood from what I was told that it was treatable. Fluid would be injected into the eye in the operating theatre; I would then lie face-down for 72 hours; after which sight would gradually be restored.

On 31st December 2009 I entered the parallel world of slow-moving NHS time. I sat rather anxiously beside a bed in Ward 1A, distracting myself in the pages of Alister McGrath's *Heresy: a history of defending the truth* as I waited to be summoned to the operating theatre. I was wryly amused and yet somehow comforted to come across a quotation from another theologian, Stanley Hauerwas – 'The church serves the world by giving the world the means to see itself truthfully'. Outside, it was snowing heavily.

I'd opted to have a local, rather than a general anaesthetic because I disliked the thought of being put to sleep – occasionally waking at night I found it hard to return to my dreams through fear of unconsciousness. I was in a place where I could do nothing but entrust myself to the skill of the specialist and in a deeper and more general way to God. And this entrusting brought me to a place where, faced with the unknown, I knew myself sustained.

Eventually, I was wheeled along the corridor into theatre; anaesthetic was painlessly administered close to the affected eye, and a green cloth with a strategic hole over the working area placed on my face.

'Do you want me to hold your hand?' said one of the attendants kindly. I declined politely but then wondered if it had been the right decision. I breathed deeply, attempting to dissolve the panic.

The operation was an unforgettable light-show. It was as though I was lying on my back looking up into a vivid multicolour planisphere, with a rainbow of bright stars and swirling nebulae of mists. All the time, the team were chatting in a relaxed way about their plans for Hogmanay.

Later, back on the ward I lay face down, skin chafing with unaccustomed pyjamas, head protruding over the bottom of the bed. At 12.30am I was wakened by one of the nursing staff, the wife of a friend, who kissed my cheek and wished me a happy New Year.

On the late morning of 1st January, Lorna and the girls wrestled the car through deep snow, coming to take me home.

*

Lying face down for the next few days, I had time to reflect. I liked to see myself as God's servant. Preaching, writing, opening eyes. My attitude had been like the Prodigal Son in Jesus' story: take me as one of your servants; I am not worthy to be called your son. Yet I had recognised the sustaining God in the hearts, hands and words of those who had helped me at Raigmore. A God who assured me 'You are my child! Let me serve you!'

*

Gradually, the black circle of fluid in the eye contracted, and then disappeared. But I was disappointed that sight in the eye was never fully restored. Where once there was a grey opaqueness, now there was vision – but it was a distorted vision – letters pulled out of shape and squeezed together so that some words were illegible.

*

One November Saturday morning four years later Lorna and I took the dog for a walk along the East Sands at Nairn. The Moray Firth was grey and sombre; a strong westerly drove sand grains in a relentless current around our knees and into Mollie's fur.

I felt heavy and disassociated. It had often been like that lately. A hot tension, a sense of energy pent up.

Later that day I sat at the computer in the study composing an email. Outside darkness had already fallen. The room seemed gloomy. I screwed up my eyes, struggling to make out what I had written.

Downstairs, I stretched out in the living room, reading a book by the progressively iconoclastic Lutheran minister Nadia Bolz-Weber – *Cranky, Beautiful Faith: for Irregular (and Regular) People*. And then I came across a word which my brain couldn't process. I look at the string of symbols. These letters signified something, I knew – but what? Panicking, I begin spelling them out, trying to coax meaning from them.

And then the moment passed and words once again uttered their comforting certainties.

I drove down to Cinnamon to collect an Indian take-away.

*

'You realise I'd have to instruct you to stop driving for a month?' the doctor said on the Monday morning.

Still feeling heavy and slow-brained, I had googled the words 'mini-stroke'.

The doctor printed out a questionnaire, and we worked through it.

I told him about the visual and cognitive issues I'd experienced.

'But was your speech affected?'

'Perhaps it was a little,' I said, not in fact sure but giving him what I felt he needed to hear. The other symptoms, he thought, could have been the fruit of tiredness alone.

'I could refer you, but....' And he made the comment about driving.

'Yes, I would like to be referred,' I insisted.

*

Later that day I watched a man older than I was parking his car beneath the overhanging trees at the edge of Culduthel Woods.

'Why is he still driving?' I thought, bitterly jealous.

And then I realised that young spirits still dance in old broken bodies.

*

The doctor had signed me off work for three weeks, and prescribed aspirin as a temporary measure. He told me that if indeed I had had a mini-stroke (a TIA, he called it – Temporary Ischaemic Attack) then I was at high risk of further strokes within the next few days.

I felt weak and mortal.

Friday, I saw the consultant at Raigmore. Lorna came along too. He confirmed, on the basis of what I had reported that I had definitely had a TIA. Yes, there was danger of a recurrence – perhaps a much more serious stroke. But in fact, what had happened might be a 'blessing,' a 'warning,' giving time for treatment. He prescribed pills for blood pressure and high cholesterol. He taught us the FAST mnemonic: 'Facial drooping. Arm weakness. Speech difficulties. Time to call emergency services.'

I was devastated, focussing on the negatives. I was entering my end of days.

At home, time hanging heavy, I felt weak both physically and psychologically my head sore and unresponsive. At lunchtimes, ITV was screening old episodes of *Doc Martin*. The gentle shenanigans at Portwen were the therapeutic highlight of my day.

*

David Wiper, the man who married Lorna and me died in early December after a long illness. We stood shivering in the bleak country graveyard at Convinth, near Beauly in fading daylight. I watched as the coffin was lowered into cold, cold earth.

*

One dark afternoon shortly after I suffered the TIA, Iain Macritchie came to visit me at home.

I looked across to where he sat under the window drinking the coffee I'd made for him.

'I really think I don't have long to live.'

And he nodded, affirmingly.

My split-second inner reaction was of indignation. 'I've just told you I think I'm coming to my end of days! And you sit nodding? You're supposed to say "No, of course you'll recover."'

But that was swept away in a tide of peace. Whatever happened, whether I lived or died, I would be OK.

And that peace was a gift of Iain's wise restraint.

THIRTY

FACING THE WINDOW
RATHER THAN THE WALL

I turned the desk to face window rather than wall, fixed uplifting posters to the blu tack stained emulsion paint and got to work.

The best thing about my new office was its proximity to the River Ness and the city centre. St Andrew's, the Episcopal Cathedral, was less than a minute's walk away.

High Life Highland, an 'arms-length' organisation was now delivering leisure, cultural and community education services for the Highland Council. Despite Max's prayer I hadn't been successful in my attempt back in 2010 to join the Council's ICT Services, but in 2012 I was assigned to the High Life Highland ICT Team based in the head office, two Victorian town houses knocked into one. My job remained much as before: I kept my specialism in library software, but was now also in touch with other services in High Life Highland helping support them in negotiations with technical providers. It was a job I was made for, and I loved it.

Initially, I shared a room at the very top of one of the town houses which in the mid-20th century had been a doctor's house. I imagined our reception area crowded with patients awaiting their consultation in the surgery, which was now the back office. I imagined the day the doc crossed the mosaic floor, early in the morning, leaving to drive to Glasgow for a meeting; and the tears that evening when his family heard what had befallen him on the road north near Glencoe. His son came to revisit the house as an old man and found me sitting in his boyhood bedroom.

Some of my colleagues at Ardross Street were Christians. It was a novelty to me to talk from time to time of faith and prayer while at work.

I felt at home there.

'Every office should have a John!' a young woman who came from another agency to weekly meetings with us said to my boss.

*

On the days when the Cathedral held a lunchtime eucharist, I went along. The building was often cold; only a handful of people present; Alec Gordon the Provost conducted the service with austere formality.

I wasn't emotionally stirred by the words of the mass; the familiarity of them after a while brought not the calm of standing in a great tradition but a struggle to concentrate. We went to the communion rail. 'The body of Christ,' Alec intoned. 'The blood of Christ.' There was no sense of the divine as I let bitter wine dissolve the fragment of wafer lingering on my tongue. In time Bishop Mark came: him you could hug after the service.

I felt that, unpromising as all this sounds, some need was met through my being there.

I remember the solemn words of 'imposition' at the Ash Wednesday Cathedral service when the Provost's finger described a cross on your brow with ash from the previous Palm Sunday's celebratory branches. 'Remember you are dust, and to dust you shall return.'

Standing outside the front door of the office, the black cross still visible on my forehead. I had meetings that afternoon. Should I wipe the stain away?

Shortly afterwards I sat down at the table in the Board Room. My forehead was ash-free.

*

We had lunch on the top floor of The Kitchen, a futuristic building shoe-horned into a small riverside site in central Inverness. Outside, the sun shone brightly on the sparkling waters of the Ness.

I retired on my 65th birthday, May 19th, 2017 and the meal with close colleagues and Lorna celebrated my liberation. Afterwards I returned home and sat in the garden, writing.

In my mid-50s, while I looked forward to the freedoms retirement in theory offered I also viewed reaching 65 with sadness and something approaching dread. It seemed to mark the ending of everything I knew, the gateway to old age and infirmity, and the journey back to dust. But as the date approached I grew generally more positive.

In my final few years in post I represented the organisation in a consortium of Scottish local authorities which went out to tender for a new library management package. I took the lead in migrating Highland Libraries across to the new platform, a process fraught with problems due to the number of parallel applications which required access to the library database. I felt this work was a parting gift, one both given to me, and given by me.

But retirement gave me a sense of deliverance and of gratitude. Each day in the early months was a gift, and I acknowledged that one or even two decades of such gifts might lie ahead. Retirement was not, I saw joyously an ending, but a beginning.

That day in May as I sat in the sunshine on the patio with my laptop, it seemed like a new birth.

THIRTY-ONE

DESTINATIONS

We sought out Grand Central Station. The concourse was curtained by imposing walls broken by multiple open arches. Puzzled, I looked around me, before walking up to the central enquiry booth. 'Where are the trains?' I asked.

'Only you, dad!' Rebecca muttered affectionately, shaking her head.

The person I'd asked, looking perplexed gesticulated vaguely at the archways which I now realised must lead to platforms beyond.

*

The April following my TIA, we had booked to go *en famille* to New York. My usual anxieties were compounded by fear of falling ill on the other side of the Atlantic so far from home. As winter turned to spring I grew more apprehensive. My energy-levels were low, my head still periodically ached. The cost of travel insurance underlined my fragility.

On Wednesdays at lunch time I was attending a Lent study group held at the Cathedral by Alex Gordon. Two days before we left for our transatlantic adventure the subject was 'The Peace' – as in the moment in the Roman Catholic and Episcopalian mass when congregants are encouraged to offer 'the Peace' to one another often (in those pre-

COVID days) shaking hands in so doing.

I mentioned that I appreciated the sense of inclusion which this gave me: but Alex gently corrected me. The primary meaning of 'the Peace,' he told me is not that we offer our peace to others, but are reminding one another of the peace God gives us all.

His words brought me a profound sense of that peace, a conviction that all would be well. This was not simply an idea but something planted within me or awakened in me, changing my perspective.

*

I tried to bear this sense of peace carefully, guarding it safe, but by the Thursday evening it was diluting. I didn't sleep well and when on the Friday morning Lorna got up first, I told her how anxious I was. Had she suggested that she go transatlantic with the girls while I remained at home, I think I might have agreed.

But as I lay there listening to water cascading in the shower I had a vivid mental picture of a map of the north of Scotland with a narrow circle drawn around Inverness. This, I understood, was my comfort zone. But then another picture came, or was given. A pair of hands held up, thumbs and forefingers touching to form the outline of a heart, and within the heart I saw our familiar dazzling blue planet, rotating gently. This and far, far more was God's comfort-zone. The whole world, sustained by God's love. If God were as at home in New York as in Inverness, then I could be too.

This image, combined with the sense of peace Alex's words had brought sheltered me in the days ahead.

*

Later that Friday, as the shuttle bus carried us across the Kingston Bridge on our way to Glasgow Airport, I was joyful, my spirit singing despite my tiredness 'Thank you, Father'.

*

I never feel completely at home when I am abroad, but there was joy as well as anxiety throughout that week in the Big Apple. The joy of being with my family as we walked in Central Park on a bright, sunny Sunday; the joy of reaching the top of the Empire State building, and sailing past the Statue of Liberty; the joy of watching an enthralling performance of *Phantom of the Opera*. From our 21st floor hotel room we could look down to the bustle of Times Square far below. We explored Macy's and Bloomingdales and New York Public Library, and had coffee in Barnes and Noble in 5th Avenue, where I bought a book I'd heard of but never read, a book I found enormously helpful, Richard Rohr's *Falling Upward: a Spirituality for the Two Halves of Life*.

I was glad to be there, yet I was glad to be going home soon.

*

On the following Saturday, we flew overnight back to Heathrow, and then caught a plane north to Glasgow.

We left the airport shuttle at Glasgow Queen Street Station. After we reached the pavement something prompted me to ask 'Has everyone got all their stuff?'

One of us had left a case on the bus, and we were able to retrieve it seconds before the driver pulled away.

I thought of the hassle we'd have had recovering that case if we hadn't checked. It seemed to me there was a 'givenness' in that gentle prompt.

Again, as we walked towards the pub in the station for a light lunch before our train north, something in me said 'Thank you, Father'.

*

One July, Lorna and I went to Orkney for ten days, driving north to Scrabster from where we took the Northlink ferry to Stromness. At times I was anxious, separated from my comfort zone by the unpredictable waters of the Pentland Firth. No visions this time of heart and spinning globe – perhaps my anxiety was not so great as to throw me completely into the merciful hands of the One I was learning to call the Great Love. But despite this, I relished being in Orkney – there was, viewed retrospectively at least, something numinous about this flat, still land.

I was struck most by the sense of community. The red stone walls of St Magnus Cathedral in Kirkwall cradled a peace which had stilled the souls of generations; the inhabitants of Skara Brae lived cheek by jowl in their small networked houses; each of the stones in the great circle at Brodgar in Stenness came from a different local area, dragged there by the people of each place to create a communal centre of worship; the Italian chapel was a testimony to community lost and found; Westray was silent the day we took the early ferry across – it seemed as though the whole island was attending the funeral at a Brethren meeting place.

I wrote in my Journal about the continuity of Orkney's many generations in terms embarrassingly similar to the quasi-Grassic Gibbon celebration of land and people which I wrote when my dad's mother died. There was a difference however in that whereas previously I had been seeking a form of immortality apart from God, now I realized that the Great Love would have been expressing compassion to the people of those islands long before the coming of Christianity.

There seemed on Orkney to be constant reminders of the gifted people, the people of insight who link two worlds, bringing God into (or recognising God's presence in) the Eden of the Orkneys. Among them were poets Edwin Muir and Robert Rendell for both of whom the islands had a prelapsarian quality.

I particularly enjoyed our day in Stromness, where we retraced the footsteps of George Mackay Brown. We saw his house, the pub where he drank, and in the museum we found the chair in which morning by morning he sat writing, caught up in what he called 'the work trance'.

I wrote to Brown as a young postgraduate student of librarianship. Could he, I asked, point me in the right direction as I researched a bibliography of his writings? To convince him of my seriousness, I hinted that, having made a beginning with this as a course project, I might continue adding to it over the years as his work developed. I knew some librarians had made a name for themselves by publishing bibliographies of significant writers. Linking my name to his in this way seemed alluring.

I enclosed a return-paid envelope, and George Mackay Brown replied patiently and helpfully in his small, crabbed writing, with a broad margin down the left hand side of the paper, a distinctive feature which I emulated for years to come. I finished my student bibliography but I did not maintain it. This is a minor regret to me – I feel that I let the poet down.

One of the girls I loved unrequitedly as a young man was passionate about Brown's work and travelled north from Lanarkshire with a group of friends to sit at his feet in that wee house in Stromness, feeding on his words, her devotion both purer and deeper than mine.

While on Orkney, I re-read Ron Ferguson's biography of Brown, and was struck by his personal fragility, his lifelong need for friendship and support as he lived and wrote and struggled with faith. I wondered as we headed homewards down the A9 from Thurso if I could do anything to support and build community for local writers and poets.

Just weeks later my colleague Merryn Glover – teacher, librarian and gifted writer whose work reflects her profound Christian insights – emailed. Would I, she asked, consider joining the Committee of Highland Literary Salon, a group which had been created some years before to encourage writers in the north and to foster creative writing. It was easy for me to say 'yes'. The group was renamed HighlandLIT (the word 'salon' might, we thought, suggest something exclusive), and we were able to encourage both established and new writers.

I appreciated the opportunity of getting to know folk who would not all call themselves people of faith. Earlier in my life, I would have erected a protective barrier excluding them (as I lacked the language and confidence to engage), and also masking my as yet largely undiscovered true self. Now I was able to be more open and real, able to connect human-to-human with people's reality, their search for meaning, as we shared fragments of our journeys, and I found joy and growth in these connections.

*

I was inspired by *Cry of Wonder* the final book by Jesuit priest and writer Gerard Hughes. In one section he writes eloquently about the benefits of spiritual retreats run on Ignatian principles, which is why I found myself in October 2016 at the Bield near Perth on a two-day silent retreat run by the Ignatian Spirituality Centre in Glasgow. For 48 hours from the Tuesday evening the small group of us were to keep silence except during two sessions with our spiritual director. I'd expected to be meeting with a priest, but in fact my mentor was as I wrote in the Journal, a delightful 'wee Glesga' wummin', a professional potter called Katy Low.

I found it hard to be silent, to listen inwardly for the whisper of God. At times I despaired, thinking God must speak to me only in the busyness of life; at times, being normally so thirled to daily agendas, I was uneasy at living whole days with little structure; at times I despised my own inclination to use what I heard as grist for the mill of my writing – 'trading on the market with the things God has given as love-gifts'; at times I'd had 'enough of silence', and filled the long hours with alternatives – reading a biography of Jimmy Carter, writing an article, visiting the current exhibition at the Bield Gallery, a display of work by artist Lorraine Nicholson whom I had known, a strong woman who struggled with depression and had taken her own life the previous year.

But nevertheless, at times there were insights which came with a powerful sense of 'givenness'.

*

On the Wednesday morning, after a silent breakfast and before morning chapel, I began journaling, simply seeking openness to the divine and writing what came. After half a page of reflections, I scribbled rather impatiently 'OK, here I am – I'm listening – what do you have to say?' And these words emerged within me (or were they dropped gently into my consciousness?): 'My Child, you are making of listening another deed, whereas I want you to listen so you will realise how much we are at one.'

Two pages later: 'Listening is allowing the well, the river of God, to rise in your heart.' And just before I went for my first meeting with Katy, I wrote 'What do I need to hear? What can I hear which will change me?' And the words came: 'My Child, is it not enough to know that the river flows, always?' And I responded 'Thank you Father!'

*

Katy gave me a particular passage to reflect on in the next 24 hours – Mark 10:46-52, the story of the healing by Jesus of a man named Bartimaeus, who had been blind from birth – and specifically to think how I would reply if Jesus asked me, as he asked Bartimaeus 'What do you want me to do for you?' (v51)

I recalled hearing that 'Bartimaeus' means 'son of Timeaeus'. I was sure that after his sight was restored he would have been known as his own person, the man healed by Jesus. This, I realized, reflected my own journey from being my parents' son, to being me-in-my-own-right, the person I was becoming. It also struck me that Bartimaeus was the outsider: the crowd assumed that the famous itinerant rabbi wouldn't be interested in him, but Jesus called him into the centre. I saw myself as the outsider, 'scarcely believing that I am welcome.'

I turned over Jesus' words in my mind: *'What do I want to do for me? Mmm! Difficult question. I want to know that you're there. I want to know that you love me. I want to be more wholly the person you'd like me to be.'*

I paused, adding *'All very me-focussed, I fear.'* And then I continued *'I suppose I have this constant sense of shortcoming. Wouldn't it be lovely to know it's OK?'*

When I was back with Katy on the Thursday morning sitting with her in the Bield gatehouse these thoughts came together and I gave my answer to Jesus' question with passion: *'I want to be my authentic self – the me I am called to be.'* There was a great liberation in discerning and articulating this.

Katy suggested one or two Bible passages I might read later that day, and then said. 'Actually, forget that. Another thing has come to me – the story of Mary anointing Jesus' feet.' (John 12:1-8) Katy then read this passage and as I wrote afterwards:

> *It came to me that as I anoint Jesus' feet – I'm not sure what exactly that involves – so Jesus anoints not just my feet, but the whole of me. He is the precious alabaster box broken for us! I am so loved by God. So enjoyed by God…..The God who calls me to enjoy God enjoys me…. See myself as God sees me. Beautiful one!*

> *Father, you actually enjoy me. Not 'Would enjoy me if…' but enjoy me now despite all my hang-ups and neuroses. That is wonderfully liberating. You enjoy me! And knowing your enjoyment, I reach out to enjoy you. Thank you, Father! No need to apply the lesson or think out the implications, at least not just now. Just enjoy, and know yourself enjoyed. Hallelujah!*

*

That afternoon, again having had enough of silence, '*I sneaked out to buy a paper. Pretty sure God would enjoy me in Tesco's as much as here.*' In the aisles, I felt like a visitor from a distant place. '*Sneaked back with The Times under my jacket.*'

Later, there was a slight edge of anxiety. '*I guess, perversely, this unusual sense of calm worries me a bit. Is something wrong that I am so calm? Slight fear of feeling suicidal because so at home with God, which doesn't really make sense. Thinking about Lorraine Nicholson.*'

This sense of being loved by God came unforced yet with an edgy, almost erotic intensity. I left the Bield feeling, as I had written on the Wednesday evening, that '*I am never doing this retreat thing again. I really think too much listening is not good in my case. Needs to be balanced by doing. Bartimaeus followed Jesus.*'

Yet those days on retreat were significant – affirming my journey, affirming God's love for me. It was both destination and point of departure.

THIRTY-TWO

LION OR LAMB?

'What's your overall impression of the week at the Casa Harului,' I asked?

Susie and Fiona sat across the table from me as we drank coffee and discussed their time in Romania. They had been part of a Hilton Church team helping run a camp for children and young adults with Downs together with their parents.

'It was the sense of love,' they said. 'You felt enveloped in love the whole time.'

*

This 'House of Grace,' of which they spoke, this place of love, became a magnet drawing my heart.

Just under a year later I was at Luton Airport with the Hilton team, waiting for our Wizzair flight to Romania. I was positive – I was trusting God to sustain me; I was one of a group of people I trusted; and I'd been encouraged by a similar visit to Bulgaria a decade earlier.

We'd flown down from Inverness that morning. I spent the afternoon drinking coffee with team leaders Susie and her husband Jonathan, playing card games with their young sons and gently debating the role of men in churches with Fiona Waite a very gifted Bible College student. She had been inspired by a book suggesting that the church was driving men away by feminizing Christian life: instead, we should recover the image of the wild man of a wild God, the Lion, courageously doing great things, contending for truth. Enough of the insipid meekness of the Lamb! I gently shared with her my own more feminine spirit, and cautioned against stereotyping either gender.

Take-off was delayed interminably. The gate was slow to open; when finally we did get on board we sat in the motionless plane for two hours. The flight was over-booked and a couple of would-be passengers had to be ejected with much protestation; the crew then decided they had to match all cabin luggage with the passengers on board, at which procedure there was mounting and vociferous protest. The bag check was completed in half-hearted haste, the stewards elbowing their way along an aisle packed with demonstrative Romanians: but had they missed something vital, I wondered? And then we'd to wait a further 45 minutes until German airspace was clear. Were all Romanian people this *loud*, I wondered?

The tension threatened to burst the carefully constructed dam of my control.

I sat in the mêlée, eyes closed, repeating quietly 'Grace, Jesus. Please show me that you love me.'

And then, at Jonathan' suggestion as I learned later, Fiona came up the aisle and crouched down beside my seat.

'Are you OK?' she said.

I smiled. 'I'm winning – just. I was remembering what you said when we were in Frankie and Benny's for tea – that you've been on some tough journeys, but you've learned to remember "I'll get there in the end."'

We touched down at a fog-shrouded Timisoara Airport at 5am local time, and were driven through a slow dawn. Eventually we turned into the long track leading to the House of Grace. The car stopped.

Mist hugged the earth in the half-light. No grace here, it seemed to me. No love. Only bleakness. I made my way through damp grass to the chalet, and found I was blessed with a bedroom to myself, with a bathroom next door. And so a long day ended.

*

The camp we were running in conjunction with a Romanian team was one of a series held annually at the Casa from spring to early autumn for children and their parents. The week was very busy – team briefings, preparing crafts for the children, helping organise evening meetings for the campers and their parents, running special events including a 'Scottish night'. My particular responsibility was to spend time with Adi, a railway engineer, the solitary Romanian dad at the camp. He spoke some English, so we were able to communicate, teaching one another how to play dominoes. I felt reasonably comfortable in Adi's company.

I learned about conditions in Romania, and about the courage of parents of children with Downs who were running services for kids like theirs which the State did not provide, and struggling to obtain, and retain funding. I also learned less savoury things about myself as I was tempted to be impatient and critical towards some of the children.

I was clearing tables after a meal helped by a young man with Downs, wiping the surfaces with a cloth. I missed a few crumbs at one corner, and was about to brush them to the floor when my friend shook his head and carefully picked them up with a paper napkin. I was chastened.

I felt accepted by the team. I respected their resolute evangelicalism while not feeling completely at home with for example their emphasis on substitutionary atonement.

*

Maria Medrea who ran the Casa and lived adjacent to it was an encouragement both in her words and in her approach to life. She told me that when she was a child, living in her parents' home at the site during the Communist era it had been an underground church. Figures would come out of the darkness in ones and twos to join in worship. Her mother spoke of a day when there would be a big house and children would come to it and be happy.

And talking to Maria about the fulfilment of that vision I realised that the love at the Casa comes at great personal cost.

One day during our week with her when Maria was taking some people to the airport her car broke down. She managed to arrange for someone else to pick up her passengers, and then waited for a friend to come with the necessary tools to effect a repair.

'Thank you, Father,' Maria prayed. 'You knew that I needed a rest.'

And she sat calmly, smiling, waiting, fully-present.

*

I struggled at the Casa with tiredness, my energy sapped by anxiety and by the relentless heat. People were kind and loving, but I did not 'feel' love. It was hard to choose joy. The sea was sighing in the pebbles beneath the Maiden Rock and I heard only sadness. As I lay in bed I could feel the panic rising. I felt far from home, unprotected, beyond the comfort zone yet with none of the assurances which had taken me to the United States a few years earlier.

I lay gently repeating 'Grace, Jesus' like a stilling mantra, a reaching-out to an unfelt presence. I visualised Sunday lunchtime, walking down the metal steps, feet touching the solid tarmac, beloved tarmac at dear, homely Inverness airport, meeting Lorna. 'Grace, Jesus.' And so at last I would sleep.

One of the Romanian team who spoke excellent English had a disability, and used a wheelchair. She told me of her frustration that the State provided a benefit for her as a disabled person, but not funding to help her into work. She was an informal counsellor in person and by phone to people in her church. She too, she told me, had psychiatric issues. Her psychiatrist had told her that she was 'perfect in imperfection'.

What I wondered did that mean? That her imperfection somehow made her truly who she was? That she was a healer precisely because of her brokenness?

*

I was due to speak at the 7.30am team meeting on the Thursday. Before it, I took one of the Valium I had with me – I felt I had tried so hard and now I needed some help.

I spoke about God's strength being made visible in our weakness and imperfections. I assured my listeners (there was a Romanian translator) that those of us gathered in the room did not all feel completely 'together'. Nor did we need to for the great God of sustaining Love was with us.

I spoke of the gift of 'the wounded healer', once more remembering the selection of J. B. Phillip's writing with that title.

But was what I said true, or was I simply whistling in the wind?

The Valium glow lingered, as Adi and I abandoned our dominoes and walked in the warm sunshine.

*

The weather was perfect on the Friday morning. The whole camp trekked from the Casa down the track to the cross at the main road and then over to the ridge beyond it which gave spectacular views across the valley.

I walked with Gabriel on one side and Grace on the other each holding one of my hands. Both had Downs. Gabriel knew a little English.

We talked, brokenly, about friends he had in Toronto, whom he hoped to visit.

Gabriel wore a cross round his neck. He pointed to it, smiling brightly. Then, letting go of my hand, he said 'Deep!' and 'Wide!' gesticulating enthusiastically to symbolise these measures. Finally, he pointed heavenwards, before seizing my hand again.

'I get it, Gabriel,' I said. 'God's love is deep, and wide.'

*

Saturday morning. Final activities. The children and their parents drove off. We changed our beds for the next team. How I struggled, sweating in the warm sun-lit room, to smoothly position that duvet into the over-large cover. Twice I had to ask Fiona for guidance. Though I'd have liked her to do it for me, I appreciated her wisdom in leaving me to tackle it myself.

There had been a misunderstanding about the time of our flight. When the person who was giving us a lift to the airport finally arrived we knew we were cutting it fine. He committed our journey to God and then drove like the clappers. I sought to entrust myself to the Great Love. I could not bear another night in Romania. Please God, no!

We took off on time and reached Luton safely. It took us a while to find the way to our airport hotel and I almost lost my temper through frustration and impatience.

*

The next day at noon, I walked down the metal steps and stepped on to the solid ground of home.

I blinked back tears of relief.

And there was Lorna, waiting to welcome me back.

And was I Lion, or Lamb?

Or both?

THIRTY-THREE

EX-EVANGELICAL

I drove nervously up the steep hill from the city for my first meeting of the monthly Men's Group to which Iain Macritchie had introduced me. Despite Iain's reassurances I wondered if I was entering the devil's den.

We met, men from different faith traditions and none, at Anam Cara, a Buddhist retreat centre high on Craig Dunain, overlooking Inverness and the Beauly Firth. I was welcomed warmly, without suspicion, without question, into an easy environment of friends. We talked about things meaningful to us, spiritual experiences. I learned a new vocabulary – shamanism, and sweat lodges and earth-centred spirituality. To my surprise, much of what was said in the course of these evenings resonated with me.

Iain's own personal spiritual framework is, he says 'hugely Christian, because of my upbringing, and the decision to inhabit that, to make that my own as a teenager, and my on-going decisions to reflect on it, to strengthen it'. And yet he is open to the stories of those whose spiritual framework is built on a different foundation.

I contributed my own perceptions to the group. As I spoke, I was aware of Iain, sitting behind me, listening intently and with appreciation.

*

Books continued to nourish me, especially by authors from more 'progressive' Christian circles. Rob Bell, Steve Chalk among others. Dave Tomlinson, whose book *The Post-Evangelical* had helped awaken me in the 1990s published *How to be a Bad Christian:…and a Better Human Being*, and its sequels about living with questions and uncertainties. And yet in all this reading of new books, I wondered if I was locked in the same cycle as I detected in my Scripture Union shop customers, forever seeking an elusive touch from the God of whom others write with such tantalizing confidence.

I suppose I was searching for the one book, the one memoir which would completely reflect my experience, thus reassuring and affirming me. But I came to realise that though books may reflect aspects of my journey, I am unique – no one else's story will totally match mine, for we are each children of a God who delights in difference.

In all this reading, I was learning new things, and yet in a profounder sense I was being shown what I already knew. The 'Yes!' moments of insight came when something I encountered expressed what I had already subconsciously grasped, bringing it into plain sight.

The US Franciscan priest Richard Rohr, founder of the Centre for Action and Contemplation was especially influential. I began *Falling Upwards* in our hotel room the day I bought it in Barnes and Noble, and soon I was an avid follower of Rohr's daily emails. In the book which is heavily influenced by Carl Jung's thought, Rohr argues that during the first part of life we are shaping our identity and seeking fulfilment in career and relationships. Our lives are shaped by the norms and expectations of family, friendship group and society. We generally embrace the religious framework we have received.

But then whether through a crisis or a process we find ourselves compelled to question everything, and have the opportunity of discovering or forging our own unique authentic identity. The paradigm shift again. For me this was a restatement of what I had read in *A Churchless Faith* about breaking through to what was labelled the 'individuative-reflective' stage of spiritual development. Rohr's book reinforced my own becoming.

I appreciated Rohr's insights from Jung. I recognised that I was working through a process of individuation, a dying and a rising. I was discovering my true identity. I was welcoming, rather than running in fear from the stuff of shadow in me. I was learning to listen for God in the deepest inner place, and understanding that the more open I am to God, the more I become fully myself: just as the Great Love calls the whole universe to find and form itself so God likes nothing better than for me to be myself.

*

My thoughts about theology kept evolving. I grew suspicious of anything claiming to be a definitive theology or a detailed statement of faith. I grew to despair of the intellectual games some theologians seemed to be engaging in, disagreeing over details in their definitions of God, striving for an unattainable certainty.

I thought of the bigness of God – an energy encapsulating the whole universe, vast beyond human understanding or ability to conceive. I thought of the wildness of God, the mystery of suffering and of 'nature red in tooth and claw'. I came to realise that everything in creation is an icon, a sacrament pointing us towards the mystery of God, a gateway through which we may pass to connect with the invisible. But God is not defined, explained, or limited by any icon.

In the same way theological ideas and insights can only be icons, which point as well as they are able to the reality beyond. Through these gateways we catch glimpses of what cannot be expressed but can, through the mediation of the icon, be experienced. For God meets us in the gateway.

I know theology is helpful for guiding us in the wisdom of past and present as we evaluate our experiences of God. But constructing over-fastidious theological arguments seems to me like trying to refine the gateway rather that enjoying a God who I suspect isn't much concerned about our theology but cares a great deal about our loving response. I believe God did not leave us an infallible book but gave us Godself in Jesus, the ultimate icon, the ultimate gateway, the ultimate incarnation.

I believe now that the Bible was written by human beings sharing details of their encounters with God, the insights they received in the course of such encounters, and their reflections on these. The Jewish people gradually came to realise that this God was not a nationalistic, local God, but a universal God, the God of all nations and all peoples, a God unlike any other. The God of grace, love, holy challenge, restoration and forgiveness. And this is the God Christians believe is seen most clearly in the life, teaching and resurrection of Jesus the Christ in whom all things are being made one.

Other than Jesus, all out gateways and icons are defective. And yet the Great Love meets us in the most unlikely of gateways and icons. We do not make something a sacrament: it is the Father who makes it so, touching our poor constructions with the fire of God's living presence.

*

For much of my life I believed that 'right' beliefs were fundamental, more important than 'right' actions, though of course my faith if genuine would express itself in compassionate living. And of course it was always good to enrich the lives of others – but what would save me was not my love but my faith in Jesus, which I construed as being identical to 'my right beliefs about Jesus'.

I'd been questioning this for some time when I heard a sermon at Hilton Church on Jesus' story about the two builders each constructing a house, one built on sand the other on deep rock-based foundations. Only the latter house survived when the great storm came.

Jesus said that that the wise deep-digging builder represents everyone who 'comes to me and hears my words and puts them into practice' (Luke 6:47) The preacher enjoined us to come to Jesus, to listen to Jesus, to express Jesus's teaching in action.

Afterwards, I wrote:

Two things surfaced powerfully as I listened to the sermon. The first is the sheer craziness of focussing on orthodoxy rather than on orthopraxis. Jesus encouraged us to come, to listen, to act – to express the love of Jesus, and to be open to the counter-cultural wisdom of Jesus. This requires not assent to a body of doctrine, to a tick-list of beliefs but a simple entrusting of ourselves to the Spirit of Love which Jesus embodied. 'Believe in me' Jesus said. Absorb within you the loaf of my constant, loving presence. Let me live through you.'

And the second thing is the craziness of living as though this life is only a preparation for the life to come. What matters, what Jesus is urging us in his teaching, is the change we can make now, as we express compassion and grace now, as we imagine a better future into existence. This is the gospel – we are loved now, we are made whole now.

And isn't the voice of Jesus prompting wherever, in whatever context of belief or unbelief, the call to live in love is heard? And isn't Jesus expressed whenever that prompting is followed?

*

At Tesco Extra at Inshes, I was stationed just inside the entrance wearing a green foodbank gilet, and handing out 'shopping lists'. I was one of a small team of folk inviting people to purchase items for the local foodbank as they did their own shopping, and collecting their donations as they left the store.

When I am shopping at Tesco, my eyes are on the shelves, on the trolley, on the people ahead as I navigate round the aisles wryly acknowledging my incipient trolley rage.

But that day I made eye contact, looking into people's faces welcomingly whether or not they accepted a leaflet. And in doing this I felt for ten minutes or so a deep sense of peace, strangely at one with these shoppers, full of love for them, young and old, fit and feeble, relaxed and fraught. And being at one with them, I felt at one with the whole of humanity.

*

I had been reading Leslie Weatherhead's book, *The Christian Agnostic* about which Harry Seawright in Peterhead had been so critical when my parents and I visited him when the book was new in the mid-1960s. My experience in Tesco reminded me of his description of an epiphany in a third-class railway carriage in London when he was a student in the early 20th century:

> *For a few seconds only, I suppose, the whole compartment was filled with light… I felt caught up into some tremendous sense of being within a loving, triumphant and shining purpose…. I felt that all was well for all mankind… All men [sic] were shining and glorious beings who in the end would enter incredible joy… I loved everyone in that compartment.*

I was uncomfortable with some aspects of Weatherhead's book. His aim was to make Christianity appear 'reasonable' to what he called 'the modern mind' as though, somehow 'the modern mind' was more discerning than the minds of previous centuries. Yet many of the opinions he quotes from mid-20th century scientists and psychologists are now hopelessly outdated. I was particularly unhappy about the ungracious language Weatherhead used to describe those who understood and interpreted the Bible in more traditional terms than he did. There is no room for arrogance in the face of God's great mystery.

But for all the book's faults, Leslie Weatherhead articulated the journey which I myself was to take, in the company of many others. This journey involves a recognition that the Bible is a book written by flawed human beings however inspired; that its story reveals over the centuries a growing conception of God as God increasingly self-reveals; that the life and teaching of Jesus should take prominence in our Bible interpretation; that moral decisions are not always clear-cut; that our lives will be judged not so much on the things we believe, as the extent to which the unsentimental self-giving love of Jesus is seen in them.

*

Richard Rohr writes much about the mystic's vision of the unity of all things. But though there were tantalizing glimpses of this unity – as I experienced that day at Tesco – I wondered how it could possibly be. How could good co-exist with evil, light with darkness when much of the Bible takes a dualistic approach?

I reflected on how impossible it is in practice to separate 'light' and 'darkness', 'good' and 'evil'. In trying to do this we create 'the other' – people we perceive as our 'enemies' who lie beyond our protective palisade. But if we're honest, we'll admit that inside the fence there is darkness as well as light, and on the far side light as well as darkness. And when I examine my heart I see not only goodness, but shadow.

I remembered the story Jesus told about a farmer who, to avoid disrupting his crops, allows wheat and weeds to co-exist in his field until harvest, when the weeds are destroyed. (Matthew 13:24-30, 36-41) Even as light and darkness co-exist in me they co-exist in the universe. To see 'oneness' is therefore to enter into the sadness and brokenness of things as well as the joy and glory. But I am writing of something I glimpse only from afar.

According to the Christian story, pure light and pure darkness met in Jesus in his dying, and the first Easter Sunday revealed a light so strong that it leaves no vestige of darkness.

And so I believe on my clearer-seeing-days that there is one benighted world, one message of hope in Jesus, and beyond a judgement which I see as restorative rather than punitive there will be one united, perfected creation.

*

Iain Macritchie is an unofficial spiritual director but also a true friend – probably the most significant of all my friends. We are similar in outlook and temperament, sensitive, creative and somewhat introverted. We chat about our families, about books and poems and theology and about our faith journeys. I almost always get up from the table feeling that I have been nourished by our conversation. The only occasions when this sense is missing is when I am projecting on to Iain my own strong negative feelings about myself.

Iain was the first person I met who invariably offered me 'unconditional positive regard'. I knew I could say anything to him. I could raise theological conundrums and doubt and struggle, and he would listen intently, unfazed, affirming, with genuine interest. I could say I was 'bloody frustrated!' and those eye-brows would not be raised.

Good counsellor that he is, Iain *never* told me what to do and I knew better than to ask. At times, he might feed back to me the substratum of meaning he detected beneath my words, to check my understanding, but also to encourage me to think. Talking to Iain I realised I must pay attention to what was rising up within me, to what the creative energies were telling me.

Deeply influential in Iain's thinking was the year he spent studying at Union Theological Seminary in New York under Ann Ulanov, the Professor of Psychiatry and Religion who was also a Jungian analyst. I had already encountered Jung in the writings of Richard Rohr, and

Jung's insights as mediated by Iain helped me better understand and befriend myself, and to find my own answer to my lifelong question – 'What does Christian faith *feel* like?'

And above all, Iain's demeanour towards me is consistently one of love and joy. As I reflect on our conversations and the regard in which I am held, healing blossoms.

*

But there were still periods of time – days, weeks, months even – when I struggled with mental health issues. God seemed absent. I would hear an evangelical sermon and my spirit would respond with reproach and guilt. I would meet strongly evangelical people and feel threatened by their very presence. I would go into the Inverness branch of the Christian bookshop chain CLC and it would seem that secure on their shelves the volumes of theology were glaring at me accusingly.

Was this God speaking to me, even though what I was experiencing differed so much from the gentle, life-affirming whisper I was so used to with its attendant gift of creative energy? Or was this merely a reflex, the fruit of a thorough past conditioning?

For a day or two I would consider withdrawing behind the safe walls of evangelicalism with its allurement of certitude. And I'd realise the impossibility of that, and hang on in the storm, functioning as normally as I could until once again the wind fell and the still voice of assurance spoke.

*

I was reading the old Journals from a decade earlier and realised that my sitting on the fence – caught between evangelicalism and a more liberal, though Holy Spirit-filled Christianity – had stretched for many years. I knew it was time to change.

So reluctant was I to sever myself entirely from the 'E-word' with its promise of security that I'd styled myself a 'Complicated

Evangelical', and even had a blog with that title. But I knew this was no longer meaningful, if indeed it ever had been. My heart had led me into a broader place: but the tyranny of five thousand sermons, hundreds of books, an early-instilled litany of 'oughts' and 'shoulds', and indeed the whole culture which had shaped my life for so long held me back.

That day, realising the need for a definitive forward step, I wrote 'I am not an evangelical,' to a friend whom I knew would understand. And I signed up to the Beloved Listener Lounge, a Facebook group for devotees of a series of podcasts called Nomad – deeply spiritual and thoughtful people who sought as I did, to ask any question on any aspect of faith with nothing off-limits, and to be welcomed and affirmed, their woundedness acknowledged. There were no prescribed orthodoxies. These people modelled not an intimidating certainty, but a humility in living with uncertainty. Their honesty, and the honesty of those like them gifted me hope and wholeness.

*

There were times when the past sought to draw me back. But even to say the words 'I am an ex-evangelical' to myself and to others was freeing.

It was as though I had left the beach on the island where I had lived for so long and climbed the gangway to the ferry's deck. The vessel had pulled away from the shore, her bows turning towards the shipping lanes. I could look over the stern with the broader vision of objectivity as the massive terrain of evangelicalism receded

It was the place I had once been, but now was no longer, and the books, the sermons, the people were no longer a threat to me. The wounds continued to heal, such was the openness and love I found on board.

As the ferry ploughed through the waves towards its mainland destination, a ceilidh band played exuberantly in the saloon.

*

But there were still triggers, especially words which, though in themselves positive produced in me a heaviness and revulsion, an inner shrinking of spirit because of their associations.

The words 'biblical' and 'scriptural': I could not hear these without feeling again a shadow of the pressure to believe and experience and act which had brought despair through my inability to conform.

'Evangelism' and 'mission' breathed life into painful memories of injunctions to save souls, to hand out gospel tracts, to bring conversations round to 'spiritual things', to talk about my faith with conviction and certainty, all of which I found a painful burden until eventually I realised that the models of being and acting I was presented with were simply not 'me'.

I shrank from the word 'church'. I knew the theory of church as a loving community, and I acknowledged and was hugely grateful for the love I was shown in churches, but I remembered too the sense of expectation that I would be active, do stuff, sign up to creeds, conform.

Even the word 'worship' was disturbing. Saying 'Yes!' to God in the heart of life, I understood. Saying 'Yes!' to God when insights were dropped into my consciousness whether or not at a church service – I understood this too. But singing hymns and songs and prayers in church mostly left me cold.

I think very gradually, Christian vocabulary is being redeemed to me as it becomes associated with more positive and life-giving connotations. On my clearer– seeing days I rejoice that all Christians, regardless of their theology are seeking God. Who am I to think that my journeying has been in any way 'better' than theirs? Regardless of theology, what matters is love, love experienced and love shared, love inspired by the Great Love which imbues the fabric of the universe. Love which sings God's song.

*

Christian Viewpoint column from the *Highland News*, March 2021 in the middle of the COVID pandemic:

Recently, I was chatting to someone about God's unconditional love. As we spoke I was filled with the utter joy of being loved and cherished, no matter what, by a Love unshakable and unchanging.

I am prone to focus on negative things, and on what I sometimes regard as my failures and inadequacy. I am prone to disturbance by bitter, critical thoughts. But the sense of being loved silences this negativism, stills my fears, calms my mind. I become confident, joyful and free.

After that reawakening to the wonder of God's love, I took our dog Ezra [Mollie died in 2019] out for a walk. Normally, caught up in my own agenda, I'm impatient of his frequent stops to sniff lamp-posts, and squirt his own territorial markers. To still my impatience, I try to focus on mindfulness, concentrating on the natural things around me, but this is simply another item on my ego's agenda, and doesn't work for long.

The instinctive response to being loved unconditionally is to love others with equal, generous abandon. Knowing myself so loved by God, I found I could set the ego agenda to one side: a sense of lovingkindness stirred within. I found myself loving Ezra, with his bright eyes, soft fur, impetuous energy; loving the other dog-walkers; loving the gnarled tree-trunks, the low sun filtering through the leaves.

Later I came across this, said by a character in Dostoyevsky's novel The Brothers Karamazov: *'Love all God's creation, the whole of it and every grain of sand in it. Love every leaf, every ray of God's light. If you love everything you will perceive the divine mystery in things.'*

At times that week, I felt like a child again, hurrying expectantly outdoors with an awakened wonder. Everything seemed lovely, brand-new, waiting to be explored. This is not childishness, but the child-like innocence which lies on the far side of perplexity, a sense that the Great Love will win out, and that in this divine Love we are utterly secure.

This sense of being both held and set free by love isn't something I can generate through words or rituals, or summon by prayer. It is a sheer gift, given when I least expect it.

And then the clarity evaporates, and I am left again in the afterglow, no longer experiencing the Love so intensely, but choosing to live in the light of being loved.

And how do I know that these moments of Love experienced are closer to reality than the times of Love seemingly absent? All I can say is that never do I find myself so complete, inwardly healed and love-filled as at those times when the Great Love whispers in my soul 'You are my beloved'.

*

I remain relatively untouched by visual art but am healed elevated and transported by classical music, and this is a very precious thing. What I really appreciate now is not the loud, angst-ridden or exultant music which inspired me as a young man but works of a gentle reflective richness especially those from the Baroque period – Bach, Handel, Albinoni. Perhaps I have now passed through the chaos of the fugue, and feel the main theme of God's love lifting me up. Certainly, I find something of the gentleness and deceptive simplicity of divine beauty in the notes of the Baroque composers who never doubted that God knows every conceivable combination of notes, and that their task was to seek and capture songs God is already singing.

*

I started this book with uncertainty over which of two stories to lead with. I've changed my mind about the ending too. I'd planned to conclude with another reference to Edmund Gosse whose childhood was in some respects similar to mine.

I would have quoted the conclusion of *Father and Son's* main section, where Gosse describes an evening during his final year at school. During the previous months he experienced a resurgence of spiritual longing and perceptiveness. He looked from a window in the school across an evening landscape of profound beauty and sensed that the time had come. Christ must surely return. 'Come now Lord Jesus,' he cried. 'Come now and take me to be for ever with Thee in Thy Paradise.' But nothing happened. The Lord did not come, and at that moment he says he realised that the Lord would never come – never invade his life, never break into history.

To which I would have added: 'I believe that what Gosse failed to realise, and what I failed to realise for so many years, was that the Lord was, and is forever present.'

But while I do indeed believe that the Lord, the great creative Spirit of Love is forever present, as a conclusion that would have been dishonest. It would I think imply that the constant presence of God is matched in my life by a constant experience of that presence, while the reality is different. Sometimes the main theme falters.

There remain struggles, doubts, times of sadness for I find that I have not been granted freedom from anxiety and depression but freedom to live with these troubles without being submerged by them. And so moments of clarity vie with seasons of uncertainty when I've wondered if I should retreat to conservative evangelicalism or whether that call to atheism or agnosticism on the Ness Islands was not a temptation resisted, but a prophecy of future freedom from Christian faith.

These times of uncertainty often have a seasonal variation, generally affecting me more in winter than in the brighter months. The very difficult passage through the COVID-19 pandemic lockdowns brought both days and weeks when in my fragility I knew myself especially sustained by God, and other times when I felt immersed in emotional numbness and accidie.

And yet it is always God the Father of Jesus to whom my deepest self cries out as it did that distant spring morning in Sandyford Henderson Church. 'Though he slay me yet will I trust in him.' (Job 13:15 AV) Where there is darkness and struggle, that deepest self chooses light, hope and joy: chooses to live in the truth temporarily obscured by my emotions, that the Lord is 'forever present'.

*

I dreamed again of the flat in Dunnet Avenue. This time however the house was occupied and in perfect condition. I was conscious that two of the occupants were just through the wall. I was in the living room, and there was a young child sitting on the floor.

Conscious that the boy might be alarmed by my presence, I got down on my knees on the carpet, and said 'You don't know me, but it's all right. I used to live here.'

I told Lorna about this the next morning while we were getting breakfast. As I was speaking, I realised that the child in Dunnet Avenue was myself.

Down on the floor beside him. 'You don't know me, but I can assure you, it's going to be all right.'

EPILOGUE

Lorna and I were listening to a couple of Nomad Podcasts on the theme of 'spiritual trauma' – emotional and psychological woundedness resulting from aspects of religious teaching, or from the expectations and behaviours of religious leaders.

I was struck, as we listened, by the deep compassion the speakers on one of the podcasts – Joy Brooks and Justin Marsh – had for their audience. Aware that some people might find the content 'triggering,' they urged listeners to find a safe space to listen, and someone to support them if necessary. To me – still feeling at times even yet that I don't deserve to be 'safe' – their concern was massively reassuring.

It seems I've been writing this book all my life, though I began actually drafting it in 2005. Having at last completed and edited the text, I planned to self-publish, and get the story out through Matador. But having sent the book to them, I twice called a halt to the publishing process, feeling deeply anxious about the project.

I struggled to understand the cause and intensity of this anxiety. Did it spring from some deep-seated fear of 'letting my parents down'? Or was I concerned about mentioning people who have been significant in my life – although I have concealed identities and written with grace? Why such profound fear? But this co-existed with a strong desire to let the story, my story be heard. Was this desire simply the fruit of a narcissistic self-projection?

I was confused. Perhaps, I reasoned, the writing of this book with the self-growth and understanding it brought was it's own blessing, leaving no need for publication. Perhaps, as I enter my 70s, I should opt for a quieter life, not going public, but seeking to show love and grace to the circle of those I encounter in church and community. Such a vision brought relief – but I thought back to earlier times in my life when I'd been lured by the easier, less-challenging option, and grown stale in it until I found my true path again.

Iain Macritchie (bless him!) and I met for coffee at Dobbies. I told him about my fear of publishing, my doubts about going ahead when there was not a clear, bubbling spring of focused creative energy welling up within me. I told him about the need I recognised to be kind to myself. Perhaps publishing is not 'right': perhaps I don't really want this, perhaps it's not 'God's will'?

Iain listened carefully as always, and affirmed the need for self-protection. But one thing he said which I didn't register at the time was that he believes God often gives us options – circumstances in which we have a free choice either way – God accompanying us in love's grace and blessing whichever we choose.

The next day, Lorna and I were driving to Aberdeen to visit Bethany on a windy, January Saturday. As we drove, we listened to the Nomad Podcasts about spiritual trauma. And I realized, perhaps as never before, that I was spiritually traumatized, as teenager and adult, by certain Christian beliefs, by the way they were presented, by the mismatch between my experiences and the claimed experiences of others, by the lack of theological nuance, by controlling church leaderships.

And I realized that my fear of publishing perhaps arose from concern about drawing down wrath upon me from those under whose spiritual gatekeeping I experienced pain, their representatives today, and most of all from the wrathful God whose fierce image they etched in my consciousness. But I also realized the importance of owning the story and sharing the story.

Stories like mine need to be told so that others may find comfort in them if they have been traumatized, and challenge if their behaviour has damaged others, and food for reflection if they have both been spiritually abused and spiritually abusing.

I realized that the gentle concern for one another that Joy and Justin evinced, and their concern for the safety of their listeners was a reflection on the great love of God who invites us into a place of peace, shalom, safety.

And it is a direct consequence of my entrusting myself to this safe place that the book you hold in your hands even exists.

ACKNOWLEDGEMENTS

I am grateful to so many people who, through their words, actions and writings have helped me on my journey. Thank you, all of you! Specific thanks are due to Steve Aisthorpe, Donald Mowat and Graham Bullen who encouraged the writing of this book, and kindly commended it – Donald in particular scrutinised the draft in detail and made very helpful suggestions from both a structural and psychiatric perspective; to Jane Wallman-Girdlestone who was so hugely inspirational, seeing it as 'a heroic tale' and suggesting the title; to everyone in the HighlandLIT writing group here in Inverness; and especially to Iain Macritchie who has become an *anam cara* to me, and wrote the generous introduction.

Above all, I am grateful to my wife Lorna, and our daughters Rebecca and Bethany for bringing me a richer life, and for believing in me.

Soli Deo Gloria

John A.H. Dempster

REFERENCES

The quotations from Stephen Fischbacher's songs on pp. 320-21 are reproduced by permission of Stephen Fischbacher.

The quotations from Billy Graham (pp. 307-8) are taken from *The Journey: How to Live by Faith in an Uncertain World* by Billy Graham Copyright © 2006 by Billy Graham. Used by permission of Thomas Nelson. www.thomasnelson.com

The lines from Frank Houghton's *Facing a Task Unfinished* are quoted on p. 258 by permission of OMF International UK.

The sentence quoted from Alan Jamieson's *A Churchless Faith* (SPCK, 2002) on p. 339 is used by permission of Alan Jamieson.

The words from C.S. Lewis on (p. 110 and p. 130) are from *A Mind Awake* by CS Lewis © copyright CS Lewis Pte Ltd 1968. Extracts used with permission.

The sentences from K. M. Peyton's *Pennington's Heir* (p. 195) are quoted by permission of Oxford Publishing Limited.

His name was Tom by Jean Rees from which the quotation on p.108 comes was published by Hodder & Stoughton Limited.

The quotation (p. 128) from *Creed for a Christian Sceptic* by Mary McDermott Shideler is reproduced under the 'Fair Use' criteria of the W. B. Eerdmans Publishing Co.

The lines from Adrian Snell's song *Goodbye October* written by Phil Thomson (p. 168) are used with permission of Adrian Snell Music.